1990

Reading People, Reading Plots

Reading People, Reading Plots

Character, Progression, and the
Interpretation of Narrative

James Phelan

The University of Chicago Press

Chicago and London

James Phelan is associate professor of English at Ohio State University. He is the author of *Worlds from Words: A Theory of Language in Fiction*, published by the University of Chicago Press.

The University of Chicago Press, Chicago 60637
The University of Chicago Press, Ltd., London
© 1989 by The University of Chicago
All rights reserved. Published 1989
Printed in the United States of America

98 97 96 95 94 93 92 91 90 89 54321

Library of Congress Cataloging-in-Publication Data

Phelan, James.
   Reading people, reading plots.

   Includes index.
   1. English fiction—History and criticism—Theory,
etc.   2. Characters and characteristics in literature.
3. American fiction—History and criticism—Theory, etc.
I. Title.
PR830.C47P47   1989   801'.953   88-20840
ISBN 0-226-66691-3
ISBN 0-226-66692-1 (pbk.)

⊗ The paper used in this publication meets the minimum requirements of the American National Standard for Information Sciences—Permanence of Paper for Printed Library Materials, ANSI Z39.48-1984.

for Katie and Michael,
two characters who wonderfully complicate
the progression of my life

Contents

Preface

A myth of origin and evolution: In the beginning, I set out to write a book about character in narrative. It seemed to me that from Henry James through E. M. Forster and Walter J. Harvey down to most recent narratologists, the study of character had always gotten too mixed up with discussions of plot or action (the what-is-character-but - the - determination - of - incident? - what - is - incident - but - the-illustration-of-character? syndrome). I intended to isolate the element, analyze its nature, and report my findings to a breathlessly waiting critical world. As the title of this book indicates, however, I too have ended by mixing up the study of character with the study of plot—what is here called progression. I have ended this way, of course, because the events of the middle of my story pushed me in this direction. The more I tried to isolate the species, the more I became convinced that the task was impossible: the only way to capture the species' dazzling variety was to link it to the chief influence on that variety—the larger context of the whole narrative created by the progression.

Once I adopted a double focus on character and progression, the study also became implicated in many other kinds of questions about the interpretation of narrative—questions about thematizing, audience, cultural codes, narrative structure, and resistant reading. Since virtually all these questions applied to every narrative I would treat, and since my conviction about the variety of character required me to treat numerous narratives, I could not reach the end of my story until I found some means to balance the investigation of the various questions against the demands of treating the numerous narratives. I found my way to a (re)solution through a strategy for managing the progression of my own argument.

The introduction seeks to acquaint the reader with the main principles of my rhetorical approach to narrative and to explain the various terms that I employ to discuss character and progression. The chapters in the main body of this study then take on a double task: each investigates a question about the relation between character and progression in a specific narrative, and each explores the connections among that question, my proposed answer, and a broader theoretical issue in the interpretation of narrative. Thus, for example, Chapter 1 looks at character and progression in *1984* and *Pride and Prejudice* in connection with an orthodox neo-Aristotelean attack on thematic interpretations, while Chapter 6 examines those elements of *A Farewell to Arms* in connection with the feminist critique of the novel presented by Judith Fetterley. There are two features of this organizational schema that have especially important consequences for the progression of the whole argument. (1) Some concepts, e.g., those about the multiple audiences of narrative, that are employed early on without much comment get examined at some length in later chapters. (2) The later chapters not only build on the work of the early chapters but they also continually recontextualize the conclusions of those early chapters.

As a result, the later explorations frequently have implications for the earlier ones. For example, after the theoretical discussion of progression in Chapter 4, there is a lot more to say about the progression of *Pride and Prejudice* than I say in Chapter 1; similarly, after the discussion of evaluating character in Chapter 6, there is a lot more to say about every narrative I examine. In order not to overtax the patience of my reader, however, I typically press on with the forward movement of the argument rather than repeatedly circling back to supplement discussions that purport to have closure if not completeness. In other words, although many of the argumentative strands of the earlier chapters are picked up in the later ones, numerous retrospective implications of the later ones are left as implications. Still, the recontextualizing effect of that forward progression is designed to reinforce one of the implicit claims of the whole study: the rhetorical transactions offered by sophisticated narratives have a complexity that many of our existing interpretive practices fail to recognize.

This last claim is closely related to a feature of the argument that is very much in evidence from the outset: this study employs a lot of terms and distinctions—some original with me, some not—as it goes about its work. I am not yet in Gérard Genette's league as a coiner of appropriately high-sounding, scientific, and expensive terms—a "mimetic function" or a "local instability" cannot even afford the entry fee to compete in the same league as a "homodiegetic narrator" or a "heterodiegetic analepsis"—but I am aware that at times my more humble inventory may itself seem overstocked. The apparent grounds for prosecution, however, are also the grounds of my defense: when I try to shave the terminological beastie with a razor borrowed from Ockham, I find it to be more clean and smooth than shaggy and rough. The defense rests, in other words, on the claim that analytical entities are not multiplied beyond necessity but are produced by the task of doing justice to the complex rhetorical transactions offered by skillfully told narratives.

I have called this narrative of origin and evolution a myth partly because it omits so much of the lived version of the story. It leaves out the indispensable help of numerous students at the Ohio State University who helped me work out my ideas about character and progression, especially Jane Zinman, Steve Jensen, Amy Goodwin, and Steve Busonik; it fails to acknowledge the provocation and good advice of colleagues at Ohio State and elsewhere who read all or parts of the manuscript at different points, especially Ralph Rader, Walter Davis, David Riede, David Richter, and Peter Rabinowitz. My simplified narrative does not account for the important influence of my friend, Jamie Barlowe Kayes, who listened and constructively responded to my harangues about most of what I say here and who in turn instructively harangued me about Fowles. The myth shamelessly neglects the pervasive influence on my thinking exerted by my colleague, James Battersby, who responded to numerous versions of my ideas with wisdom, generosity, and an active pencil, and who has engaged me in a decade-long conversation about literature, interpretation, and critical argument from which I have profited immensely. To all of these people, I want to express my gratitude for making the story of this project too complicated to narrate. The greatest omission in the myth is the role of Betty Menaghan, my partner in love and logistics, who directly and indirectly shared—and felt—all the progressions and regressions of the writing (and the waiting). To her, I am grateful beyond words—even beyond narrative.

Some of the material in this book has appeared earlier in somewhat different form. Portions of the Introduction are to be found in "Thematic Reference, Literary Structure, and Fictive Character: An Examination of Interrelationships," *Semiotica* 49 3–4 (1984): 345–65, and in "Narrative Discourse, Character, and Ideology," *Reading Narrative: Form, Ethics, Ideology*, ed. James Phelan (Columbus: Ohio State University Press, 1988), pp. 132–46. This latter essay also contains a small part of Chapter 6. A portion of Chapter 1 appeared in "Character, Progression, and the Mimetic-Didactic Distinction," *Modern Philollology* 84 (1987): 282–99. And some of Chapter 2 is to be found in "Character in Fictional Narrative: The Example of John Marcher," *Henry James Review* 9 (1988): 105–13. I gratefully acknowledge permission to reprint this material.

Introduction
Character, Progression, and the Rhetorical Interpretation of Narrative

I

Some twenty years ago, in a critical age more innocent than our own, David Lodge advanced the argument that everything in a novel could be explained by reference to an author's choice of language, and that therefore character is only a convenient abstraction from verbal signs. Part of Lodge's argument involved the following "watch, I'll-show-you" demonstration:

> If I wish to describe an actual person, Mr. Brown, I might be able to choose between calling him *tall* or *big*, *dark* or *swarthy*. . . . But I could never "choose" between calling him *tall* or *short*, *dark* or *fair*. If he is a character in a novel, however, I can choose to describe him as tall and fair, or short and dark, or short and fair, or tall and dark. I can also call him Mr. Green or Mr. Grey or by any other name. I could conceivably call him all these things for a special literary effect: *Mr. Brown, or Green as he was sometimes called, was short, but tall with it. His fair-complexioned face was swarthy. As one of his friends remarked, "Grey is a difficult man to pin down."* [1]

In an earlier book, I have argued at some length that Lodge's example actually works against his case because it shows that character cannot be fully explained by reference to language alone.[2] The passage describes a particular chameleon-like character, and though the character may still be in process (indeed he may always be in process), the representation of him in the first two sentences puts constraints on the language of the third. If that sentence is to remain a summary that also adds to the description, there are countless things the friend cannot say, including, for example, "Brown is an easy man to pin down." My claim in short is that Lodge's attempt to collapse character under language actually shows that character can put constraints on language.

Since in the earlier book my focus was on the role of language in

1

fiction, I pursued those implications of the claim most relevant to my developing argument that language played a great variety of roles, ranging from the crucial to the incidental, in the achievement of fictional effects. Now I want to consider some other implications of Lodge's passage and my reading of it. What else can we conclude about character in imaginative literature besides the fact that it is or at least can be a nonlinguistic (or translinguistic) element? In one respect, of course, Lodge's commentary on his demonstration is very much on target: this description does not refer to a real person.[3] Furthermore, Lodge's setup and execution of the description foreground its artificiality: Brown-Green-Grey is neither real nor the image of a real person but rather is a construct, designed as an amusing display of authorial ingenuity which will also make Lodge's argumentative point about the importance of language in fiction. Although our awareness of, say, Hamlet, or Huck Finn, or Clarissa Dalloway, as made-up is not foregrounded to the degree it is with Brown-Green-Grey, we can recognize that such an awareness is part of our apprehension of them as characters. Part of being a fictional character, in other words, is being artificial in this sense, and part of knowing a character is knowing that he/she/(it?)[4] is a construct. I will hereafter call the "artificial" component of character the *synthetic*.

Lodge's example, I think, gets its punch from the interaction of this synthetic component with something else, namely, Brown-Green-Grey's possession of recognizable traits: his being short, tall, swarthy, fair; his having surnames. In other words, the description creates its effect by playing off—and with—the way characters are images of possible people. Lodge gives Brown-Green-Grey traits that normally help us identify a person, but by giving this character two or three traits where one is usually present and by having the second and third contradict the first, Lodge takes away as he gives: this person is not really a person. To identify the concept implied in the phrase "this person," I propose that we recognize a second component of character, what I will hereafter call the *mimetic*.

If we were to abstract Lodge's example from its context, and ask what is the point of describing such a character, we could no doubt generate a variety of answers: it is a comment on the way the times require us to perform multiple social roles; it is a response to all those male poems about the inconstancy of women, suggesting that men are fickle through and through; it is a paean to the complexity of even the most ordinary individual. I am not interested here in choosing any of these answers as superior to the others, and, indeed, I shall later return to discuss why all in one important way miss the mark. But I am interested in what this ordinary ability to generate such answers suggests about literary character. The ability is no doubt connected with what Jonathan Culler has identified as that part of literary competence called "the rule of significance"—"read the poem as expressing a significant attitude concerning man and/or his relation to the universe."[5] (Thus, my later question will in effect be why we would be incompetent to follow that rule here.) More pertinent to my purposes here, the ability to generate such statements of significance reveals another component that character may have. In each statement, Brown-Green-Grey is taken as a representative figure, as standing for a class—the individual in modern society, men, the ordinary human, respectively—and his representativeness then supports some proposition or assertion allegedly made by Lodge through his text. This exercise suggests, then, that character also has a *thematic* component, while my claim that each of the three statements of significance somehow misses the mark suggests that this component may not always be developed.

In summary, this further consideration of Lodge's colorful creation indicates that character too can be multichromatic, that it is a literary element composed of three components, the mimetic, thematic, and synthetic, and that the mimetic and thematic components may be more or less developed, whereas the synthetic component, though always present, may be more or less foregrounded.[6] The logical next questions are whether the synthetic, by virtue of its ineradicable presence, ought to be privileged in our theoretical account of character and whether we can determine under what general conditions the mimetic and thematic components get more or less developed. Again it will be useful to work with a specific case in which the creation of a character is the focal point of the text. So I move from Lodge's Brown-Green-Grey to Browning's Duke of Ferrara, a more complex creation than our flexible friend.

In an essay on issues facing contemporary American criticism, Jonathan Culler offers in capsule form the structuralist view of character, one suggesting that critics should turn away from what I have called the mimetic component of character and privilege the synthetic component: "The most intense and satisfying reading experiences may depend upon what we call involvement with characters, but successful critical investigation of the structure and effects of a novel, as a literary construct, may require thinking of characters as sets of predicates grouped under proper names."[7] Culler's discussion in *Structuralist Poetics* of Todorov's and Barthes' work on character clarifies this view by shedding light on what he means by predicates. Todorov, he says, "proposes to treat characters as proper names to which certain *qualities* are attached during the course of the narrative. Characters are not heroes, villains, or helpers; they are simply subjects of a group of predicates which the reader adds up as he goes along."[8] In *S/Z* Barthes treats Sarrasine as "the meeting place of turbulence, artistic ability, independence, violence, excess, femininity, etc."[9] Note first that Culler's conception of character as a collection of predicates does not go beyond interpretation—the predicates (or qualities) sometimes must be inferred from seeing a proper name associated with speech, thought, or action, or indeed, with speech associated with another proper name. By simultaneously depending at least in part on interpretation and denying any importance to the mimetic component, Culler does bring the thematic component of character (and then by extension of narrative in general) into an almost equal prominence with the synthetic. One consequence of Culler's conception is that it can resolve many critical disputes about particular characters by declaring that such disputes are themselves the result of a common category mistake. Applying Culler's conception to, say, the notorious dispute about whether the governess in *The Turn of the Screw* is sane or insane, we could conclude that the dispute stems from the mistaken assumption that the character is a representation of a possible person. Jettisoning that assumption, we could then more properly understand the character as the meeting place of both sane bravery and insane paranoia.

Applying this view to Browning's poem yields the following results. Through the use of pretended speech acts, Browning has made "Ferrara" the meeting place of many predicates or qualities: imperiousness, power, unscrupulousness ("I gave commands; Then all smiles stopped together"); vanity ("She thanked . . . as if she ranked / My gift of a nine-hundred-years-old name / With anybody's gift"); possessiveness ("None sets by / That curtain I have drawn for you but I"); appreciation of beauty ("I call that piece a wonder now;" There she stands / As if alive"). In addition, two rather incompatible qualities meet under "Ferrara": "mental instability," a quality inferred by concluding that the emissary from the Count is an inappropriate audience for the speech acts of the poem; and "boldness," a quality inferred by concluding that the emissary is an appropriate audience. Since the poem is Browning's creation of a character, this delineation of predicates gives us the major structural elements of the whole. The full structure results from the intersection of this larger set of predicates with a smaller set grouped under "my last duchess," a set whose most important members are friendliness, beauty, openness to pleasure. The poem reveals the character of the Duke by indicating how the set of qualities associated with his name dominates over the set associated with "my last duchess."

If we analyze the poem according to a conception of character that gives weight to the mimetic component, we get markedly different results. As Ralph Rader has pointed out in an analysis that assumes the importance of the mimetic component, Browning's task is to create the *illusion* that we are not reading a poem but overhearing part of a conversation.[10] More specifically, Browning seeks to make the Duke's speech appear to be motivated entirely by the dramatic situation, even while it paints a complete portrait of him—complete, that is, within the limits of the implied dramatic situation. In sum, the Duke is a character whose mimetic component is overtly emphasized while his synthetic component, though present, remains covert. At this stage of the analysis, his thematic component does not figure prominently, but I will later discuss its place in the poem.

It may seem odd to argue that the synthetic remains covert when we are reading a poem written in rhymed couplets, but a short thought experiment suggested by Rader will help justify the point. Who is responsible for the rhymes, Browning or the Duke? The fact that we instinctively answer "Browning" indicates the kind of involvement with the Duke we have: we have only his voice but we do not hear *him* rhyming. The synthetic is there but it remains covert. To the more general question of whether a poem will always appear more synthetic than prose, I answer, not necessarily. Whenever we read a title page which tells us that the work is a novel, we know we are reading something as synthetic as any poem. But neither this knowledge nor our perception of line breaks, stanzas, and rhymes necessarily prevents our participating in the mimetic illusion. To participate in the illusion is to enter what Peter Rabinowitz has called the narrative audience; to remain covertly aware of the synthetic is to enter what Rabinowitz has called the authorial audience.[11] In other words, the authorial audience has the double consciousness of the mimetic and the synthetic, while the narrative audience has a single consciousness of the Duke as real. I will be discussing the nature of—and the relation between—these audiences in more detail in later chapters; for now let me just note that the authorial audience is the ideal audience that an author implicitly posits in constructing her text, the one which will pick up on all the signals in the appropriate way. When I speak about "our" responses in the pages that follow, I am referring to the responses of this audience. The narrative audience is that group of readers for whom the lyric, dramatic, or narrative situation is not synthetic but real. For the mimetic illusion to work, we must enter the narrative audience. To enter it in Browning's poem is to imagine oneself an invisible eavesdropper who hears and sees just this part of the interview between the Duke and the envoy.

Within the general conception of "My Last Duchess" sketched

above, we must choose between the view of the Duke as mentally unstable and the view of him as extremely bold. Is the Duke's confession of his crime against his last duchess an unwitting self-revelation or a purposeful warning? I follow Rader in concluding that it is a purposeful warning whose purpose will be accomplished only if it does not appear to be a warning. The Duke must not appear to be warning for the same reason that he never openly objected to the frequent smiling of the duchess: "E'en then would be some stooping; and I choose / Never to stoop." This hypothesis about the Duke's character is superior to one that says he is out-of-control for two main reasons, one general, the other specific. First, it gives a definite, positive motivation for this speech in this situation, whereas the alternative is a *faute de mieux* account (I can't see any reason why the Duke would say this to the envoy from the father of his next wife, so he must be crazy). Second, this conclusion more adequately explains the rather elaborate business the Duke goes through before the main revelation.

> I said
> "Fra Pandolf" by design for never read
> Strangers like you that pictured countenance,
> The depth and passion of its earnest glance,
> But to myself they turned (*since none puts by*
> *The curtain I have drawn for you but I*)
> *And seemed as they would ask me, if they durst*
> How such a glance came there; so, *not the first*
> *Are you to turn and ask thus.*
>   (ll. 5–12; emphasis mine)

The inference is that the Duke is acting with premeditation here: he is determined to make the envoy "sit and look at her" so that he can tell his story and thereby give his warning-sans-stooping.

Furthermore, this hypothesis, with its emphasis on the relation between the overt mimetic and covert synthetic components of the Duke, allows for some important insights about Browning's control of the whole, a control which is perhaps most impressive in the conclusion:

> Will't please you rise? We'll meet the
> Company below then. I repeat,
> The Count your master's known munificence
> Is ample warrant that no just pretence
> Of mine for dowry will be disallowed;
> Though his fair daughter's self, as I avowed
> At starting, is my object. Nay, we'll go
> Together down, sir. Notice, Neptune, though

Taming a sea-horse, thought a rarity,
Which Claus of Innsbruck cast in bronze for me!

(ll. 47–56)

It is here at the end that we learn for the first time that the Duke's auditor has come on business relating to the Duke's next marriage. This delayed disclosure is of course a direct consequence of the mimetic imperative: as the poem is constructed, any prior definition of the situation by the Duke would seem an obvious contrivance by Browning. As Browning follows the mimetic imperative, he also increases the effectiveness of the poem as a constructed object. The details illuminating the dramatic situation function not just as exposition but also as climactic strokes in the portrait of the character. The Duke's horrible imperiousness has been revealed in his account of how he handled the Duchess. But the sheer audacity that accompanies that imperiousness and adds substantially to its horror is made known only when we realize the audience and the occasion for the Duke's speech.[12] In addition to making this exposition an effective device for the achievement of completeness in the poem, Browning makes it contribute substantially to the arresting quality of the portrait he is drawing. Because the full dimensions of the Duke's character dawn upon us only gradually and only in retrospect, they dawn upon us more powerfully. Finally, these concluding realizations are brilliantly set off by the last two lines of the poem, in which the Duke symbolically encapsulates his purpose ("Neptune taming a sea-horse"), even while, as Rader also points out, he seems to insist that he has been talking only about art throughout the whole monologue.

Comparing the analysis based on Culler's conception of character with the one based on a conception that gives weight to a mimetic component, we find some interesting results. Despite their considerable differences, both analyses offer worthwhile insights into the poem. Choosing between them is also a matter of choosing the kind of knowledge that one wants from a theory of character. Culler suggests that his conception will lead to a better understanding of the "structure and effect" of works. I think that the parallel analyses indicate that his claim is misleading. The structuralist analysis does not yield any substantial account of the effect of the poem and has little to say about the specific structure of the whole. Instead, it identifies the basic elements out of which the structure of both the text and the character are created; this identification of basic elements is both the weakness and the strength of the analysis. By identifying the basic elements, the structuralist can indicate something about the materials out of which the mimetic analyst will build his account, but such an indication comes at the price of failing to offer any well-developed interpretation of its own.

The mimetic analysis, on the other hand, commits one to developing an account of the structure and effect of a work. Judged by that shared criterion, it does offer a superior way of theorizing about character. But the differences in the results of the analyses suggest that, Culler's reference to structure and effect aside, the methods are not always competitive and that each could be used for a different critical purpose. Where the structuralist analysis tends toward the inclusive (e.g., in its identification of semantically incompatible predicates), the mimetic tends toward the restrictive: it chooses among incompatible traits, it tries to build as precise a portrait of the character as possible. Where the structuralist remains suspicious of the emotional involvement that comes from viewing the character as a possible person, the mimetic analyst regards that involvement as crucial to the effect of the work. In short, where the structuralist seeks an objective view of the text, one which foregrounds the text as construct, the mimetic analyst takes a rhetorical view, one which foregrounds the text as communication between author and reader. Since I want my theory to account for the structure and effect of texts by accounting for such communication, I shall pursue the rhetorical (and mimetic) view here.

The consequences of choosing the rhetorical over the structuralist conception of character become even greater as we consider the role of the thematic component within the rhetorical conception of Browning's poem. Whereas the Duke has been defined for the structuralist as the meeting place of many thematic qualities, the rhetorical analysis to this point has neglected the thematic component of the Duke's character. Does the Duke have a role in the structure of the poem that leads to our abstracting thematic conclusions from it? The best answer, I think, is yes and no. On the one hand, it is fairly easy to construct thematic propositions that are implied or reinforced by Browning's creation of the Duke, propositions that would go right along with the structuralist conception of the character.[13] A partial list would include: to execute one's spouse for her friendliness is horrible; to possess beauty by killing it is reprehensible; power corrupts; men (frequently) treat women as possessions that exist for the sole purpose of giving them pleasure. On the other hand, these propositions are not conclusions that the poem itself leads one toward in the way that, say, Golding's *Lord of the Flies* tries to lead the reader toward the conclusion that humans are inherently evil. Instead, these propositions are in effect taken for granted by Browning. The powerful effect of his portrait does not depend on his demonstrating the truth of these assertions; rather these are general propositions whose truth Browning presumes independently of our reading the poem and on which he relies to make his portrait more arresting.

We can usefully distinguish between the thematic elements of a character like the Duke and of one like Jack in Golding's novel by making a distinction between a character's *dimensions* and his or her *functions*. A dimension is any attribute a character may be said to possess when that character is considered in isolation from the work in which he or she appears. A function is a particular application of that attribute made by the text through its developing structure. In other words, dimensions are converted into functions by the *progression* of the work. Thus, every function depends upon a dimension but not every dimension will necessarily correspond to a function. The Duke has many thematic dimensions (attributes that may be considered for their potential to contribute to thematic assertions) but essentially no thematic function: the work progresses not to make assertions but to reveal his character. Golding's Jack has many thematic dimensions— his lust for power, his willingness to destroy nature for his own advantage, his greater concern with short-term advantage than long-term good, and so on—that all contribute to his main thematic function of demonstrating the strength of inherent evil in humans. The distinction between dimensions and functions allows us to see why applying the rule of significance to the case of Mr. Brown-Green-Grey would be an act of literary incompetence. Lodge's character, like Browning's, has thematic dimensions—he is male and chameleon-like, he resists fixities, and so on—but no thematic function: the text achieves closure before it develops the thematic potentiality of these dimensions.

The distinction between dimensions and functions also applies to the mimetic and synthetic components of character, though, as we shall see, it has a greater relevance to the mimetic. Furthermore, it allows me to resituate the importance of the mimetic component within the general rhetorical approach to character I have been defining. The distinction between dimensions and functions is based on the principle that the fundamental unit of character is neither the trait nor the idea, neither the role nor the word, but rather what I will call the *attribute*, something that participates at least in potential form in the mimetic, thematic, and synthetic spheres of meaning simultaneously. Thus, the rhetorical theorist need not stipulate in advance that the characters in a given work will be represented people, or themes with legs, or obvious artificial constructs. The theorist only commits himself to the position that a character may come to perform any of these functions or indeed all three of them to varying degrees within the same narrative.

An analogy with the way speakers use utterances may clarify the distinction between dimensions and functions. Most utterances contain a potential for signification greater than the signification actualized, if only because most utterances do not take advantage of the signifying potential of the sounds used to make them. Nevertheless, a speaker may take advantage of this signifying potential by shaping his utterance in such a way that its sounds call attention to themselves. The teacher who bids good morning to his class in rhymed couplets conveys an attitude with those rhymes that is simply not present in a prosaic greeting. Or to take a more standard example, recall how Pope in "An Essay on Criticism" reinforces his dictum about sound echoing the sense by exemplifying his point in his own lines:

> Soft is the strain when Zephyr gently blows,
> And the smooth stream in smoother numbers flows;
> But when loud surges lash the sounding shore,
> The hoarse, rough verse should like the torrent roar.
> When Ajax strives some rock's vast weight to throw,
> The line too labors, and the words move slow.
>   (ll. 366–71)

Similarly, when an author creates a character, she creates a potential for that character to participate in the signification of the work through the development of the character in three spheres of meaning; that potential may or may not be realized depending upon the way the whole work is shaped.

At the same time, we need to remember that, as we read, characters do not come to us first as attributes which we recognize as dimensions which then become transformed into functions as we look on in wonder, but that they come to us already in the process of being shaped into functions, or (especially within the mimetic sphere) as already functioning. When we read, "Miss Brooke had that sort of beauty that seemed to be set in relief by poor dress," or "Emma Woodhouse, handsome, clever, and rich, seemed to unite in her person the best blessings of existence," we are immediately encountering characters who are already performing mimetic functions. The point, in other words, is that my rhetorical theory of character is claiming to offer analytical distinctions that allow us to understand the principles upon which works are constructed rather than claiming to offer a blow-by-blow description of what happens when we read.[14]

II

This sketch of a framework for a rhetorical approach to character also indicates the conditions that must be satisfied for that sketch to develop into an adequate working theory of character in narrative. (1) We need to explore further the nature of the three components, including the relation between dimensions and functions. (2) We need to investigate the range of relations among the three different functions. (3) We need to investigate the nature and variety of narrative progression so that we can better understand the mechanisms by which dimensions get converted into functions. Fully satisfying these conditions will be the task of the later chapters, but here I can take some initial steps toward satisfying the first and third conditions.

Mimetic dimensions, as we have seen, are a character's attributes considered as traits, e.g., the Duke's maleness, his position of power, his imperiousness, his boldness, and so on. Mimetic functions result from the way these traits are used together in creating the illusion of a plausible person and, for works depicting actions, in making particular traits relevant to later actions, including of course the development of new traits. In works where the traits fail to coalesce into the portrait of a possible person, e.g., Swift's creation of Gulliver, or some modern works intent on destroying the mimetic illusion, a character will have mimetic dimensions without a mimetic function. Moreover, within the creation of a possible person, a particular trait might serve only to identify that character, e.g., the detective who always eats junk food, and the trait might not (though it often will) have any consequences for his later actions—or for our understanding of them. In such a case, the character has a mimetic dimension that is incidental to his or her mimetic function: the plausibility of the portrait would remain without the trait and the rest of the work would be essentially unaffected by its absence.

Silently underlying this discussion of the mimetic component are some messy problems. First, all this talk about characters as plausible or possible persons presupposes that we know what a person is. But the nature of the human subject is of course a highly contested issue among contemporary thinkers. Although this study of character can have consequences for that debate, I shall not take it up directly here. Not only would such a discussion require lengthy excursions into biological, philosophical, psychological, sociological, and economic territories that would preclude the exploration I have just begun but, more important, such a discussion is not a necessary preliminary to the rhetorical study I am undertaking. For that to be justified, it is enough that authors write with some working notion of what a person is and with some belief that characters can (or indeed, cannot) represent persons and that as readers and critics we can discern these ideas in the work. At the same time, this principle means that for certain works we may need to invoke the findings of psychology, sociology, economics, biology, and/or philosophy because authors may be drawing on (or perhaps anticipating) these findings in their representations of the mimetic components of character. Thus, for example, it seems to me necessary to know something about the psychoanalytic understanding of character to enter the authorial audience of *Light in August*: certain features of the representation of Joe Christmas as a possible person that are rendered comprehensible by that knowledge remain virtually inscrutable without it. On the other hand, we do not need such an understanding to enter the authorial audience of, say, *Tom Jones* or *Pride and Prejudice*: the characters in these works, though perhaps susceptible to psychoanalytical interpretation, are constructed and offered to us on different principles.

The second problem is related to the first: how to specify adequately the criteria by which to judge a given representation of a character as plausible or not. For the most part, such a representation is a matter of conventions and the conventions change over time as both ideas about persons and fictional techniques for representing persons change. Modern readers may have a hard time finding Pamela Andrews a possible person but Richardson's contemporary readers (*pace* Henry Fielding) did not. Thus, I think that for my purposes flexible, shifting criteria are superior to fixed ones. Since my goal is to understand the principles upon which a narrative is constructed, I shall seek to make my judgments according to what I know or can infer about the conventions under which a given author is operating. Furthermore, we ought to recognize from the outset that it is very easy to call any character's plausibility into question by abstracting the character's behavior from the situations which influence it. Is it really plausible that a man who has been king all his life would be able to learn anything about himself by giving up his kingship and then hanging around on a heath in a storm with a fool, a disguised friend, and someone pretending to be mad? Come off it, Mr. Playwright. Finally, in addition to judging plausibility in connection with the whole web of circumstances surrounding a character's actions, I will out of respect for the variety of human behavior and experience seek to err on the side of generosity rather than of parsimony in judging plausibility: the dividends that might accrue to our remaining open to the idea that such and such a person could exist and behave in such and such a way in such and such a situation are more rewarding than the satisfaction we might get by initially questioning the plausibility of such a creation.

Thematic dimensions, as we have seen, are attributes, taken individually or collectively, and viewed as vehicles to express ideas or as representative of a larger class than the individual character (in the case of satire the attributes will be representative of a person, group, or institution external to the work). Just as characters may be functioning mimetically from our first introduction to them, so too may they be functioning thematically, but just as the full mimetic function is often not revealed in the initial stages of a narrative, so too may thematic functions emerge more gradually. In works that strive to give characters a strong overt mimetic function, thematic functions develop from thematic dimensions as a character's traits and actions also demonstrate, usually implicitly, some proposition or propositions about the class of people or the dramatized ideas. Usually, the narrative will then use these functions to influence the way we respond to the actions of the character, and sometimes the progression may make these functions crucial to the work's final effect, even if the work is not organized to convince us of a particular proposition. We shall see an example of such a narrative shortly, when I turn to discuss Lardner's "Haircut." In works where the artificiality or the synthetic nature of characters is more overt, thematic dimensions get developed into functions somewhat differently: the representative quality of the traits or ideas will usually be explicitly revealed in the action or the narrative discourse. Golding's initial description of Jack connects Jack's physical appearance with the conventional image of Satan. Thus, Jack's physical attributes immediately give him a thematic dimension that is of course later converted into a thematic function.

The distinction between the mimetic and thematic components of character is a distinction between characters as individuals and characters as representative entities. In attaching the notion of "plausible person" to the mimetic component, I do not mean to imply that my own working concept of a person precludes representativeness. It seems to me that our understanding of people in life also commonly has a thematic component: we see the traits that others possess as defining a type of person or a set of ideas and attitudes that are not peculiarly their own. We say, "He's a sixties flower-child," or "She's a radical feminist," and imply that the identities of these people can be summed up by a set of ideas or values associated with those descriptions. At the same time, we (i.e., those of us sharing a fairly widespread, though less than universal, belief about how to treat other people) commonly regard ourselves as more enlightened, more open, more tolerant, if we refrain from making any quick leaps from traits to themes. Indeed, we label those who leap from skin color or sex to assumptions about a person as racist or sexist. As I have already suggested in the discussion of "My Last Duchess," we must also resist the automatic ascription of traits to themes in literature. In both cases, then, the problem arises not from thematizing itself but from doing so prematurely or carelessly, i.e., without sufficient attention to the relation of the trait to the rest of the person or character and the situation and actions in which he or she is engaged.

On the other side of this similarity between people and literary characters, there is, of course, a significant difference: however much we may wish that Ronald Reagan or Howard Cosell or the next door neighbor were just an artificial construct, each of them is undeniably organic, just as Elizabeth Bennet and Prince Hamlet of Denmark and Hester Prynne are undeniably synthetic. One consequence of the difference, I think, is that we are given a greater license for thematizing in literature; though we must remain wary of hasty jumps from trait to theme, we are likely to be invited to make more considered ones. Because literary characters are synthetic, their creators are likely to be doing something more than increasing the population, more than trying to bring another possible person into the world. They are likely to be increasing the population in order to show us something about the segment of the population to which the created member belongs.

As this point implies, the ineradicability of the synthetic component marks it off from the mimetic and thematic components: in the synthetic sphere dimensions are always also functions. Synthetic dimensions will always be synthetic functions because they will always have some role in the construction of the work; this role may be extraneous or disruptive, the character's other components may interfere with the success of the synthetic function, but the function cannot be eliminated. Furthermore, although every mimetic and thematic function implies a synthetic function, not every synthetic function implies a mimetic or thematic one. The unnamed emissary in "My Last Duchess" has a mimetic dimension by virtue of his status relative to both the Duke and the Count, but he has no functions other than the synthetic one of being the appropriate addressee for the Duke's veiled warning. (The Count, of course, is a character with mimetic and thematic dimensions but no corresponding functions.) Nevertheless, it does make sense to distinguish characters like the Duke of Ferrara whose synthetic status remains covert and those like Christian in *Pilgrim's Progress* whose synthetic status is foregrounded. Although this distinction is not strictly parallel to the distinction between dimensions and functions for the other two components, it does capture a similar phenomenon: the development of a potentiality in the character into an actuality. The means by which the synthetic component can be foregrounded are many and diverse, but one is especially noteworthy because it exploits the artificiality of the *material* out of which the character is made. An author can focus the reader's attention, through a narrator, another character's speech, or even an action, on the character's name or the descriptions of the character so that we regard the character as symbolic rather than natural. When I construct a narrative in which Smoothtalk meets Bumpkin on a bustling boulevard in Urbia, then I am inviting my readers, fit and few as they may be, to regard the characters as constructs designed for some thematic purpose.

III

Progression, as I use the term, refers to a narrative as a dynamic event, one that must move, in both its telling and its reception, through time. In examining progression, then, we are concerned with how authors generate, sustain, develop, and resolve readers' interests in narrative. I postulate that such movement is given shape and direction by the way in which an author introduces, complicates, and resolves (or fails to resolve) certain instabilities which are the developing focus of the authorial audience's interest in the narrative. Authors may take advantage of numerous variables in the narrative situation to generate the movement of a tale. In general, the story-discourse model of narrative helps to differentiate between two main kinds of instabilities: the first are those occurring within the story, instabilities between characters, created by situations, and complicated and resolved through actions. The second are those created by the discourse, instabilities—of value, belief, opinion, knowledge, expectation—between authors and/or narrators, on the one hand, and the authorial audience on the other. To recognize this difference in kind I reserve the term "instabilities" for unstable relations within story and introduce the term "tension" for those in discourse.[15] Some narratives progress primarily through the introduction and complication of instabilities, whereas others progress primarily through tensions, and still others progress by means of both. In examining progression, we are also involved in considering narratives as developing wholes. In order to account for the effect of, say, a complication of one instability, we will need to consider the previous development of that instability and its relation to other instabilities or tensions as well as the way it is disclosed to the reader. To do a similar analysis for all such complications would lead one to an analysis of the whole narrative. The point, in other words, is not that all parts of a narrative are directly concerned with instabilities or tensions, but rather that all parts of a narrative may have consequences for the progression, even if those consequences lie solely in their effect on the *reader's understanding* of the instabilities, tensions, and resolution. Let me illustrate this conception of progression, and some of its consequences for the way in which I shall seek to develop my rhetorical theory of character by a look at a short narrative that progresses both by tension and instability. I choose Ring Lardner's "Haircut" in part because, as a narrative analogue to the dramatic monologue, it also fits in with the progression of examples in this chapter.

Just as the poet in a dramatic monologue seeks to create the illusion that his audience is not reading a poem but overhearing part of a conversation, so Lardner seeks to create the illusion that his audience is not reading a story but overhearing a barber's rambling monologue to a new customer. Lardner builds the illusion in large part by emphasizing the haphazardness of the barber's speech—Whitey frequently shifts topics with no more transition than a "Well" or a "But I was going to tell you." Like the poet in the dramatic monologue, Lardner needs to sustain the illusion of unartistically delivered speech even as he arranges it for maximum effect. But there is a significant difference between Whitey's narrative and most dramatic monologues: while the speaker in a dramatic monologue may or may not talk directly about himself, the movement of the poem is typically a movement toward the disclosure of his character, whereas the movement of Whitey's narration is toward the disclosure of events involving other characters, particularly Jim Kendall, Julie Gregg, Paul Dickson, and Doc Stair. Significantly, however, the first major instability among these characters is not introduced until after the halfway point of Whitey's narration, when he says that "Jim was like the majority of men, and women too, I guess. He wanted what he couldn't get. He wanted Julie Gregg and he worked his head off trying to land her."[16] Indeed, at this juncture, the narrative divides neatly into two parts; everything before this point serves to disclose information about the four chief actors and their environment, information that is necessary for the authorial audience's understanding of how and why they act as they do in the focused narrative of related events that follows this point. The apparently scattered information of the first half is brought into a coherent relationship as we draw upon it to infer the means and motives behind the central events of the story, Jim Kendall's humiliation of Julie Gregg and his subsequent death in what Whitey regards as an accident. This arrangement makes the second half of the story move with economy and power to its climax, but it raises some interesting questions about the first half: What does Lardner do there to propel the reader forward, and what happens to that principle of propulsion after the shift to a different principle just after the halfway point?

In the terms introduced above, the initial principle of movement in "Haircut" is the tension between Whitey and the authorial audience: Whitey's judgments of Jim Kendall as a "card" (p. 25), as "kind of rough but a good fella at heart" (p. 24), are at odds with our much harsher judgments, and we read on in part for the pleasure of communicating with Lardner behind Whitey's back, in part to take in what he tells us about his small town, and in part to see how the portrait of our unreliable narrator develops. In other words, in the absence of any clear direction to the potential instabilities introduced in this first half of the narrative, Whitey becomes much like the speaker in a dramatic monologue: he is as much the focus of our interest as anything he tells us.

Now what emerges from the tension and our interest in Whitey is a clear, if limited, mimetic portrait: he is a small-town barber who is garrulous, loves a laugh, is well-liked, and most significantly, for this is the source of the tension, is morally obtuse. He is unable to detect the cruelty of most of Jim Kendall's practical jokes and unable to differentiate between such acts as Jim's kidding Milt Sheppard about the size of his Adam's apple, and Jim's falsely promising his wife and children that he would take them to the circus. In addition, Whitey has attributes that mark out a thematic potentiality: he is shown to be a representative of his own small town and thus of a small-town mentality. Whitey's occupation and personality make his shop the base of Kendall's operations, and indeed, the first joke of Jim's that Whitey tells about is directed at Whitey himself, and the barber is able to reply in kind. The occupation further identifies Whitey as a representative male—he is a man serving other men, talking and joking with them in a space where the women are excluded. In addition, Whitey seems to know and get on with everyone, and his nickname accentuates his status as one of the gang.[17] Finally, Whitey's very role in the narrative, passing on the gossip of the town to its new inhabitant, emphasizes his place as representative male.[18]

The initial movement by tension has many consequences for the narrative after it shifts to its movement by instability. First, our understanding of Whitey's obtuseness operates to create one of the dramatic ironies of the narrative: given what we know of Whitey, we have little trouble seeing that his report of Jim Kendall's death as accidental misses the truth of that event by a country mile. We are quickly able to discern that Paul Dickson, urged on by Doc Stair's angry remark that anyone who could pull anything like Kendall's trick on Julie Gregg "ought not to be let live" (p. 32), had deliberately shot Kendall when they were out duck-hunting. We can discern further that Doc Stair as coroner took advantage of Paul's reputation as "cuckoo" (p. 27) and "a half-wit" to declare the death accidental because that declaration would better serve the cause of justice than the truth would. The dramatic irony—and part of the effect of the story—arises, as Brooks and Warren say in *Understanding Fiction*, from the fact that the biter is bitten[19] and from the fact that Whitey is blind to the complicated "trick" played on Jim by Paul Dickson and Doc Stair. But the effect produced by the ending is more than ironic satisfaction, and to describe the way that effect comes about I need to introduce one last distinction, that between completeness and closure.

Closure, as I use the term, refers to the way in which a narrative signals its end, whereas completeness refers to the degree of resolution accompanying the closure. Closure need not be tied to the resolution of instabilities and tensions but completeness always is. For example, in a narrative entitled "Diary of Disastrous December," which has 31 chapters, each of which is headed by the date and which follow each other in chronological order, the very inscription of 31 December at the head of the last chapter will be a strong signal of closure. Whether the narrative will have completeness will depend on how the instabilities and tensions are worked out in that (and of course previous) chapters. In a narrative in which a character sets out from home on a dangerous journey and returns at the end, the return itself will function as a sign of closure and the condition in which he returns will be a step toward completeness, indicating how the initial instability is resolved; the degree of completeness will depend upon whether and how the later instabilities have been resolved. In "Haircut," Lardner provides closure by signaling the end of the customer's turn in the chair. He provides completeness by using Whitey's final words, including the signal of closure, to provide final resolution to the instabilities by altering the authorial audience's understanding of the resolution that has already been narrated. This altered understanding is a result of Lardner using Whitey's final lines to convert the thematic dimension of Whitey's character into a thematic function. These lines create the second main consequence of the initial progression by tension as Lardner reemphasizes the tension between Whitey and the authorial audience and more subtly recalls his representative status:

> Personally I wouldn't leave a person shoot a gun in the same boat I was in unless I was sure they knew somethin' about guns. Jim was a sucker to leave a new beginner have his gun, let alone a half-wit. It probably served Jim right, what he got. But still we miss him round here. He certainly was a card.
> Comb it wet or dry? (P. 33)

This ending creates an effect more chilling than satisfying first because Whitey's judgment of Jim ("It probably served Jim right, what he got") is made for a reason that misses the mark as widely as his judgments about Jim's character. The chill gets deeper when we reflect that Whitey as representative spokesman can confidently report Kendall's death as accidental and blithely talk about missing the old card only because Doc Stair's declaration has been accepted by the townspeople. And they have accepted the judgment because, like Whitey, they believe that Paul Dickson is a half-wit, a belief based not on Paul's recent behavior but on his having been given that label years ago. Whitey's final comments reveal that the whole sordid episode, begun with Kendall's pursuit and humiliation of Julie Gregg and ended by Paul Dickson's murder of Kendall, has transpired in front of the townspeople's eyes without their recognizing its sordidness. Because no one has been intellectually or morally sensitive enough to understand what happened in the case of Jim Kendall, it is not at all unlikely that a similar sequence of events could occur again. The insensitivity of the good-natured Whitey and by extension of the townsmen he represents is nicely underlined by the story's final sentence, or rather by the swift and matter-of-fact transition from the account of Kendall's death to the business at hand: "Comb it wet or dry?" Like Browning in "My Last Duchess," Lardner is able to make the final signal in the progression contribute to both its closure and completeness, that is, both indicate the narrative's end and reinforce its final effect. From this point, extrapolations to the significance of the story for Lardner's view of both the viciousness and stupidity of small town life are rather straightforward. The more general point I want to emphasize is that Lardner uses both the initial movement by tension and its consequences for the characterization of Whitey to transform the progression of the whole from the tale of a trickster tricked to a tale emphasizing the chilling implications of that event.

Indeed, Lardner's conversion of Whitey's thematic dimension into a thematic function affects the authorial audience's understanding of the resolution still further. Given that Lardner has encouraged us to establish a general pattern of inverting Whitey's judgments, we may initially conclude that our obtuse friend is right for the wrong reason when he says that Jim got what he deserved. Once we begin thinking about how Lardner is using Whitey to reveal ideas about the American small town, we will soon reflect enough to question whether Jim's punishment fits his crimes: despite Jim's cruelties, murder in cold blood seems an excessive punishment. Furthermore, Whitey's representative obtuseness allows Lardner to leave murky the relation between Doc Stair's decision to call the death accidental and his own role as the agent, however unwitting, behind Paul's action: Is Doc simply protecting himself? Has he become another version of Kendall by playing upon the stupidity of the townspeople in his declaration that the death was accidental? Or is he a fit instrument of justice, someone who regrets what he said to Paul but also acknowledges, with Lardner's approval, that justice is better served through his lie than through putting Paul—and perhaps himself—on trial? Lardner's technique does not allow us to answer these questions with any confidence, but this uncertainty adds to rather than detracts from the completeness of the story. The murkiness is appropriate because it contributes further to the unsettling, chilling experience of the narrative, especially the way its ending causes the authorial audience to reconsider its understanding of Whitey, Doc, Jim, Paul, Julie, and the town in which they live. Lardner's view of the viciousness and stupidity of the small town is not accompanied by any easy judgments about its simplicity or transparency.

This claim that the ambiguity about Doc's motives contributes to rather than detracts from the completeness of the story perhaps requires further explanation. With the conversion of Whitey's thematic dimension into a function, the progression gives new importance to the thematic sphere in the story as a whole. Thus, when the ambiguity about Doc contributes to our understanding of Lardner's view of small-town life it contributes to the completeness. If Doc Stair were the protagonist, if the progression centered on instabilities surrounding him and his motives, then this ambiguity would most likely be a sign of incompleteness: some major instability would not be resolved. In Lardner's story, however, the instabilities are resolved; it is the authorial audience's understanding of the resolution that is revised and completed in an appropriate way by our reflections on the residual ambiguity and Whitey's inability to resolve it.

IV

In addition to illustrating the interconnections between character and progression, this discussion of "Haircut" also suggests some guidelines for the next—and largest—step in this study. That step is to develop the theory of character from the framework sketched here through an examination of the range of relations among the mimetic, thematic, and synthetic components of character. Because progression and character are so closely interrelated, I can best encounter the variety of narratives necessary to explore that range by choosing a group of works whose characters collectively raise a multitude of questions about the interrelations of their components and whose progressions follow a variety of different principles. In analyzing these principles of progression as part of explaining the relations among the components of character, the study will adumbrate a theory of progression as well. Furthermore, since, as we have seen in the earlier discussion of Culler and Rader, questions about character and progression are inextricably tied to larger theoretical issues in the interpretation of narrative, my questions about specific characters and progressions need to be linked to more general theoretical questions about the interpretation of narrative.

More specifically, I shall proceed by making a loose division of the main problem of character into two parts and then conclude with a demonstration of how the solutions to the problem can be built upon as we extend the reader's role in the rhetorical transaction of narrative beyond appreciation into resistance. The first part will take as its dominant focus the mimetic-thematic relation, the second will more fully incorporate the synthetic. The division between these parts must be loose because, as the framework sketched above indicates, though the synthetic component can sometimes remain in the background of the work and its analysis, it is nevertheless always present. Furthermore, when in Part II I want to focus on the synthetic-thematic and synthetic-mimetic relationship, the third component will necessarily exert its influence as well.

I have chosen to begin with the mimetic-thematic relationship because it immediately connects this study to a central theoretical issue in the interpretation of narrative, one that clearly involves those who call themselves theorists and those who abhor that label: the practice of thematizing the particulars of the text. Thematizing has been both attacked and celebrated in recent years, and I shall reconsider its pleasures and problems by considering the relation between the mimetic and thematic components of Winston Smith's character in *1984* and of Elizabeth Bennet's in *Pride and Prejudice* in connection with Richard Levin's powerful neo-Aristotelean attack on thematizing. I shall argue that Levin offers a useful corrective to facile thematizing, but that his attack goes too far. In addition, I shall try to demonstrate that the relations between the mimetic and thematic components of Winston Smith and Elizabeth Bennet represent two frequent but distinct developments of these components. The study will turn next to the relation betweeen the mimetic and thematic functions of John Marcher in "The Beast in the Jungle," examining these functions in connection with the celebration of thematizing offered by Robert Scholes in *Textual Power*. My analysis will focus especially on Scholes's twin claims that interpretation proper is thematizing and that the generalizing movement of thematizing ought to continue until one reaches the broadest cultural code one can find applicable to the text. I shall want to modify both claims as I try to show that the analysis of narrative progression complicates the notion that interpretation equals thematizing and that in James' narrative the mimetic functions of the characters do indicate that the generalizing movement of thematizing should stop before we reach the broadest code possible.

In Part II, I shall consider three narratives that foreground the synthetic component of character in different ways and to different degrees. These different kinds of foregrounding also induce further theoretical reflections about the concepts of progression and of audience that I have introduced here and will employ throughout. In *The French Lieutenant's Woman*, the foregrounding of the synthetic occurs through Fowles's exploitation of the differences between the assumptions that the narrative and authorial audiences make about their reading. In *Great Expectations*, the foregrounding occurs through Dickens's wonderfully inventive way with outlandish characters such as Wemmick. In *If on a winter's night a traveler*, the foregrounding occurs through the text's extreme self-reflexiveness.

In discussing Fowles's novel, I shall try to complete the consideration of the mimetic-thematic relationship by accounting for the influence of the synthetic component of character upon it, while also investigating the relations among the audiences of narrative. In considering *Great Expectations*, I shall re-examine my concept of progression by comparing my ideas about textual dynamics with those of Peter Brooks in *Reading for the Plot*, who wants to "impose psychic functioning on textual functioning," and demonstrates the results of that imposition with his own reading of Dickens's novel. Brooks's theory will require me to develop further the ideas about the relation between text and audience that underlie my rhetorical theory, and that are the foundation of this study's claim to offer a more adequate account of what Brooks in his subtitle calls "design and intention in narrative." In examining *If on a winter's night a traveler*, I shall take up the question of audience once again, because Calvino's attempts alternately to blur and emphasize the differences among real readers, narrative readers, and authorial readers indicate that even these distinctions among audiences may not be sufficient to account for the complexity of communication in some narratives, especially his.

In Part III, I shall take up the problem of resisting characters (and authors), as I examine the relations among the components of Catherine Barkley in Hemingway's *A Farewell to Arms*. I shall situate my discussion in the context of Judith Fetterley's feminist critique of Hemingway in *The Resisting Reader*,[20] but it will draw upon virtually all of the principles that have been argued for and demonstrated in Parts I and II. That is, the discussion will reconsider both Fetterly's critique and any more positive view of Catherine by investigating all of Catherine's components and their role in the progression of the whole. Since the evaluation of Catherine must be connected with the evaluation of Frederic, and since that issue is connected with the evaluation of Hemingway's beliefs about the world, the discussion will ultimately address the problems inherent in that last kind of evaluation as well.

By the end of Part III, the range of relations among the components of character and the varieties of narrative progression will have been amply demonstrated; in addition, different kinds of responses to those narrative representations will have been illustrated and argued for. Yet I would make no claim that my nine sample texts represent all the possible relations among the components of character or the full variety of progressive principles. In the concluding chapter, therefore, I will sketch how the analysis might be extended to three especially interesting cases without undertaking a full-bore analysis of any. First, I shall consider the relations among the components of character in a nonfiction narrative such as *The Armies of the Night*, focusing specifically on how Mailer's (re-)creation of himself, his own "mimetic" portrait, is a consequence of the synthetic functions that he wants his character to perform. Second, in a discussion that will pick up on the principles I see underlying Dickens's use of Wemmick, I shall examine the functions of some minor characters in the multiple-plot progression of *Middlemarch*. Third, I shall finish the analysis of character and progression by sketching an account of what happens in a work like *Mrs. Dalloway* where the progression is more lyric than narrative, where the movement is one of gradual revelation of a character yet is still something very different from a dramatic monologue.

Finally, the conclusion will draw together the findings of this book and reconsider both the theory's predictive power and its flexibility for considering new cases, new possibilities of narrative communication. The point to make here is that in taking up questions both theoretical (about thematizing, progression, audience, ideology, evaluation) and practical (about protagonists and secondary characters, Jane Austen and Italo Calvino, Hemingway and Henry James, realism and metafiction), this study does propose to survey a wide territory of narrative theory. It will not offer a full view of every square mile, but it does seek to provide glasses that will enable the reader to discern both the broad outlines of that territory and some close-up views of numerous especially significant sites.

I   The Mimetic-Thematic Relationship and the Thematizing of Narrative

1 Character, Progression, and Thematism: The Cases of *1984* and *Pride and Prejudice*

I

The interpretive maneuver most widely practiced by contemporary critics can be summarized in a two-word slogan: "Always thematize!"[1] To follow the slogan as we begin to look at the relations among the components of character would of course be to give pride of place to the thematic function: the importance of thematizing derives from the assumption that a narrative achieves its significance from the ideational generalizations it leads one to. The same assumption leads one to conclude that the component of character contributing to those generalizations is the most important. More succinctly, if a fictional narrative can claim to work upon the world, then it must base that claim upon its ideational significance, much of which will be carried by the characters.

Yet amid the widespread practice of thematic criticism, there continue to be occasional cogent protests against it, most often on the grounds that it is frequently reductive, that typically it moves one away from the richness of response authors and texts invite their audiences to have. The most forceful protesters have been neo-Aristoteleans, and their alternative practice leads them to give pride of place to the mimetic function of character.[2] For them, narratives are typically representations of actions involving human agents for the purpose of moving their audiences in a particular way. Such emotional responses can also depend crucially on the ideational content of the work, but in the neo-Aristoteleans' view the ideational content is less often made central than the thematists would have one believe: a character is a represented person and the emotions we feel about that character are the emotions we feel about people in life. Although people may have representative significance, they typically cannot be adequately summed up by their representativeness. And the same goes for literary characters.

This disagreement provides a useful starting point for investigating the relation between the mimetic and thematic components of character because it indicates how the relation is connected both to ways of reading and to claims for the importance of literary narrative. Furthermore, although adjudication itself matters less here than investigating the relation between the mimetic and thematic components of character, the attempt to adjudicate will require me to make some careful discriminations about the connections among those components of character and the general progression of a narrative. I shall eventually argue that in order to account for the complex relations of the mimetic and the thematic components of character the alternatives presented by the thematists and the anti-thematists need to be transcended. This argument, however, cannot proceed simply by saying that each side has a piece of the truth and that we need to synthesize those pieces. Instead, it will cause me to reexamine the nature of character and to complicate what I have said in the introduction about the relation between character and progression. I shall begin with an analysis of a work that both the thematists and the Aristoteleans would regard as dominated by theme: Orwell's *1984*. After proposing an explanation of the relation between Winston Smith's functions and the progression of the narrative, I will take up the issues of the dispute as they apply to Elizabeth Bennet's character in *Pride and Prejudice*, a novel about which the thematists and anti-thematists would disagree.

II

What Murray Sperber said in 1980 about the criticism of *1984* remains true today: despite all the attention Orwell's novel has received, its detailed structure has yet to be sufficiently analyzed.[3] For this reason, my account of the progression will be fairly detailed. One of the striking features of that progression is that after Orwell introduces the first major instability in Chapter 1—Winston's thoughtcrime, his beginning his diary—he does not significantly complicate that instability until the eighth and last chapter of Book One, when Winston returns to Mr. Charrington's shop, the place where he bought the diary. This feature is made all the more striking because, with the exception of the segments given over to *the book* of the brotherhood, the remainder of the narrative rather tightly follows the line begun with that crime and continued with Winston's developing relationships with Julia and O'Brien. Analyzing how the narrative progresses in Book One will also illuminate the relationship between Winston's mimetic and thematic functions.

Apart from the introduction of the first instability, the narrative in the first book progresses largely by the introduction and partial resolution of a significant tension. "It was a bright, cold day in April and the clocks were striking thirteen."[4] This first sentence creates a gap between the narrative audience that already knows the year of the action and is already familiar with clocks striking thirteen and the authorial audience for whom these facts are either unknown or unfamiliar. Mark Crispin Miller's discussion of this first sentence[5] points to the significance of April in the British literary tradition from Chaucer to Eliot, a significance which further emphasizes the peculiarity of the weather for the season. Since the authorial audience would be presumed to know that tradition while the narrative audience, located in time after the Party's alteration of the past, would not, the mention of April further emphasizes the gap between the two audiences. This gap also signals a tension of unequal knowledge between author and authorial audience: he and his narrator surrogate know all about this world but plunge into the narrative without orienting us. The tension is heightened as the first few paragraphs work in this gap between narrative and authorial audiences and make references to a poster of someone called Big Brother; a preparation for something called Hate Week; a telescreen; INGSOC; Thought Police; the Ninth Three-Year Plan; and the Ministry of Truth. Our reading is driven in part by a desire to reduce this tension.

Of course the experience of beginning a narrative and being asked to read as if we shared knowledge that we do not actually possess is a common one. Such an experience does, I think, always produce a mild tension, but that tension is often quickly resolved. My claim about *1984* is that the initial defamiliarizations emphasize the tension (the difference between it and other narratives that carry the illusion of occurring in our world is a matter of degree) and that this tension is not—indeed cannot be—quickly resolved. This cognitive tension is both like and unlike the ethical tension that we saw in "Haircut." It functions to propel us forward in the narrative, but because of other signals we are given about Winston as a mimetic character, it orients us toward the acquisition of information that will influence our judgments, expectations, desires, and attitudes about the characters and the instabilities they face. In general, cognitive tension functions in this way in narratives with a strong mimetic component. In narratives like the classic detective story, where the mimetic component is restricted, cognitive tension can be the primary source of the progression. (Of course in such narratives, the cognitive tension does not manifest itself in a gap between authorial and narrative audiences but between both of them and the author.) Ethical tension is typically a sign that the narrative has a strong mimetic component; it is itself one mechanism through which authors induce readers to form judgments, set up expectations, develop desires, adopt attitudes, and so on.

After introducing the major instability of Winston's thoughtcrime (an incident to which I shall return), Orwell's narrative progresses by reducing the tension: rather than immediately showing how the first thoughtcrime leads Winston into a related series of actions, Orwell shows us Winston going about his business in his world, occasionally punctuating the accompanying disclosures about that world by returning to scenes of Winston writing in his diary. By the end of Book One, Orwell has reduced much—though not all—of the tension and simultaneously complicated our understanding of the major instability. In addition, through his references to Julia and O'Brien he has laid the groundwork for further development of the instability.

One of the major ways in which the progression by tension complicates the initial instability is to affect our expectations about Winston's success in eluding the Thought Police. By the end of Book One, we certainly still hope that he will, but we have strong reason to think that he will not. In addition, through maintaining the technique of the opening paragraphs and through representing Winston in numerous contexts, Orwell has also revealed most of Winston's major attributes. The narrative then returns to the progression by instability.

More specifically, before Book One is over, Orwell shows us Winston with his neighbors, Mrs. Parsons and her rabid children; Winston submitting to the morning exercises (Physical Jerks) beamed over the telescreen; Winston working at the Ministry of Truth, where his job is to alter records, especially those contained in newspapers; Winston undergoing the trials of eating lunch in the Ministry's cafeteria; Winston reflecting on the Party's control of the past through its handling of the counterrevolutionaries Jones, Aaronson, and Rutherford; Winston roaming about the proles' quarter of the city until he once again finds himself in Charrington's shop. Through these various scenes Winston frequently reflects on the social and political organization of his world as it impinges on—or indeed, determines and controls—the particular activity he is engaged in; occasionally, Orwell gives us Winston's thoughts about incidents in his own past life such as his vague memory of his mother sacrificing herself for him, and his unhappy marriage to Katherine, who despised sex but thought of procreation as their duty to the Party.

The world revealed through these scenes and incidents is a curious mixture of efficiency and inefficiency, a world with sophisticated technology and a poor standard of living. Telescreens can both transmit and receive, and individuals can be watched vigilantly by the Thought Police, but elevators frequently don't work and food is barely palatable. Winston can rewrite newspaper articles and the historical record can be swiftly altered, but the streets don't get cleaned, and decent medical care for such things as Winston's varicose ulcer seems to be nonexistent. Above all, Oceania in 1984 is a world dominated by the Party and the social structure it has imposed on the province. The basic principle of this structure, we soon learn, is state control over the individual. The relatively poor standard of living signifies both one way of exerting control—it keeps the Party members extremely dependent—and one way the system is execrable.

The telescreens, the enforced Physical Jerks, the ubiquity of Big Brother, the ritual of the Three Minutes Hate, the existence of the Spies and the Thought Police, the creation of Newspeak, the abolition of written laws without the abolition of punishments: all these Party innovations testify to its elaborate—and largely successful—efforts to control the lives of its members. Mrs. Parsons's fanatically loyal children terrorize her. Winston's thought that his friend Syme, a dedicated worker on the new edition of the Newspeak dictionary, will be vaporized simply because he understands the intended effects of the impoverished language points to the truth that, ironically, Syme has himself articulated: "Orthodoxy is unconsciousness." Winston's memories of his mother and his wife indicate how the Party has destroyed the most intimate relationships: Winston thinks that the kind of sacrifice his mother made "had been tragic and sorrowful in a way that was no longer possible. Tragedy, he perceived, belonged to the ancient time, to a time when there were still privacy, love, and friendship, and when the members of a family stood by one another without needing to know the reason. . . . Today there were fear, hatred, and pain, but no dignity of emotion, no deep or complex sorrows" (p. 22). He was not able to develop any deep emotions in his own marriage because Katherine had been so unconsciously orthodox that she could not experience such emotions. Finally, Winston's excursion among the proles illustrates how the Party keeps them occupied with work on the one hand and bread and circuses on the other.

The extent—and success—of the Party's control is sketched more fully in the information about Winston's job, in his remembrance of what happened to Jones, Aaronson, and Rutherford, and in his attempt to find somebody who can remember the time before the Party was in power. As we see Winston at work, we see how the Party controls history. Winston's remembrance of the three counterrevolutionaries dramatizes the consequences of that effort: to control history is to control reality. Although Winston's photograph of the three counterrevolutionaries is concrete evidence that the official version of their history is false, he could not do anything public with that evidence. Furthermore, thinking back to his brief possession of the photograph, Winston muses that the "photograph might not even be evidence." Finally, the impossibility of recapturing history is dramatized in Winston's futile attempt to get the old prole to answer his questions about the past.

By the end of Book One, our knowledge of Winston's world is not complete, but the tension between Orwell and the authorial audience is greatly diminished: we know the kind of world we are reading about, and this knowledge has significant consequences for our understanding of the initial major instability and of Winston's character. We come to understand that to begin the diary is to rebel against the Party, not merely because the diary contains exclamations like "DOWN WITH BIG BROTHER!" but also because the act of writing is an act of individual consciousness and autonomy. Simply by sitting down to write, indeed, by contemplating that act, Winston is guilty of thoughtcrime; he is asserting his selfhood against the Party, which wants to deny that selfhood. The central issues of the whole narrative are gradually defined in the course of Book One: can Winston elude the Thought Police and go on writing the diary, and more important, can he have any sustained existence *as an individual* in this totalitarian society? As the form of the second question indicates, the progression of Book One leads us to read Winston thematically: he comes to represent the individual citizen, and what he does and what happens to him matters to us because of what these things imply about the possibility of individual freedom in totalitarian society. This movement of Book One gives thematic prominence to certain of Winston's attributes, even as Orwell's handling of the point of view emphasizes his mimetic function.

By the end of Book One, the most salient attributes of Winston's character to emerge are his name, his age, his habit of thinking by subconscious association, his intelligence, his concern with the past, his love of beauty, his hatred of the Party, and his optimism; furthermore, though Winston is distinguished from his associates by his intelligence and his resistance to the Party, he is not given any great powers of action—he is a man more ordinary than extraordinary. The first chapter of the novel, indeed its first three paragraphs, establish Winston's name and age—and as noted above in a somewhat different way, they immediately signal to the authorial audience that his world, despite its similarities to our own, is a synthetic construct. Our awareness of the fictionality of the world naturally brings the synthetic component of Winston's character into the foreground of the narrative. This foregrounding combines with other aspects of Orwell's presentation to emphasize some of Winston's thematic dimensions. When we learn in the sixth paragraph that he lives in London, and when the later progression encourages us to regard him thematically, his name and age take on further associations. Combining the extremely common British surname with the first name of England's greatest hero of the 1940s identifies him as what a typical male British citizen of 1984 would be—if there were still a Britain. Since he is thirty-nine, he was born in 1945, and, we can infer, was named for Churchill. The last name, though, emphasizes his ordinariness: this is not Winston Churchill, but Winston Smith. I shall return to the significance of this point after discussing the way Orwell handles the conclusion of the narrative.

Later in the narrative, after Orwell reveals how the Party is destroying the past, and especially after Winston becomes involved with Julia, his age takes on a thematic significance that further defines his representative status. His conversations with Julia indicate that the next generation simply cannot envision life without the Party. Having grown up with the Party as a fact of life, Julia takes it so much for granted that it constrains her ideas of rebellion; until she meets Winston, her goal in life is to manipulate the Party's system rather than overthrow it. She, for instance, pretends to be a rabid member of the Junior Anti-Sex League so that she can have a cover for her various sexual liaisons. Winston, in contrast, with his dim memories of life before the Party, can envision life without it. His response is to do whatever he can—keep his diary, get involved with Julia, attempt to join the Brotherhood—to resist the Party's repression of individuals. His optimism allows him to hope that such resistance may eventually lead to the Party's overthrow, even as his intelligence reminds him that such an outcome is unlikely. This disparity between Winston and Julia clearly marks him off as a member of the last group of citizens to remember life without the Party, the last group that could use that connection to the past as a motive for rebellion. "Who controls the past controls the future." As the narrative progresses, Winston's name and age combine to make him a figure of "the last man in Europe," a phrase that Orwell considered using as the book's title.[6] Consequently, the stakes of the instabilities are raised: Winston's story is not just an exemplary case of what happens when the individual rebels against the totalitarian state but also an account of how the Party responds to one of its last apparently serious threats.

Despite the elements of the opening chapter that foreground its synthetic status, and despite the movement of Book One that places Winston's actions into a broad thematic context, Orwell's initial treatment of Winston himself is directed toward emphasizing his mimetic function. Orwell's own statement about the book aptly describes the effect of the opening pages: "it is in a sense a fantasy but in the form of a naturalistic novel."[7] Orwell relies greatly upon the manipulation of point of view to establish Winston's mimetic function. Winston is consistently the focalizer in the narration; we see things as Winston sees them, though frequently the voice used to express Winston's vision is the narrator's.[8] "Outside, even through the shut window pane, the world looked cold. Down in the street, little eddies of wind were whirling dust and torn papers into spirals" (pp. 3–4). It is Winston who is up at his window looking "down" at the "little eddies of wind," but it is the narrator who describes the wind in those terms. In addition to emphasizing the mimetic function of Winston's character, this technique has other important effects in the progression, but these can be better understood after we look at the progression in Book Two.

At the end of Book One when Winston returns to Mr. Charrington's shop, Orwell begins to shift the main principle of movement from the resolution of tension to the complication of instabilities. Winston builds on his initial "crime" of buying the diary by buying the hundred-year-old glass paperweight, and he begins to think about returning again and again to the shop, even about renting the upstairs room. Book Two opens with Julia's approach to him, and soon they are in love with each other and united against the Party. In addition, O'Brien makes his approach to Winston, and the lovers soon join the Brotherhood. Meanwhile Winston rents Charrington's upstairs room, and he and Julia begin meeting there. With each step, the magnitude of their rebellion and the exercise of their individual freedom (one equals the other) increase, and so of course does the danger that they will be captured. "We are the dead," they remind themselves without fully believing what they are saying. Having established the overarching thematic background in Book One, Orwell here designs the trajectory of the main action around our mimetic interest in Winston and his struggle. And as Orwell confines us to Winston's vision through the point of view, he has us participate in the trajectory of Winston's own emotions in the main action: Like Winston, we not only take pleasure in his relationship with Julia and in his finding an apparently kindred spirit in O'Brien, but we also come to desire deeply the total overthrow of the Party.

At the same time, from the information in Book One about the power of the Party, we develop a strong sense that this positive outcome is not possible. When Winston and Julia are arrested by the Thought Police, we share his feeling that such an event was inevitable, but our knowledge offers no solace for the disappointment we feel. Moreover, even the appropriate surprise of discovering Mr. Charrington to be a member of the Thought Police does not fully prepare us for the new developments of the progression in Book Three, developments that are dependent in large part on Orwell's management of the point of view and that in turn contribute to the emphasis on Winston's mimetic function. Book Three resolves the instabilities by tracing the conversion of Winston's rebellion into his total defeat. Although such a resolution has been implicit in the narrative from early on, Orwell is able to maximize its power by suddenly showing us that the tension between his knowledge of the world and ours has not been resolved as fully as we thought. In consistently restricting us to Winston's vision, Orwell does not give his own authority to Winston's conclusions about the world; we need to recognize that those conclusions are always subject to later revision. In fact, it is because he handles the technique this way that Orwell can legitimately "surprise" us with the truth about Charrington and O'Brien. At the same time, Orwell counts on our erroneously accepting some of Winston's conclusions. For example, in Chapter Two Orwell depicts Winston thinking about the ubiquity of Big Brother: "Even from the coin the eyes pursued you. On coins, on stamps, on the covers of books, on banners, on posters, and on the wrapping of a cigarette packet—everywhere. Always the eyes watching you and the voice enveloping you. Asleep or awake, working or eating, indoors or out of doors, in the bath or in bed—no escape. Nothing was your own except the few cubic centimeters inside your skull" (pp. 19–20). Although we are still clearly being given only Winston's vision here, we are inclined to share it and Orwell does nothing to alter that inclination. The inviolability of one's mind is one of the supposed truths of our world, Winston's thoughtcrime has not yet brought down any punishment on him, and the rhetoric of the passage makes the final sentence a mere concession. We are being told by both Winston and Orwell about the limited freedom the individual has; we accept what we are told, including what the passage regards as the single small exception. Although the rest of Book One tells us a great deal about Winston's world and about the power of the Party, it is not until the very end of the narrative that we learn that even those few cubic centimeters are not one's own. Indeed, the Party's power extends far enough to control not only what one does, not only what one thinks, but also what one feels.

I shall return to discuss the resolution in some detail but even here we can recognize some important effects of the delayed resolution of the tension. In relieving so much of the tension in Book One, Orwell gives us the illusion that we know the worst. When we learn that even our extensive knowledge of the Party's mechanisms of control has underestimated its power, our revulsion from such a totalitarian state becomes even greater—and so too does the effectiveness of the narrative as a warning. In this way the tension is crucial to the mimetic (and emotional) effect of the ending, which in turn Orwell uses to reinforce the thematic point about the threat of totalitarianism.

In general, Orwell's handling of Winston's character follows the pattern outlined here: he emphasizes Winston's mimetic function, increases our involvement with his progression toward his fate as itself an emotionally affecting experience,[9] and then ultimately subordinates that function and our involvement to his communication of a larger thematic point. The relation between the mimetic and the thematic is fairly clear for such attributes as Winston's concern with the past and his love of beauty;[10] perhaps the least obvious and most dramatic illustration of the general pattern occurs in what Orwell does with Winston's attribute of associative thinking, which is itself a significant part of his psychological portrait. Here Orwell immediately establishes this attribute as a significant mimetic trait, but he does not develop its full thematic significance until the final pages of the narrative.

Winston's attribute of associative thinking is established simultaneously with the introduction of the first major instability. Winston's first diary entry describes his trip to the "flicks" the previous night. During the war films, which were depicting various people being shot or hit with bombs or otherwise violently obliterated to the great approval of most spectators, one proletarian started shouting her objections to the film. Winston breaks off his account after saying that the police turned her out; then we are told, "He did not know what had made him pour out this stream of rubbish. But the curious thing was that while he was doing so a totally different memory had clarified itself in his mind" (p. 8). That memory turns out to be a look from O'Brien during that morning's Two Minutes Hate, a look that Winston interprets as a signal that O'Brien is on his side. Winston never figures out the connection between the two events, but Orwell expects his audience to recognize that the scene at the flicks clarifies the scene during the Two Minutes Hate because in each an individual acts in opposition to the hysterical mob surrounding him or her. Orwell never does anything else with Winston's instinctive connection between the two events; and consequently, the association becomes significant largely for the way it adds a psychological complexity to Winston's character. Furthermore, at this stage of the narrative, this important attribute does not have any thematic function.

As the narrative develops, Orwell places this attribute in a rather complex relationship with Winston's optimism. When Winston begins his diary, he tells himself that he is thereby making himself one of the dead; but as I noted above, this admission does not become a conviction until he is actually captured. Instead, he goes on with his acts of rebellion, becoming more and more hopeful about the possibility of eventual success with each passing day. Yet Orwell shows us, through Winston's habits of associative thought, that in another part of himself Winston senses that his optimism is based upon a denial of certain perceptions. In Chapter 7 of Book One, for example, Winston gazes at a portrait of Big Brother which forms the frontispiece of a children's history textbook: "The hypnotic eyes gazed into his own. It was as though some huge force were pressing down upon you—something that penetrated inside your skull, battering against your brain, frightening you out of your beliefs, persuading you, almost, to deny the evidence of your senses" (p. 55). Then he consciously resists these conclusions as his optimism gains the upper hand: "But no! His courage seemed suddenly to stiffen of its own accord." And then: "The face of O'Brien, not called up by any obvious association had floated into his mind" (p.55). Although the vision of O'Brien comes hard upon the heels of his renewed courage, the narrator's comment about the absence of any obvious association directs the audience to supply that association: Winston subconsciously links O'Brien and Big Brother.

In case we have lingering doubts, Orwell shows us at the end of the next chapter that the association can also move in the other direction: Trying to think of O'Brien, whom he now regards as the eventual audience for his diary, Winston focuses on the memory of O'Brien's saying in a dream, "We shall meet in the place where there is no darkness." The nagging presence of the telescreen interferes with his thoughts, and then "The face of Big Brother swam into his mind, displacing that of O'Brien" (p. 70). This reinforced association of the two occurs in the last paragraph of Book One, and thus provides an ominous backdrop to the apparently positive developments of Book Two. Again, though, the general point is that Orwell is using the attributes to increase the psychological realism of his treatment of Winston and thereby to increase the extent of our emotional involvement in his unfolding story.

Before I turn to how Orwell makes the attribute of associative thinking function thematically, I need to expand on my earlier assertion that this attribute is part of Orwell's attempt to create a realistic individual psychology for Winston—even as Orwell leaves it to us to piece together the workings of that psychology. Recall Winston's initial thought after breaking off his first diary entry: "He did not know what had made him pour out this stream of rubbish" (p.8). Later in the narrative Orwell supplies us with the answer: in recounting the scenes where the mother in the movie vainly tries to protect her child who burrows into her and where the proletarian mother in turn tries to protect her children from having to watch such a movie, Winston is recalling his own mother's attempts to protect his sister—and more generally himself as well. The first time he sleeps after beginning the diary, he dreams of watching his mother and sister sink in the bottom of a ship while he is able to stay up and out in the light; later, when Julia brings chocolate to their first tryst, it stirs up "some memory which he could not pin down, but which was powerful and troubling" (p.81). Still later, during one of his visits to the room above Charrington's shop with Julia, he dreams of his mother again and this dream allows him to pin down the earlier memory: it is a memory of the last time he saw his mother, and how on that occasion his own ravenous hunger drove him to take for himself his sister's lesser share of chocolate. What is most vivid in the memory is how Winston's mother embraced and tried to protect his sister, and how even after he snatched her chocolate, his mother went on trying to protect and comfort her. Winston draws a very significant moral at that point: "he did not suppose, from what he could remember of [his mother], that she had been an unusual woman, still less an intelligent one; and yet she had possessed a kind of nobility, a kind of purity, simply because the standards that she obeyed were private ones. Her feelings were her own, and could not be altered from outside. . . . If you love someone, you loved him, and when you had nothing else to give, you still gave him love. . . . The terrible thing that the Party had done was to persuade you that mere impulses, mere feeling were of no account, while at the same time robbing you of all power over the material world" (pp. 109–10).

Yet the significance of Winston's dreams and memory for the narrative are not exhausted in this moral, because they reach beyond these insights to affect our understanding of what happens in Book Three.[11] The whole sequence—journal entry, dream, dim memory, second dream, clear memory—works like the associative thought processes to emphasize Winston's realistic psychology. The particular nature of the dreams and memories adds a significant dimension to our understanding of how and why Winston's betrayal of Julia breaks him. When, faced with imminent attack from the ravenous rats, Winston shouts "Do it to Julia!" he violates something at the core of his values because it is at the core of his own existence: the feeling that he is alive because the woman who brought him into the world and loved him had sacrificed herself for him. Both the power and the repulsiveness of the Party are emphasized by our understanding that Winston had no choice but to act as he did.

The ending of the narrative then takes these attributes of Winston's character that have been working to emphasize his mimetic function and converts them into thematic functions. In the last chapter, Winston has become a figure reminiscent of Jones, Aaronson, and Rutherford. In Chapter 7 of Book One, Orwell describes Winston's recollection of the day he saw the three of them in the Chestnut Tree Café.

> It was the lonely hour of fifteen. . . . The place was almost empty. A tinny music was trickling from the telescreen. The three men sat in their corner almost motionless, never speaking. Uncommanded, the waiter brought fresh glasses of gin. There was a chessboard on the table beside them, with the pieces set out, but no game started. And then, for perhaps half a minute in all, something happened to the telescreens. The tune that they were playing changed, and the tone of the music changed too. There came into it—but it was something hard to describe. It was a peculiar, cracked, braying, jeering note; in his mind Winston called it a yellow note. And then a voice from the telescreen was singing:
>
> "Under the spreading chestnut tree
> I sold you and you sold me
> There lie they, and here lie we
> Under the spreading chestnut tree."
>
> The three men never stirred. But when Winston glanced again at Rutherford's ruinous face, he saw that his eyes were full of tears. And for the first time he noticed, with a kind of inward shudder, and yet not knowing *at what* he shuddered, that both Aaronson and Rutherford had broken noses. (Pp. 52–53)

In the last chapter, Winston sits in the same café, and again it is almost empty at "the lonely hour of fifteen." From time to time, an "unbidden" waiter comes and fills Winston's glass with gin, which has become "the element he swam in," while he fitfully plays a solitary game of chess and listens to the telescreen. He recalls his last, cold, painful visit with Julia, a visit in which they confessed that they had betrayed each other. And then:

> Something changed in the music that trickled from the telescreen. A cracked and jeering note, a yellow note, came into it. And then— perhaps it was not happening, perhaps it was only a memory taking on the semblance of sound—a voice was singing:

"Under the spreading chestnut tree
I sold you and you sold me—"
The tears welled up in his eyes.
(P. 195)

The expected inferences are clear: the song is the Party's way of mocking Winston for betraying Julia, just as it had been mocking Jones, Aaronson, and Rutherford for their own versions of mutual betrayal. More generally, what has happened to Winston in the Ministry of Love is just a variation on what always happens to thought-criminals. Winston has come to represent the inevitable failure of the individual to resist the totalitarian state. Nevertheless, at this point the instabilities created by Winston's rebellion and the Party's response to it are not entirely resolved: the tears are a sign that he is still attached to his former attitudes, that he regrets his betrayal of Julia. If he were to die now, he would die hating Big Brother—and thus, by his own earlier definition, achieve some measure of victory. Orwell works toward the resolution of the instability by following the progress of Winston's thoughts.

First, he gives us one more instance of Winston's associative thought process. Winston's thoughts of the alleged war in Africa— "He had the map of Africa behind his eyelids. The movement of the armies was a diagram: a black arrow tearing vertically southward, and a white arrow tearing horizontally eastward, across the tail of the first" (pp. 195–96)—trigger a subconscious association with a childhood memory. He thinks of an afternoon spent playing with his mother a game called Snakes and Ladders, a game in which the tiddlywinks move vertically and horizontally. "Soon he was wildly excited and shouting with laughter as the tiddlywinks climbed hopefully up the ladders and then came slithering down again. . . . His tiny sister, too young to understand what the game was about, had sat propped up against a bolster, laughing because the others were laughing. For a whole afternoon they had all been happy together, as in his earlier childhood." Then Winston's training at the Ministry of Love takes over: "He pushed the picture out of his mind. It was a false memory" (p. 196).

This reaction to the memory is sharply different from Winston's reactions to his previous memories. As we have seen, those lead him to reflect on the Party's elimination of the human bonds that develop in a social order that allows privacy, friendship, and love. His pushing the memory away signifies a very crucial step in his defeat: under the pressure of his training, he is betraying not only his own prior belief in the integrity of the past but also the bonds that were part of his early private life and part of his identity. His rejection of the memory is also crucial because it represents his own conscious attempt to control his subconscious. In presenting the memory, Orwell is reminding us that Winston's mind has worked in ways that were beyond his control. In presenting Winston's first memory of a happy time during this afternoon of his own dull unhappiness, Orwell is showing us again the power of Winston's subconscious. But when Winston reacts by denying the validity of the memory, his defeat is all but complete.

The final steps come with the telescreen's announcement of Oceania's victory in Africa. In representing Winston's response here, Orwell indicates that Winston's memory is not so easily pushed away; instead, it is perversely transformed and applied to Winston's present situation. Wildly excited in memory, he becomes wildly excited in the present: "in his mind he was running, swiftly running, he was with the crowds outside cheering himself deaf" (p. 197). Happy and content in memory, no longer at odds with his mother and sister, he becomes happy and content in the present, no longer at odds with the Party.[12]

> Ah, it was more than a Eurasian army that had perished! Much had changed in him since that first day in the Ministry of Love, but the final indispensable, healing change had never happened until this moment . . . sitting in a blissful dream, he was back in the Ministry of Love, with everything forgiven, his soul white as snow. He was in the public dock, confessing everything, implicating everybody. He was walking down the white-tiled corridor, with the feeling of walking in sunlight, and an armed guard at his back. The long-hoped-for bullet was entering his brain. (P. 197)

He is ready for the last step of his transformation, the final perverse twist the Party's training produces on his specific memory and his general consciousness.

> He gazed up at the enormous face. Forty years it had taken him to learn what kind of smile was hidden beneath the dark mustache. O cruel, needless misunderstanding! O stubborn, self-willed exile from the loving breast! . . . But it was all right, everything was all right, the struggle was finished. He had won the victory over himself. He loved Big Brother. (P. 197)

This passage appropriately closes and completes the narrative because it not only signals the end of Winston's rebellion but also indicates the extent of the Party's ability to control the individual. It is able to manipulate not just behavior, not just thoughts, but also emotions. It is even able to control the workings of the subconscious mind. In achieving this completion, the narrative transforms the thematic dimension accompanying Winston's trait of associative thinking into a major thematic function. That trait now exists not only to give Winston mimetic plausibility but also to demonstrate the extent of the totalitarian state's power. If it can effect such a transformation in a mind like Winston's that frequently operated in a way that was beyond his own conscious control, its power is enormous indeed. The narrative's warning about totalitarianism becomes even more urgent.

Orwell's handling of vision and voice in the final pages sheds further light on the relation between the mimetic and the thematic functions of Winston's character there. Previously, as the narrative has presented the world of 1984 through Winston's vision, the authorial audience has been asked to share virtually all of Winston's evaluative comments. Here for the first time, our evaluations are diametrically opposed to his. Indeed, since we have been traveling with Winston so closely throughout the narrative, if Orwell had not been so insistent on the state's control over the individual, we ourselves might have felt betrayed by Winston in this passage. Even within the final passage Orwell takes steps to block that response. In the sentence represented by the ellipsis above, the narrator leaves Winston's vision and describes him from the outside: "Two gin-scented tears trickled down the sides of his nose" (p. 197). The outside view provides a comment on his internal elation; we see him not as triumphant but as pathetic. The emotions generated by our vision work to support our own opposition to the totalitarian system that reduced Winston to this state. Again, in short, Orwell develops the mimetic response and then subordinates it to his thematic purpose.

This reading of the ending and the way it affects both the previous mimetic characterization of Winston and the indictment of totalitarianism suggest a further conclusion about Orwell's use of mimetic and thematic elements of Winston's character. At first glance, it may seem surprising that Orwell does not make Winston a man with greater powers of action. If he is to be a figure of the last man in Europe who succumbs to the power of the state, and if his losing struggle is to be as tragic as possible, then, we might argue, Orwell ought to have made him more formidable. Although I believe that such a strategy might have also been effective, I think that Orwell was constructing the narrative along different lines—and toward a different kind of effectiveness. For Orwell the greater power of the totalitarian state is finally a foregone conclusion. He builds some suspense about whether Winston can succeed in his rebellion by restricting us to Winston's point of view for most of the narrative and by not fully resolving the tension about the nature of the totalitarian state until Book Three, but the greater emphasis in the narrative is on what the state does to the individual, common man. In this respect, Winston's mental life is of more significance than his powers of action. By showing us what the state does to an individual with such a mental life, an individual who finally is not a serious threat to the Party, Orwell places the burden of his indictment precisely on the dangers that the totalitarian state poses for Everyman.

In conclusion, the narrative progression of *1984* eventually gives the greatest weight to the thematic functions of Winston Smith's character, but the effects of those functions also depend crucially on Orwell's ability to make Winston function as an effective mimetic character. At the same time, the progression develops different thematic functions from different attributes: his age and his ordinariness make him a certain kind of representative figure; his love for the past is used to develop the thematic point about the connection between the Party's control of the individual and the Party's control of history; his associative thinking is used to develop the thematic point about the Party's control over the thoughts and feelings of the individual. Moreover, all these separate functions work together as part of the narrative's exploration of the threat of totalitarianism. In this respect, we might say that the separate functions eventually run together in a Grand Central Function as Winston becomes the embodiment of individual actions and desires that the totalitarian state seeks to crush. The narrative of *1984*, in other words, presents one form that the mimetic-thematic relationship can take. More generally, it presents one remarkable example of how one component of character can be subordinated to another without that subordination restricting the component, for Orwell can only communicate the full thematic significance of Winston's character through his extended development of his mimetic component.

III

The most immediately relevant part of these conclusions for the discussion of *Pride and Prejudice* is that the thematists would claim that they apply, *mutatis mutandis*, to Elizabeth Bennet. For them, Elizabeth is a character whose individuality is joined to a representative function, and their analyses seek to explain the precise nature and significance of that function. In order to understand why the neo-Aristoteleans object to that practice, let us look at some thematic readings of the novel and the case against such readings.

In *The Improvement of the Estate* Alistair Duckworth sets forth a well-executed example of thematic reading. He argues that through her representation of Elizabeth Bennet's education Jane Austen communicates her vision of a "properly constituted society."[13] According to Duckworth, Austen insists that such a society "emerges only from the interaction of cultural discipline and individual commitment, and only when inherited forms receive the support of individual energy do they carry value. Conversely, however, . . . individual energy must be generated within social contexts, for, lacking social direction and control, it turns too easily to withdrawal from society, or to irresponsibility and anarchy" (p. 132). Duckworth maintains that this dialectic between cultural discipline and individual energy is played out through Austen's representation of Darcy and Elizabeth respectively. "Only when Elizabeth recognizes that individualism must find its social limits, and Darcy concedes that tradition without individual energy is empty form, can the novel reach its eminently satisfactory conclusion" (p. 118). Duckworth's reading focuses on how Elizabeth's recognition comes about, on how Darcy both possesses and learns to modify a "proper pride," and on how the same dialectic between individual energy and social control is at work in other elements of the novel, especially in the motif of laughter. For Duckworth, in short, though Austen is writing a comedy, what is important in the comedy is not the characters as people but the characters as ideas. Furthermore, his particular thematic view of *Pride and Prejudice* exemplifies a general thematic view of comedy, one that sees the genre as largely an affirmation of societal values as it depicts individuals becoming integrated into a social community.

Susan Morgan's reading of Elizabeth's character provides a useful second look at thematism because Morgan explicitly sets her reading in opposition to Duckworth's. "To understand *Pride and Prejudice* in terms of some ideal blend of the individual and the social is to speak of finalities about a writer who herself chooses to speak of the possible, the continuous, the incomplete."[14] More specifically, "if Mr. Darcy is to represent society and Elizabeth a rebellious individualism, how can we account for the fact that the first breach of society's rules is made by Mr. Darcy, when he insults Elizabeth within her hearing at the Meryton ball?" (p. 80). For Morgan the central issue of the novel is the relation between freedom and intelligence, or more particularly, involvement and perception, and this issue receives its fullest expression through Austen's presentation of Elizabeth's character. Like her father, Elizabeth initially believes that "understanding, intelligence, and perception depend on being independent of their objects" (p. 83), and she wants above all to be an intelligent observer. Yet the action of the novel shows Elizabeth learning that she is never fully detached from but "always involved" with the objects of her perception (p. 84). Even after the essential lesson is learned through Darcy's letter, Elizabeth makes mistakes of perception and judgment—as in her decision not to expose Wickham—but "the difference is that Elizabeth no longer sees her world as a place of easily discovered folly from which in self-defense as much as in amusement she must stand apart if she is to see the truth. She has come to value the connections and particularities which inform truth and to understand the lesson of Hunsford that a lively intelligence is personal and engaged" (p. 104). With this new attitude, Elizabeth comes to discover her own affection for Darcy, an affection which leads to her expression of gratitude for what he did on Lydia's—and her family's—behalf and from there to Darcy's second proposal. Morgan finds this story of a heroine giving up her freedom from being involved to be "most appropriately a love story" (p. 83), but, like Duckworth, Morgan clearly locates its value and the importance of its characters in the ideas they represent.

Presented with this disagreement between Duckworth and Morgan, Richard Levin would respond by saying "a pox on both your houses." Levin's attack on thematism occurs in *New Readings vs. Old Plays*, a book whose project is to examine "in some sort of rigorous way, the basic assumptions, techniques, and consequences" (p. ix) of three interpretive approaches to Renaissance drama—the ironic, the historical, and the thematic.[15] Since he follows his plan of isolating assumptions, techniques, and consequences, his case against thematic readings of Renaissance drama also applies to such readings as Morgan's and Duckworth's. Because Levin's argument amplifies and updates such early attacks on thematism as Keast's and Crane's,[16] it offers me the opportunity to examine some problems with both thematism and anti-thematism as they influence our understanding of a character such as Elizabeth Bennet.

Levin's case against thematism derives much of its force from his implicit application of the neo-Aristotelean distinction between mimetic and didactic works to thematic criticism. The distinction divides all works into one of two general classes: those organized mimetically, that is, to represent characters in action for the sake of the emotions generated by that representation, and those organized thematically, that is, to represent characters in action for the sake of some ideational purpose such as convincing the audience of the truth of some proposition or ridiculing objects external to the representation. In one respect, Levin's argument is that the thematists typically treat mimetic works as if they were didactic, though, as will be evident, he would find some of the methods of thematism inappropriate for many didactic works as well.

The major flaw Levin finds in the thematic approach is contained in what he identifies as its major assumption: literary works representing characters and actions are not *really* about those characters and actions but rather about some abstract idea such as jealousy, irresolution, ambition, honor, appearance and reality, the individual and society, perception and involvement, and so on. The basic technique of thematic reading, employed by both Duckworth and Morgan, and called the thematic leap by Levin, follows naturally from this assumption: "it consists of seizing upon some particular components of the drama and making them the representatives or exemplars of the general class, which then become the subject of the play and the critic's analysis" (p. 23). Duckworth and Morgan make the leap not from any single component alone but from character and incident considered together; in this respect, their critical reasoning is both more complex and more typical than Levin's description would suggest. But his essential point remains unaffected by this modification.

Levin argues that the procedure is flawed because it is arbitrary: the work itself does not provide a sufficient basis for the thematist to choose one general idea rather than numerous others, and thus the critic may leap from the particulars to a multitude of possible thematic platforms. The first problem that this arbitrary leap creates for the thematist is one of showing why his or her thematic interpretation should be preferred over others. Levin contends that a thematist has only two ways to solve the problem and both are unsatisfactory. A thematist can claim greater centrality for his reading by claiming either that the chosen theme corresponds to more parts or aspects of the work than previous thematic interpretations—this is Morgan's strategy with Duckworth's reading—or that it encompasses the previous candidates for thematic center. The problem with the second strategy is that either the relation between abstractions cannot be so easily ordered (does the thematic pair freedom and intelligence encompass perception and involvement or vice versa or neither?) or the move up the ladder of abstraction has nowhere to stop. The problem with the first strategy is that it may well show some flaws in a rival reading without validating the proposed one. When Morgan "corrects" Duckworth's reading, she gives the appearance of providing greater support for her own; but that support is finally insufficient because the central theme Morgan claims to find—the relation between perception and involvement—also exists at too great a distance from the particulars. Levin concludes this part of his case against thematism by asserting that when we examine the various themes purported to be central to any one work, "we will have to conclude that any or all or none of them could be considered central, which is equivalent to admitting that the concept of central theme has no real meaning here" (p. 41).

Levin extends his objections to thematism by criticizing the typical way thematists build their positive case for their reading, i.e., their thematic analyses of structure. These analyses, Levin explains, come in "two basic varieties, which might be called the homogeneous and the dialectical" (p. 42). In the homogeneous account, which might be described as "the same damn thing over and over again," all the elements of a work—imagery, characters, incidents, plot, etc.—directly embody or mirror or encapsulate the central theme. In dialectical accounts such as Duckworth's and Morgan's, the various parts of the work are regarded as heterogeneous and in interaction with each other, an interaction that, in the thematist's view, is designed to exemplify the central idea. The dialectical account of structure itself takes two basic shapes, one schematic, the other sequential. In the schematic reading, exemplified by Duckworth, the basic opposition of two ideas is reflected at various levels and in various elements of the text—thus, for Duckworth, the motif of laughter participates in the dialectic between individual and society—and this opposition is consistently resolved in the same way. In the sequential reading, exemplified by Morgan, the thematist assumes that the thematic structure has a "distinct temporal movement which corresponds to the play's line of action" (p. 49). The typical pattern here is for the critic to identify a basic conflict between two ideas and then to argue that the action of the work dramatizes and finally resolves the conflict.

Levin identifies two main problems with the homogenizers: (1) in most cases these critics have to ride roughshod over differentiations which exist in the "literal structure" of the literary works; (2) the unity found by these critics is of the most general—and easy—sort: "it is like the unity of a heap of pennies, which may be called 'one' only in the sense that every object in the heap partakes of penniness; and it is a nominal unity because the number or arrangement of the pennies can be changed without affecting the oneness of the heap or its penniness" (p. 46).

The chief difficulty Levin finds with the dialectical accounts of structure is that they inevitably introduce distortion of the textual facts. His point in effect is that these readings take the "high priori" road, manipulating those facts to fit the conceptions rather than letting the conceptions emerge, *if possible*, from the facts. The distortion is all but inevitable because the thematic assumption renders the literal facts relatively inconsequential. For the thematist "the particular facts of the play take on significance only as they 'symbolize' or 'embody' the one governing Idea floating above them that gives the play its meaning" (p. 52). Morgan herself shows that Duckworth's thematic conception distorts details of Darcy's characterization. Levin, in turn, would point out that Morgan's thematic categories lead her to some distortions, or at least inconsistencies, the most obvious of which involve Elizabeth's attitudes toward Wickham. Morgan declares that "because Austen depicts both Elizabeth's credence and her feelings in the familiar and suspect language of sentimental fiction we must conclude that Elizabeth no more seriously believes Wickham's tale than she believes she is in love with him" (p. 91). Later, however, Morgan argues that "the worst moment of Elizabeth's objectivity is her letter to Mrs. Gardiner telling of Wickham's defection to Miss King. Her sisters, she says, are more hurt than she for they 'are young in the ways of the world, and not yet open to the mortifying conviction that handsome young men must have something to live on, as well as the plain.' It is a terrible sentence, terrible in its distance from her feelings, its self-satisfied realism, its 'way of the world' " (p. 98). Morgan herself, Levin would maintain, is manipulating Elizabeth's feelings to keep them traveling smoothly along her high priori thematic road.

In concluding his attack, Levin observes that the chief disadvantage of thematism is the very process of abstraction upon which it is based. The process is so disadvantageous because it requires the critic to operate at a considerable distance from the imaginative experience offered by the work and consequently to have little to say about that experience. Thus, instead of enabling us to enrich and refine our understanding of our experience, thematism removes us from that experience and often distorts it.

Levin's argument, even as presented in this truncated version, is damaging to the thematists: thematic leaping is methodologically unsound because it encounters so little resistance from textual gravity; because it is not adequately grounded in texts, it cannot make good its claims to offer insight into their structure. However, as Levin's own comments on the rivalry between thematic readings instruct us, the fact that thematic reading is unsound does not necessarily mean that his alternative—eliminating almost all talk of themes—will itself be satisfactory. Furthermore, in considering the limits of his alternative, we need to ask whether he has overdone his attack.

Concerned as he is with criticizing other modes of analysis, Levin gives only a brief sketch of his positive neo-Aristotelean program. He does, however, offer a fuller sketch of his ideas about character as he considers a possible problem in his argument. In insisting so strongly that characters as possible people are part of the literal particulars of a work, Levin is vulnerable to the charge that he ignores the role of general ideas in our experience of character. Aware of the risk, Levin openly maintains that characters can have or participate in what he refers to as a universal dimension. (I might note in passing that the reference is misleading since the universal, upon closer scrutiny, is usually a culture-bound phenomenon and sometimes a class-bound one.) "Although I have been arguing that the kind of play we are dealing with presents the particular actions of particular characters, those actions and characters must incorporate some more general component or we could not understand them, much less be moved by them. We could never 'recognize' Lear, for instance, if we could not relate his personal traits and thoughts and feelings to general ideas or categories, derived from our past experience (both real and vicarious), which we bring to the play—ideas of kingship, fatherhood, age, rage, love, and many other abstractions including even appearance and reality" (pp. 75–76). The trouble with the thematists, for Levin, is that they "reduce or assimilate the particulars to these general ideas." Or "in other words, they solve the problem of the relationship of the particular to the general in literature by sacrificing the former to the latter. But our actual response to these plays appears to be just the opposite—we use the general ideas to understand the particular actions and characters, which are the primary focus of our attention. For we do not see Lear as the representative of the ideas we bring to bear upon him; although we recognize him by means of these ideas, we at the same time recognize that he is not completely contained under them, that he is something unique in our experience" (p. 75). For Levin the universality of characters refers "not to the inclusiveness of the idea or class they represent but to the breadth of their appeal. . . . And this is not a function of the typicality of the characters, but of their richness, complexity, roundedness, completeness, depth, uniqueness—all the terms we employ to distinguish a successfully individualized character from a class stereotype" (p. 76).

This sketch has a certain appeal, but finally it also fails to do justice to the question of universality, and in that failure shows the constricting effect of the mimetic-didactic distinction. Levin's argument seems to exclude possibilities without even considering them, perhaps because the distinction does not allow them to be seen, or perhaps because to take these possibilities seriously would jeopardize the validity of the distinction. General ideas, Levin says, can be used to recognize a mimetic character like Lear, but then their work is finished. Indeed, if one believes in the mimetic-didactic distinction, their work *must* be finished; if their work continued, the general ideas would then be a significant part of the plot, and the movement of the work would have to be conceived as not just a movement of action but also a movement of thought. If, however, we look at the problem of universality without any prior commitment to the mimetic-didactic distinction, we can remain open to the possibility that our experience of Lear may depend on Shakespeare's representation of his rich individuality, on our *bringing* ideas of kingship, fatherhood, age, rage, love, and so on to the play and also on the way the play *makes active use* of these ideas in its representation of the protagonist and then emphasizes them or downplays them in the progressive unfolding of his struggle. That Lear is a character who is more than the embodiment of general ideas does not necessarily mean that he is not also such an embodiment. In short, Levin's belief in the mimetic-didactic distinction leads him to present an either/or choice when a both/and solution is more likely to be adequate.

Perhaps even more troubling is that Levin's commitment to the distinction hinders him from making useful discriminations even among so-called mimetic works. It is possible that in some works the appeal of character may be based on the process of invoking and transcending general ideas that he describes, whereas in others it may be based on the process of invoking and staying with general ideas that I have described. Although Levin's case against thematism still remains persuasive, we need to recognize that if the thematists solve the problem of the relation between the general and the particular by sacrificing the particular to the general, Levin solves it by sacrificing the general to the particular. Indeed, the both/and approach to the problem of the general and particular as it applies to character seems more in keeping with the principles enunciated by the founding father of Levin's critical school when he claimed that poetry was more philosophic than history because it would recount not what Alcibiades did and suffered but what such and such a man would do and suffer according to the laws of probability and necessity.

As we turn to consider what the both/and approach to character means for our understanding of Elizabeth Bennet's character, we ought to be wary of simply concluding that we need a reading of *Pride and Prejudice* that consists of equal parts thematism and mimesis. My turn away from that recipe and into the novel will follow the progression, giving a special emphasis this time to the movement generated by the opening chapter.

IV

That chapter introduces two different kinds of instabilities, one local, the other global. A local instability—in this case, Mr. Bennet's apparent refusal to go call on Mr. Bingley—generates the narrative progression for a scene or two and is then quickly resolved, while a global instability—in this case, Bingley's moving into the neighborhood—is one that gets complicated by later action. Each instability in this chapter has a significant effect on the authorial audience's expectations about the ensuing narrative, but those effects can only be appreciated by looking both at their relation to each other and at the influence exerted by Austen's handling of the devices of disclosure—the narrator's commentary and the dialogue between the Bennets.

The global instability is introduced in the third sentence of the chapter which is also the first line of dialogue, "My dear Mr. Bennet, . . . have you heard that Netherfield Park is let at last?" The famous first sentence—"It is a truth universally acknowledged that a single man in possession of a good fortune must be in want of a wife"—and its less famous but equally important follow-up—"However little known the views or feeling of such a man on his first entering a neighborhood, this truth is so firmly fixed in the minds of the surrounding families that he is considered the rightful property of some one or other of their daughters"[17]—provide us with a general pattern of social attitudes and behavior, a particular instance of which we now infer that Mrs. Bennet will supply. The local instability, introduced with Mr. Bennet's uncooperative reaction to his wife's news, is foregrounded in the chapter, but even as Austen takes us through the various thrusts and parries of the Bennets' conversation, she directs our attention beyond their drawing room toward the possibilities and questions raised by Bingley's arrival: What are his views upon settling at Netherfield? Does Elizabeth, whom Mr. Bennet singles out as his favorite, share either her mother's or her father's views toward the marriage market? How interested are the Bennet daughters in getting married? Just what difference will Bingley's presence make for the family and the neighborhood in general? And so on.

This development of the global instability within the complication of the local one is a sign of Austen's characteristic narrative economy, but we need to ask what she gains by being economical in this way. The local instability is after all resolved swiftly and easily in the beginning of the next chapter when the narrator tells us that Mr. Bennet was among the first to call on Bingley and had always intended to visit him. First, the humor with which the dialogue is conducted—and which is topped off by the resolution of the local instability—helps establish our expectations about the progression of the whole narrative. We are reading comedy with an edge here. The ironic first sentence is bright and sparkling but not entirely light. And this description applies as well to Mr. Bennet's voice in the dialogue, which in part merges with the narrator's voice. While the edge is maintained, Mrs. Bennet's reactions to some of Mr. Bennet's speeches indicate that although he is not making her happy, his opposition is not seriously threatening her welfare: When he jests that Mr. Bingley might like her better than her daughters, she replies, "My dear, you flatter me. I certainly *have* had my share of beauty, but I do not pretend to be anything extraordinary now" (p. 2). And the resolution of the dialogue gives Mr. Bennet, with whom we have sided, the last word. Although we could not yet predict with full confidence that the global instability will always be treated within the boundaries of this particular comic context, the first chapter does make a substantial contribution to the stability of that context.

Perhaps more important, by foregrounding the local instability, Austen is able to raise at the outset of the narrative important ideational concerns that we then pay attention to as the narrative develops. In fact, part of the edge in the comedy results from the introduction of these issues: the importance for a young woman in this society to be well-married, the openly acquisitive attitude toward single men displayed by a member of established family. Austen also uses the way that the Bennets play out the positions taken in the opening ironic statement to affect our immediate judgments and our understanding of much that happens later. Mrs. Bennet of course repeats much of the language of the narrator's introduction—"a single man of large fortune;" "I am thinking of his marrying one of [our girls]"—and so comes to represent one of those who do not get the irony of the opening because she lives by the creed Austen is ironically undercutting. By having Mr. Bennet take the narrator's view of the marriage market, Austen can then use his brief phrase about Elizabeth to arouse our expectations about her eventual importance in the global instability introduced in the chapter: when the surrogate for the narrative voice affectionately singles her out as more sensible than the others, we take greater notice of her.[18] By the same logic of voices, Mrs. Bennet's denial of Elizabeth's superiority functions to confirm it.[19] Finally, by presenting the global instability by means of the dialogue between this ill–matched couple, Austen makes a further reflection on the values of Mrs. Bennet: The values and concerns of the majority in the marriage market begin at the bank and stop at the altar. Although we may get a marriage plot here, the narrative has no illusions about the inevitability of marital bliss. Thus, the first chapter begins a progression that is generated by the seemingly autonomous acts of individual characters but that immediately implicates those acts in an exploration of thematic issues. The precise relation of the mimetic and the thematic is of course not yet clear, but the chapter gives a strong signal that both will be significant parts of the progression.

The economical and subtle craft of the first chapter remains in evidence throughout the rest of the narrative, but by the standards of modern narratives its general movement is fairly straightforward—and readily seen. Some basic instabilities of character and situation are introduced in the opening chapters; these instabilities are further complicated as the narrative progresses until a turning point is reached, and then the instabilities are resolved with the establishment of a new stable situation. But note that even this general description of the progression indicates an important difference from the movement of *1984*. Where the initial movement of Orwell's narrative is provided by the arousal and resolution of tensions, a movement that places the later action clearly within a broader thematic context, the movement here is generated through instability and consequently follows the mimetic and thematic interests without clearly subordinating one to the other.

More concretely, Elizabeth's fortunes begin to fall almost as soon as she meets Darcy and has her pride injured by him (Vol. I, chapt. 3); they continue to fall as she continues her misjudgments of his character and endorses Wickham's view of him; and finally, they hit bottom in the first proposal scene (the exact halfway point of the narrative) in which she proudly refuses Darcy, accusing him of ruining Wickham's life and Jane's happiness. Elizabeth's fortunes begin to change after the proposal, when Darcy is able to alter her opinion of him through his letter explaining his conduct and, as we learn later, is also able to alter his arrogance; the reversal continues as her feelings for Darcy are further altered, first, by her visit to Pemberly, which brings renewed contact with Darcy and the discovery of his changed manner, and second, by her discovery of his role in Lydia's marriage to Wickham; then, Elizabeth reaches a state of final happiness—as defined by the novel—in her marriage to Darcy.

Within this general pattern, Austen accomplishes three tasks that significantly affect the way we respond to the developing narrative: (1) she subordinates the initial global instability—Bingley's moving into Netherfield and becoming attracted to Jane Bennet—to a later one—Darcy accompanying Bingley and injuring Elizabeth's pride; consequently, the complication and resolution of that first instability contribute to the complication and resolution of the more central one involving Elizabeth and Darcy; (2) she reassures us that Elizabeth's fortunes will never be irrecoverably damaged; (3) she exploits the ensuing gap between our perception of Elizabeth and her situation and her own perception of herself and situation. These last two steps allow Austen to represent Elizabeth reflecting on the serious negative consequences of her rash judgments while never threatening our own sense that the consequences will not be disastrous.

As my longer look at the first chapter indicates, the omissions in this description are enormous, but my purpose here is simply to offer a sketch of the progression that will provide a useful background for a closer look at the relation between the mimetic and thematic components of Elizabeth's character. As we look at her character, we shall be required to consider the progression more closely.

Elizabeth's character is composed of these main attributes: she is the twenty-year-old daughter of a gentleman and of a woman whose father was in trade, a twenty-year-old who possesses (1) a greater degree of independence from the norms governing the marriage market, including a greater independence from the influence of rank and social prestige, than anyone else in her social sphere; (2) "more quickness of observation" than all her sisters and "less pliancy of temper" than Jane (p. 9); (3) "a lively, playful disposition which delights in anything ridiculous" (p. 7); (4) a strong pride in her own abilities; and (5) a capacity to be honest with herself about her own faults. To this list of frequently noted attributes, I would add two less often commented upon: a capacity for feeling emotions of all kinds that exceeds what any other character has; and a tendency to give immediate voice to her emotions. We see these linked attributes throughout the narrative. They appear, for example, in the ardor with which she meets Wickham's account of Darcy's injuries to him, and in the agitation she feels after reading Darcy's letter, but they are probably most evident on three occasions: (1) in her response to Charlotte's news that she is to marry Mr. Collins: "Engaged to Mr. Collins! my dear Charlotte— impossible!" (p. 87); (2) during the first proposal in her angry response to Darcy's haughtiness; and (3) in her surprising outpouring of her grief to Darcy after she learns of Lydia's flight with Wickham.

These attributes also exist as mimetic traits that coalesce to make Elizabeth not just a plausible person but also one of the most lovable characters in English fiction: the independence and the pride give free rein to the quickness of observation and the playful disposition, even as her honesty and her capacity for feeling show us that she is more than just light and bright and sparkling. When one adds to this combination of traits the fact that she acts effectively in a world where most of the real power is wielded by men, one has a good understanding of her appeal. Yet this is not the whole story of her character. For just as the foregrounded mimetic interests of the novel's first chapter are located within some larger thematic concerns so also do most of Elizabeth's mimetic traits simultaneously perform thematic functions. And these thematic functions do much to determine the complex effect produced by the progression of the whole novel.

Elizabeth's independence from the norms of the marriage market is most clearly seen for the first time in her refusal of Mr. Collins's proposal, despite the importunities of her mother and the possible solution it offers to the problem of the Bennet estate being entailed to him. Because Collins himself is such an odd mixture of pride, obsequiousness, and bad judgment, the thematic significance of Elizabeth's independence does not begin to appear until Charlotte accepts his proposal. Once Charlotte's acceptance shows us what even a highly sensible, perceptive, and intelligent woman would do when facing the prospect of spinsterhood in this provincial society, and once that acceptance makes Elizabeth feel that their friendship has been permanently altered, Elizabeth's stand for independence becomes not just a natural choice for any woman but a choice for a certain kind of woman. Elizabeth's independence, clearly endorsed by Austen even as she treats Charlotte with sympathy and understanding, comes to represent one kind of admirable stance toward the marriage market—one that rejects the views of a Mrs. Bennet and a Charlotte, and instead insists on dealing in the market on one's own terms rather than on those of the men or of the society in general. Where Winston Smith's thematic function evolved from his status as a representative person of a certain age, value-system, and ability, Elizabeth here becomes a possible person who embodies an abstract idea.

The thematic function of Elizabeth's independence is then a very important part of the first proposal scene. With Charlotte's action as a backdrop to this scene, which occurs in her house, and with Darcy's expectation that she could not possibly refuse him, we come to appreciate how rare and admirable an act it is for a woman of Elizabeth's age and social position to reject an offer of marriage from a gentleman of Darcy's income and social consequence. To be sure, Elizabeth is not thinking of these things at the moment of her refusal—she is too angry with Darcy's manner of expressing himself, too prejudiced against him even to consider his offer tempting. But "she is not insensible to the compliment of such a man's affection" (p. 131), and we remain aware of this thematic background. Indeed, I think that the presence of this thematic function here helps explain why Elizabeth, in spite of her seriously prejudiced view of Darcy, nevertheless remains essentially admirable in the scene. She is wrong in her judgments of him, wrong because her wounded pride has made her eager to believe Wickham's slander and ready to give Darcy all the blame for Jane's disappointed hopes about Bingley; yet, even apart from Darcy's unattractive haughtiness, Elizabeth's distinctive strength overshadows these misjudgments.

Since the principle underlying Austen's use of Charlotte will be one that we will return to in the discussion of Wemmick in Chapter 4 and of Fred Vincy and Mary Garth in the conclusion, it is worth a further look. Except in the mechanical sense of allowing Austen to bring Elizabeth and Darcy within the same social circle after Bingley's departure from Longbourn, Charlotte's decision to marry Collins does not directly affect the complication of the instabilities between Elizabeth and Darcy. Its more significant contribution to the progression is to alter the authorial audience's understanding of those instabilities, an alteration that emphasizes the thematic component of Elizabeth's mimetically motivated action. In short, Charlotte's decision is a crucial part of the progression, even though it does not directly affect the outcome of the main action. Austen's use of Charlotte here thus illustrates what we might call the Principle of Indirect Affective Relevance.

The narrative brings the thematic function of Elizabeth's independence to the foreground when Lady Catherine comes to Longbourn to order Elizabeth to give up any idea of marrying Darcy. Elizabeth's ability to stand up to Lady Catherine—indeed, to get the better of her—is impressive without being surprising, and at first the scene appears to be merely giving us the pleasure of watching Elizabeth overmatch Lady Catherine while reinforcing the point about her admirable independence. But with Austen's characteristic blend of narrative economy and appropriateness, the scene becomes a step toward the engagement of Darcy and Elizabeth after Lady Catherine informs Darcy of the "perverseness and assurance" (p. 253) with which Elizabeth responded to her attempted persuasion. Because Elizabeth's trait of independence thus becomes one means by which she achieves her happiness, the thematic function resulting from this trait is further developed. Austen asks us not only to admire this kind of woman but also to believe that such a woman may in fact achieve a fate commensurate with what she deserves.

The first conclusion we may draw, then, is that Austen's representation of Elizabeth as a consistently mimetic character is fused with her use of that character in exploring and exemplifying thematic issues. We not only bring general ideas to this work and its characters, but, contrary to what Levin claims, the work itself takes up some of those ideas and develops them in its progressive unfolding of the characters in action. The second conclusion we may draw is that this recognition provides a superior account of the problem of the "universal" than either Levin's or the thematists'. The representative component of literature is a result neither of the direct correlation between particulars and general ideas nor of rich individuality alone but rather of characters whose mimetic and thematic dimensions both get converted into functions. Elizabeth, then, can be both a representative of the idea of individual independence and a possible person, without either function restricting the other.

This conclusion may draw further validity from a third one which can be quickly seen by a brief consideration of the thematic functions resulting from almost any one of Elizabeth's other attributes. Take, for example, her pride in her own abilities. Even novice thematists will be be able to tell us that Elizabeth serves to exemplify both the strengths and weaknesses of pride. On the one hand, the pride enables her to maintain her independence, but, on the other, it is the source of most of her misjudgments in the narrative: she is willing to believe Wickham because Darcy has injured her pride; then once set on the track of believing in his villainy she has too much pride in her own judgment to question her belief until she is given the severe jolt of Darcy's letter. This rather obvious thematic function together with the presence of the function of Elizabeth's independence and the functions of her other attributes shows that Elizabeth's mimetic and thematic functions have a complex relationship—or at least one noticeably different from that between Winston Smith's mimetic and thematic functions. In Elizabeth's case, the thematic functions do not combine into a single function or even into a hierarchy of functions supporting one central point, but instead are rather disparate.

The concept of a central theme for this novel is a misleading one not because all the themes one may claim to find in it are the result of arbitrary leaping from particulars to generalities but because the progression of the novel generates a multiplicity of diverse themes, which move in and out of the foreground of the narrative at different points in the progression. As for so-called universality, the "richness" of a character that Levin appeals to as a sign that such universality is a function of mimetic individuality can now be reconceived as equally the product of multiple thematic functions.

This conclusion indicates that the mimetic-didactic distinction is far too rigid to account for the complexity of effects generated by a narrative such as *Pride and Prejudice*. Indeed, given that *Pride and Prejudice* is a virtual paradigm case of what the neo-Aristoteleans call an "action" as distinct from an "apologue" (the terms are from Sheldon Sacks)[20] such as *1984*, my analysis suggests that the concept of the action needs to be revised. For Sacks, the thematic material of an action was important for the way it affected our involvement in the mimetic illusion offered by the narrative, but it was only the apologue that made thematic assertions for their own sake. My argument is that the thematic material of a so-called action like *Pride and Prejudice* can be made important for its own sake, whenever the progression converts the thematic dimensions of the characters into thematic functions—in other words, in most narratives. As the brief comparison of Elizabeth's functions with Winston's suggests, this revision does not completely collapse the distinction between action and apologue because it is only in the apologue that the thematic assertions will coalesce into a central one or at least into a clear hierarchy. The revision, however, does make the gulf between the two forms much narrower than Sacks originally described it.[21]

More concretely, the multiple thematic functions of Elizabeth are so much a part of the progression that to see them as working only to influence what the neo-Aristoteleans call our "expectations and desires" about Elizabeth and Darcy is to offer an inadequate account of the progression of the novel. That progression is not just one of action but also one of thought. To be sure, the progression of thought does increase the power of the emotions we feel about Elizabeth and Darcy, but the thematic functions of Elizabeth's character play such a large role in our understanding of the significance of her union with Darcy that they merge with our interest in the characters as people. Consequently, the union of Darcy and Elizabeth is a union of people and an affirmation of ideas and issues that each, especially Elizabeth, has come to represent.

To do further justice to the complexity of the progression and of Austen's treatment of Elizabeth, I want to explore one more element of the relation between the mimetic and thematic components of her character. Consider Elizabeth's linked attributes of feeling deeply and reacting quickly, especially as they reveal themselves in the scenes where they are most dramatically exhibited, her outburst to Charlotte, her angry response to Darcy's first proposal, and her almost instinctive revelation to him of the news of Lydia's disgrace. Although the first scene has a limited function in the narrative, serving primarily to reinforce the difference between Elizabeth's and Charlotte's attitudes toward the marriage market, the other two have very large functions, bringing about significant changes in Darcy's character and Lydia's situation. However, I believe that the ways in which these two scenes function in the progression do not result in a conversion of this dimension of Elizabeth's character into a thematic function.

This claim may be somewhat surprising since in both cases Elizabeth's spontaneous overflow of powerful feelings eventually aids in bringing about her final happiness. Darcy not only hears her accusations about her pride but comes to acknowledge their justice;

he not only seeks to give her immediate relief in her sorrow over Lydia but he acts to make the best of the bad situation, which in turn earns her gratitude, deepens her affection, and ultimately leads to the second, successful proposal. But unlike the case of Elizabeth's independence and her scene with Lady Catherine, the narrative does not do anything to give the credit, as it were, to Elizabeth's deep feelings and frank expressions; it works instead to make us see that it is Darcy who is responsible for his self-improvement and for the salvaging of Lydia's respectability. In other words, Elizabeth's reactions in these' scenes provide the occasions for significant changes or the revelation of such changes in Darcy's character.[22] One way to understand the lack of any significant thematic function of these deep feelings is to reflect that had Darcy been different, had he been what Elizabeth thought he was, her outbursts would have simply driven him and Elizabeth further and further apart.

This discussion also illustrates further the differences between a dimension and a function. Certainly part of Elizabeth's attraction for Darcy (and for us) is this twin capacity for feeling deeply and speaking quickly, and to that extent her attribute can be seen as participating in the thematic sphere—behind such attraction must be some authorial recommendation. But just as Browning gives the Duke of Ferrara attributes that cause us to take a negative attitude toward him without making it a purpose of the poem to alter our feelings about people with those attributes, so too Austen gives Elizabeth these positive attributes without developing them into thematic points about feeling and reacting. In both cases, the authors seem to take our response for granted. If this analysis is accurate, then, in the terms I have been using, Austen gives Elizabeth an attribute that gets converted by the progression into a significant element of her mimetic function but that does not get converted into a thematic function. Consequently, a significant part of our experience of Elizabeth's character remains chiefly in the mimetic sphere—a realization that gives special force to the statement that just as she is more than a possible person she is also more than a vehicle for carrying ideas. Furthermore, this point also reinforces my initial claim that an adequate account of character in this novel cannot be derived from a recipe calling for equal parts thematism and neo-Aristoteleanism.[23]

To what extent do this account of the novel's progression and the counterargument to Levin's anti-thematism weaken the case against Duckworth and Morgan? In one sense, not at all. Their thematic analyses still appear to be reductive and selective and to invite distortion of textual particulars. But the charge that their procedure is completely arbitrary needs to be withdrawn. What each critic has done, in effect, is to take one or two attributes of Elizabeth's character—for Duckworth, her relative independence from the influence of social prestige and her inferior social status; for Morgan, her lively, playful disposition and her quickness of observation—to suggest ways that these attributes combine with other elements of the work to get converted into thematic functions, and to argue that the novel is structured around them. It is the last step in their procedure that involves the thematic leap and that causes all the problems: the novel cannot be adequately described as structured by Austen's exploration of these ideas. Since, however, the first steps have a "literal" connection to Austen's representation of Elizabeth, we can, I think, understand much of the appeal and continued vogue of thematic criticism for *Pride and Prejudice*—and, by extension, for numerous other narratives.

One of the points that the argument so far has kept returning to is the crucial role of narrative progression in the developing relationship of a character's mimetic and thematic functions. In order to extend our consideration of the variations on that relationship, I will turn in the next chapter to a narrative whose progression is very different from Orwell's and Austen's: "The Beast in the Jungle." As I consider James's novella, I shall also take up some further problems associated with reading and interpreting the thematic function of character, problems that will require further reflection on different ways of marching under the critical banner, "Always thematize!"

The Thematic Function and Interpreting by Cultural Codes: The Case of "The Beast in the Jungle"

I

In *Textual Power*, Robert Scholes offers an account of thematizing that provides an instructive contrast to the one I have developed in the preceding chapter, because the two accounts raise the question of when the generalizing movement of thematizing should appropriately stop. As I noted in the introduction, and as my discussions of Browning, Lardner, Orwell, and Austen implicitly indicate, my approach to character and progression leads its practitioner to be concerned with drawing a circle around the thematic functions of characters, with being able to say not only "these are the appropriate generalizations, and these are not" but also "just this much generalizing and no more." Scholes represents a perhaps more widely held view—in any case, he presents himself as describing current institutional practices. Scholes not only enlists under the banner of thematizing but becomes a gung-ho recruiting officer: "interpretation proper," he asserts "is the thematizing of a text."[1] Furthermore, since for him thematizing is the practice of generalizing from textual particulars to cultural codes, the habit of broadening the thematic range of such particulars is to be cultivated: in this way, the text's connection to multiple—and more widely encompassing—codes is revealed, and in that revelation the interpreter will also uncover the grail of contemporary criticism—the ideology of the text.[2]

Scholes illustrates his method with Interchapter VII from Hemingway's *In Our Time*:

> While the bombardment was knocking the trench to pieces at Fossalta, he lay very flat and sweated and prayed oh jesus christ get me out of here. Dear jesus please get me out. Christ please please please christ. If you'll only keep me from getting killed I'll do anything you say. I believe in you and I'll tell every one in the world that you are the only one that matters. Please please dear jesus.

The shelling moved further up the line. We went to work on the trench and in the morning the sun came up and the day was hot and muggy and cheerful and quiet. The next night back at Mestre he did not tell the girl he went upstairs with at the Villa Rossa about Jesus. And he never told anybody.

Scholes works by finding oppositions in the text—trench against Villa Rossa; Jesus against the girl—and then connecting these opposiions to

the larger cultural entities of which they may be seen as instances. Trench and Villa are tokens of the greater cultural types, War and Love, whose iconography has been charted through countless images of Mars and Venus, and been embodied in countless literary characters. What is important in connecting Interchapter VII to this great cultural code or topos is that Hemingway has brought the icon down into the muck as far as he can. Venus is a hooker and Mars is a boy blubbering at the bottom of a trench. (P. 34)

Scholes's thematic interpretation (a phrase, we might note in passing, which would strike him as a redundancy) continues for another page and we will look at its principles in detail later, but for our present purposes the point is clear: the generalizing move of thematizing reaches its end only after one reaches a cultural code that is both basic and broad.

With this view of thematizing and its implicit challenge to what I have said so far as a backdrop, I want to turn to James's "The Beast in the Jungle," a narrative which, I shall argue, goes very far in the restriction of the thematic function of its protagonist. I shall then take up the challenge Scholes offers and the broader question that challenge presents: when does thematizing appropriately stop? The answer to that question, I shall argue, depends less on any abstract rule than on the particular relation between the mimetic and thematic functions of character established by the progression of individual works.

II

James's treatment of John Marcher is a natural focus for questions about the relation between the mimetic and thematic functions of character because that treatment poses in an especially suggestive way the problem of the relation between character as individual and character as embodiment of an idea. On the one hand, Marcher and what happens to him are, if not unique, then at least highly unusual, but on the other hand, he seems to represent an attitude toward life—waiting for it to happen—that makes him a very representative figure. To understand the relations between these components more fully, it will again be useful to start by examining the progression of the narrative.[3] I will give special emphasis to four points of the novella: section I, where Marcher becomes reacquainted with May Bartram; section II, where Marcher discovers that May's knowledge of his special fate exceeds his own; section IV, where Marcher fails to understand May's offer and thus misses the chance to escape his fate; and section VI, where Marcher learns the truth about his life.

One of the most striking features of the tale is the narrowness of James's focus: Marcher and May are the only characters given any substantial attention, and despite the fact that the narrative traces the lives of Marcher and May from their thirties until their deaths, James gives them each only a few attributes. Section I of the narrative, recounted primarily but not exclusively with Marcher as the center of consciousness, begins with a sentence that establishes a tension between the narrator and the authorial audience: "What determined the speech that startled him in the course of their encounter scarcely matters, being probably but some words spoken by himself quite without intention—spoken as they lingered and slowly moved together after their renewal of acquaintance."[4] The sentence raises numerous questions: not only about who "they" and "him" are and what the speech was, but also why he was startled, what the significance of his being startled is, and whether it has any connection with the renewal of their acquaintance. The startled response suggests an instability, but the dominant effect of the sentence is to establish the tension. James, of course, quickly resolves this tension as he moves the narrative back a few hours and recounts the meeting of Marcher and May at Weatherend that led to the "speech that startled him." Given that quick resolution, we might well wonder why James begins with this local tension.

This beginning allows James not only to employ the dramatic method that he favors but also to guide our interest, our suspense in that drama in a rather pointed way. Unlike Marcher, we do not worry that the ensuing "sketch of a fresh start" (p. 67) with May will fail to develop into a larger picture. We wonder instead just what the nature of the particular startling utterance will be. This orientation to the "sketch" heightens our interest in both the previous acquaintance and present meeting of Marcher and May: as we learn about the less-than-startling past and somewhat bumbling present, we invest both with more significance because we regard them as a prelude to the startling speech. Furthermore, although this opening sentence leaves us willing to accept Marcher's interpretation that the cause of the startling speech is unimportant, we are also alerted to look for that cause. Thus, when May "saves the situation" (p. 67), a number of effects are created. First, Marcher's egoism is highlighted: the cause of the speech that startled him is not as he supposes in something he said but rather in May's own decision to "suppl[y] the link" (p. 67). Marcher's egoism on this occasion also suggests the reason why he told May his secret ten years before and why he then forgot that he did. Regardless of whether the egoism fully explains this behavior, the behavior itself further emphasizes the trait. This awareness in turn complicates the instabilities of the situation brought about by May's eventual promise to "watch with" Marcher.

The first global instability established at this point in the narrative is whether anything will happen to Marcher: will he be right about his expectation of the "coming catastrophe," and if so, what will that catastrophe be? The second instability raised at this point stems from May's involvement in Marcher's sense of his fate: what difference will her decision to wait make for Marcher and what difference will it make for her? Indeed, this instability is given further importance in the narrative by the simple fact that James chooses to begin at this juncture. We are not being told the whole of Marcher's life but rather that part of it that began with May's decision to wait with him. Like Marcher's egoism, this element of the narrative contributes to the third major instability: what will be the progress of the relationship between Marcher and May? This instability takes on even greater interest in light of Marcher's dismissal of May's suggestion that the grand fate he envisions for himself is to fall in love. Considering the three instabilities all at once, we can see that as James brings Marcher and May together he establishes—and begins to intertwine—two directions for the narrative movement: outward from May and Marcher to the "coming catastrophe" and inward to the relationship between Marcher and May itself.

Section II adds a new instability to the progression, one that interacts with the previous instabilities to tighten the intertwining of the inward and outward directions of the narrative. In addition, James's technique introduces a significant tension into the narrative, one that is not fully resolved until its final paragraphs. At the end of the first section, May had asked Marcher whether he was afraid of what was in store for him—indeed she had asked him three times before he answered that he didn't know but that she could tell him herself if she watched with him. At the end of this section, May can answer her question: "You're not afraid." Her continuation of her thought, however, signifies that she now has a new relation to Marcher's impending fate even as it complicates both Marcher's and the audience's relation to it. "But it isn't . . . the end of our watch. That is, it isn't the end of yours. You've everything still to see." Marcher correctly infers that she has already seen something he has not. "You know something I don't." "You know what's to happen" (p. 88). "You know, and you're afraid to tell me. It's so bad that you're afraid I'll find out." May, for her part, has the last word in the scene: "You'll never find out" (p. 89).

This conversation complicates the progression in numerous ways. First, it gives a new twist to Marcher's obsession: not only does he wait now, he eagerly wants to know what May knows—and this desire will continue to drive him even after her death. Second, the conversation alters Marcher and May's relationship: although in one respect she continues as Marcher's subordinate, supportive watcher, in another sense she has become his superior. She is now in a position to use or not use her superior knowledge as she deems best. It is from that position that she gives the narrative its next major development in section IV. Third, the conversation creates a tension of unequal knowledge between the narrator and the authorial audience. The narrator does leave Marcher's vision in section II, but what he tells us about May and what he shows of her consciousness is hardly full disclosure:

> So, while they grew older together, she did watch with him, and so she let this association give shape and colour to her own existence. Beneath *her* forms as well detachment had learned to sit and behaviour had become for her, in the social sense, a false account of herself. There was but one account of her that would have been true all the while, and that she could give, directly, to nobody, least of all to John Marcher. Her whole attitude was a virtual statement but the perception of that only seemed destined to take its place for him as one of the many things necessarily crowded out of his consciousness. (Pp. 82–83)

Although we may suspect that the content of her virtual statement concerns her feelings about Marcher, we cannot yet be entirely sure what those feelings are. Furthermore, even if we knew for sure what they were, we would not know what May—and the narrator—know about Marcher's coming fate. But this minimal disclosure does remind us that we could—if the narrator once again exercised the option of entering May's consciousness, this time to show her reflecting on her knowledge. We read on in part to find out what May knows and to discover whether Marcher himself will ever find out. Thus, at the end of section II, we find Marcher still looking outward toward the beast, May now looking only at Marcher himself, and ourselves looking in both directions but with a greater interest and concern for the relation between the outward and the inward. What will May's knowledge, whatever it is, mean for their relationship? Section IV provides the answer, as it also resolves some of the tension and further complicates the instabilities.

Pressed by Marcher to tell him what she knows, May tries to use that knowledge to have him avert his peculiar fate. Afraid that he has been mistaken, worried that he will have been "sold" (p. 97), Marcher seeks reassurance: "I *haven't* lived with a vain imagination, in the most besotted illusion? I haven't waited but to see the door shut in my face?" (p. 105). May at first provides that reassurance and then attempts to alter his perception of their situation, by in effect getting him to stop looking outward toward the beast and to start looking inward at the two of them and especially at her as someone other than a fellow-watcher.

> "However the case stands *that* isn't the truth. Whatever the reality, it *is* a reality. The door isn't shut. The door's open."
> "Then something's to come?"
> She waited once again, always with her cold, sweet eyes on him. "It's never too late." She had, with her gliding step, diminished the distance between them, and she stood nearer to him, close to him, a minute, as if still full of the unspoken. . . . It had become suddenly, from her movement and attitude, beautiful and vivid to him that she had something more to give him; her wasted face delicately shone with it, and it glittered, almost as with the white luster of silver, in her expression. . . . [T]hey continued for some minutes silent, her face shining at him, her contact imponderably pressing, and his stare all kind, but all expectant. The end, none the less, was that what he had expected failed to sound. Something else took place instead, which seemed to consist at first in the mere closing of her eyes. She gave way at the same instant to a slow, fine shudder, and though he remained staring . . . she turned off and regained her chair. It was the end of what she had been intending, but it left him thinking only of that. (Pp. 105–6)

When May tells him, upon leaving the room a few minutes later in the company of her nurse, that what has happened was "what *was* to" (p. 107), we can recognize that Marcher's failure even to see her offer—to move his eyes inward, as it were—constitutes the springing of the Beast. Yet we still do not know everything that May and the narrator seem to know. She is acting out of some hope here, not out of confident knowledge that he will fail to see what she means. Just as some but not all of the tension is removed, so too some but not all of the instabilities are resolved. The narrative has now given answers to two of the three major questions raised at the end of the first section. Marcher has been both right and wrong in his expectation of some catastrophe: there is no Beast external to him but there is one of his own making that causes him to miss his chance for a life beyond his waiting and looking outward. May's decision to wait with Marcher has given him his chance to escape his fate, but he has been too blind to see it. It has given her something to live for but it has also exacted a great toll upon her—she has loved without return and she has been unable even to get Marcher to see the extent of that love.

In effect, the outward-facing instability has now been subsumed by the inward-facing one. With May's death shortly after this scene, Marcher faces new thoughts about his relationship to her: "how few were the rights, as they were called in such cases, that he had to put forward, and how odd it might even seem that their intimacy shouldn't have given him more of them. The stupidest fourth cousin had more, even though she had been nothing in such a person's life" (p. 114). At this point, however, he still looks outward and only indirectly moves toward clarifying his "rights" toward, his understanding of, and his feeling for May, as he tries to discover what she knew that he did not. He comes to accept the idea that the Beast had sprung, and devotes himself to discovering what it was and how it affected him.

The remaining instabilities and tensions are simultaneously resolved in section VI, when Marcher, through his observation of the true mourner, is finally able to see outside himself, and thus articulate for himself his failure with life in general and May in particular. Marcher and the authorial audience now finally come to know what May knew and had indirectly tried to tell him: "he had been the man of his time, *the* man, to whom nothing on earth was to have happened" (p. 125); "the escape would have been to love her" (p. 126). The insight does bring new knowledge to Marcher, but the knowledge comes too late to enable him to change the established pattern of his whole life:

This horror of waking—*this* was knowledge, knowledge under the breath of which the very tears in his eyes seemed to freeze. Through them, none the less, he tried to fix it and hold it; he kept it there before him so that he might feel the pain. That at least, belated and bitter, had something of the taste of life. But the bitterness suddenly sickened him, and it was as if, horribly, he saw, in the truth, in the cruelty of his image, what had been appointed and done. He saw the Jungle of his life and saw the lurking Beast; then, while he looked, perceived it, as by a stir of the air, rise, huge and hideous, for the leap that was to settle him. His eye darkened—it was close; and, instinctively turning, in his hallucination, to avoid it, he flung himself, on his face, on the tomb.(Pp. 126–27)

This ending provides the appropriate final twist to Marcher's story because the hallucination reenacts the Beast's springing in his life—the Beast is not external but of his own making—and because Marcher's reaction to it is in keeping with his life. Just as he is not capable of maintaining the feelings evoked by his "horror of waking," he is not capable of dealing with the hallucination. He turns, as he has always been turning since the day at Weatherend on which the narrative opened, to May. But this time his turning ends with a parody of an embrace as he flings himself face down on her tomb.

Although James's portrait of Marcher is restricted to just a few salient attributes, he does give us a sufficiently deep and coherent portrait for Marcher to have a significant mimetic function. In addition to his obsession with being singled out and his virtually boundless egoism, his main attributes are an active imagination and a desire to discover the truth of things.[5] The obsession and egoism are apparent on every page, the imagination shows itself in the very first section as Marcher is able to penetrate "to a kind of truth [about May] that the others were too stupid for" (p. 63), and the desire for the truth is evident in the quest he commits himself to after May's death. What is striking, however, about these attributes is that they all serve Marcher's obsession with being singled out: the obsession is made possible by the egoism and the imagination, and it takes much of its direction in the narrative after section two from his desire to know the truth—indeed, after May's death it is what enables him to go on living.

If this account is accurate, then we have here an analogue in the mimetic component to what we saw in the thematic component of Winston Smith in *1984*. Just as the different thematic functions of Winston's character contribute to one central thematic point of the narrative, so too do the different traits of Marcher contribute to a central trait of his character—his obsession with being singled out. In this respect, Marcher is different from the Duke of Ferrara, Winston, Whitey the barber, and Elizabeth Bennet: all five characters have a recognizable mimetic function and thus appear to be coherent selves, but only Marcher can be adequately described by reference to one central trait. More generally, he is rare among protagonists of realistic fiction in that his mimetic component can be adequately described in a single statement: he is the man who fails to live by waiting for life to come to him.

Viewing Marcher's mimetic component this way allows us to supplement Wayne Booth's explanation of one very striking feature of the narrative.[6] Booth argues that James's handling of the center of consciousness narration allows him both to make Marcher's egoism plain and, by having the reader travel with Marcher, to generate sympathy for him. Now we can also say that the response is a result of James's ability to make the egoism subordinate to the more central matter of the obsession, a trait which does not preclude sympathy the way egoism does. Thus, even as the authorial audience remains acutely aware of Marcher's deficiencies, we remain at least partly sympathetic to him throughout the narrative, and find the suffering brought on by his final illumination to be moving in a way that we associate with tragedy.[7]

What happens in the mimetic sphere is mirrored in the thematic sphere: this obsession is the only attribute that the progression converts into a function—demonstrating the regrettable consequences of waiting for life to come to you. The thematic dimensions corresponding to the attributes of egoism, imagination, and desire for truth, like Elizabeth's attributes of feeling deeply and speaking quickly and like all the Duke of Ferrara's attributes, are not individually crucial in any of the turns taken by the progression. Instead, although James takes a negative attitude toward Marcher's egoism and a positive attitude toward the imagination and the desire for truth, he always gives us these attributes in the service of the obsession, and consequently, that attribute is always crucial to the progression, as we can see by reflecting again on those points of the narrative we examined most closely. When May agrees to wait with him, Marcher in effect looks past her and outward toward the Beast. When May's knowledge outstrips his, he can still think only of what his fate will be. When May makes her offer, he cannot recognize it, because he cannot understand how she can be referring to anything but the outward-looking instability, and of course he cannot understand that because he is obsessed. When Marcher experiences his illumination, he is in effect first realizing that he has been obsessed and then realizing the consequences of that obsession.

If this analysis is accurate, then James has effected what I believe is a rare fusion of the mimetic and thematic functions of the protagonist. Not only is neither function subordinated to the other but the line between them becomes blurred: to be Marcher is to be this obsessed man and to be this obsessed man is to fail to live. The relation between the mimetic and thematic functions here is different from that relation in the case of Elizabeth Bennet, precisely because of the narrowness of James's portrait. Although our concern with Elizabeth as a possible person merges with our concern for the ideas she comes to represent, the very multiplicity of her traits and thematic functions works against the degree—and finally, the kind—of fusion we have here. Elizabeth's thematic functions do not fully define her character, and her mimetic component is not just the other side of any single thematic function. By making Marcher a character with a central trait, by orchestrating the progression around the influence of that trait on Marcher's actions, and by guiding our judgments of those actions, James makes the mimetic and thematic functions of the character virtually interchangeable.

The one aspect of the synthetic component that becomes prominent in the narrative supports this fusion, though it does so by reinforcing the thematic function. Like Austen in *Pride and Prejudice*, James seeks to keep the synthetic components of his characters in the background—with one exception: he expects the authorial audience to recognize the way that their names call attention to their constructed status, a recognition that emphasizes the thematic function of the characters even as it encapsulates their mimetic portraits. "May" connotes both the sense of possibility and the sense of new life in the spring, both of which the inexorably marching Marcher misses, and thus, in effect dooms himself to live at winter's end. To be Marcher is to be obsessed with the next season and therefore perpetually dormant.

Another way of expressing the point about Marcher's mimetic and thematic functions is to notice the consequences of the narrative's resolution for the two functions. During Marcher's moments of illumination, the narrative reaches its mimetic high point, and everything that happens is perfectly consonant with Marcher's mimetic function: his imagination and desire for truth, acted upon by the true mourner's ravaged look, enable him finally to look inward, to understand and articulate for himself how egoistic he has been, how he has consequently deluded himself, how May had lived while he has failed to and how he has missed the opportunity she offered. Indeed, his truthful review of his life is so painful that it leads his imagination finally to the horrible hallucination of the springing of the Beast, whom he is appropriately unable to face. At the same time, the scene effectively concludes the development of Marcher's thematic function for, as noted above, it is only here that the authorial audience's knowledge of Marcher catches up with May's and the narrator's. Consequently, when he articulates for himself what his life has been, Marcher also finishes articulating its meaning for us: "It was the truth, vivid and monstrous, that all the while he had waited the wait itself was his portion" (p. 125). Finally, the closing action of the narrative, the imagined springing of the Beast and Marcher's failure to meet it, dramatically enacts the consequences of a life that has been missed. In short, the resolution scene simultaneously brings the two functions to their high points, as the strokes developing one also serve to develop the other. Again the result is the fusion of the functions.

III

In order to appreciate the differences between Scholes's view of thematizing and the one underlying my discussion so far, we should at least sketch some of the things that Scholes's principles would lead him to say about James's narrative. The principles are revealed in Scholes's four-step process of interpretation, a process that he summarizes as the production of text-upon-text.[8] "The first things to look for are repetitions and oppositions that emerge at the obvious or manifest level of the text" (p. 32). Then, "the next step is the crucial one. To accomplish it we must ask what these oppositions 'represent,' or as our institutional vocabulary usually phrases it, what they 'symbolize' " (p. 33); in other words, this step "involves connecting the singular oppositions of the text to the generalized oppositions that structure our cultural system of values" (p. 33). Third, "the act of interpretation involves both making the cultural connection (seeing the resemblance [between the text and the general cultural code it participates in]) and understanding the unique quality of this particular version of the larger instance (that is, noting the difference)" (p. 34). Fourth, to reach the "ultimate interpretation" we "must move from noting the cultural codes invoked to understanding the attitude taken toward those codes by the maker of this text" (p. 34).

The central opposition in "The Beast" is that between Marcher and May, and the force of the opposition becomes clearer if we give more attention to their names than I have done above. The May/Marcher opposition contains others: woman/man; spring/winter; possibility/predetermination; life/death. The central repetition of the narrative is the springing of the Beast, and this repetition yields further oppositions within the similarity of Marcher's creation of the Beast: reality/illusion; ignorance/knowledge; spring/fall; escape/doom; life/death. Furthermore, the oppositions of the characters can be mapped on to the oppositions of the repetition: May represents reality, knowledge, and escape (as well as spring and life), while Marcher represents illusion, ignorance, and doom (as well as fall, winter, and death). These oppositions, not surprisingly, link the story with numerous general cultural codes. The opposition between appearance and reality links the story with a general code about the opposition between the truth about one's self and one's romantic perception of oneself. The opposition between escape (or possibility) and predetermination (or doom) links the story with a general Western theological code about the opposition between free will and predestination. The oppositions between escape (or possibility) and predetermination (or doom) and between life and death link the story with a cultural code about the full life versus the empty one. For the sake of clarity, I will pursue only this last link in steps three and four, but I will return to the issue of multiple codes after the illustration.

In our own day we quickly encapsulate the values of the code about the full life by invoking—and keeping current—an expression such as "it is better to have loved and lost than never to have loved at all" (the sneaky appeal of the cynical popular advice, "if you can't be with the one you love, love the one you're with," derives in large measure from its carrying along some values of this code). In nineteenth-century literature, the code is probably given its most forceful expression in Tennyson's "Ulysses" (1842):

> I will drink
> Life to the lees. All times I have enjoyed
> Greatly, have suffered greatly, both with those
> That loved me and alone; . . . .
>
>   (ll. 6–9)

> How dull it is to pause, to make an end,
> To rust unburnished, not to shine in use!
> As though to breathe were life. Life piled on life
> Were all too little . . . .
>
>   (ll. 23–26)

> Though much is taken, much abides; and though
> We are not now that strength which in old days
> Moved heaven and earth, that which we are, we are:
> One equal temper of heroic hearts,
> Made weak by time and fate, but strong in will
> To strive, to seek, to find, and not to yield.
>
>   (ll. 65–70)

James himself gives direct expression to his own belief in the values of this code when in *The Ambassadors*, a work published in the same year as "The Beast," he creates Strether's famous injunction to little Billham: "Live all you can: it's a mistake not to. It doesn't so much matter what you do in particular so long as you have your life. If you haven't had that what *have* you had?"[9] In his Preface to the New York Edition, James underlines the importance he placed upon this value by identifying Strether's speech to Billham as the germ of the whole novel. In the terms of this code, Marcher is a severely reduced, inverted version of Ulysses, an unwily version of the Homeric original seeking false adventures among the leisured upper-class. Rather than drinking life to the lees, this genteel warrior idly waits for it to be served to him; when he does finally experience "something of the taste of life," its "bitterness . . . sickened him" (p. 126); his peculiar striving then leads him to find something illusory and, when he finds it, he yields. May, by contrast, is a Penelope transforming herself into a more genuine Ulysses, because in her waiting she lives. She has suffered greatly, both with him she loved and alone; she has finally had to yield before finding what she has been seeking, but she has remained strong in will throughout her watching with Marcher.

James's attitude toward Marcher is made plain through the very inversion of the ideal represented by Ulysses, through Marcher's being a negative example of what Strether tells Billham. At the same time, the sympathy James nevertheless generates for Marcher suggests that James may have been worried that his own choice to spend so many hours of his life writing may have been a choice for the empty rather than the full life.[10]

Scholes no doubt could execute the method more elegantly, and if comprehensiveness rather than contrast were my goal, I would attempt to carry out its last two steps for other textual oppositions as well. But I believe that this application has done its necessary job of illustrating the important difference between his broad thematizing and my more restricted kind. Before discussing that difference further, I should explain why the difference between his multiple thematic generalizations and my single one does not offer grounds for significant debate, while the difference in the degree of generalization does. The difference between the multiple and the single arises largely out of our different projects: Scholes wants to interpret the whole text, and he believes that all interpretation is thematizing, so he is concerned with all the ways that the text invites thematizing. I want to understand the thematic function of the protagonist, and so my discussion of thematizing is more narrow, less concerned with the all the sources of thematic assertion in narrative. I do of course claim to speak of the whole by speaking of progression, and in that way I can acknowledge the existence and the relative importance of thematic assertions arising out of other elements of the text. In other words, I would not claim that the only theme in the whole narrative is the one associated with Marcher's thematic function—May has thematic functions as well, and the action itself, as Michael Coulson Berthold points out, does play upon the theme of "too late."[11] My claim instead is that the progression puts Marcher's thematic function at the center of the whole text. The thematic functions of May's character (e.g., representing a life of active commitment) are subordinated by the progression to Marcher's, and the idea of "too late" is a natural corollary of Marcher's thematic function.

In general, my extended attention to the thematic functions of characters is not meant to imply that the attributes of characters and the roles they play in narrative progression are the only sources of a narrative's thematic statements. Such statements can arise out of the action itself—if, for example, all characters regardless of their attributes meet the same fate, then the implied thematic statement about the kind of world in which they live is not carried by the characters themselves. Thematic statements can also arise independently of character and action, as in the narrative commentary of, say, *Tom Jones* or *Vanity Fair*, where the narrator not only does the usual job of reinforcing the thematic points made by character and action but goes beyond them to independent assertions. At the same time, of course, the extended attention I give to the thematic functions of character is meant to recognize that character is typically a very important source of a narrative's thematic component. I shall return to the issue of multiple thematic assertions after I examine my differences with Scholes over the appropriate methods of thematic generalizing.

Despite the ultimate differences between Scholes's semiotic framework and my rhetorical one, those frameworks share enough for our differences over the degree of thematic generalization to be genuine disagreements. Both frameworks want to account for what Scholes calls reading, interpretation, and criticism, for, that is, a first-order understanding of the text, a second-order understanding of the claims on the reader the text makes, and an evaluation of those claims.[12] More succinctly, both frameworks are concerned with the way texts work on readers and the way readers may exercise power over texts. What we have are two sometimes converging, sometimes diverging ways of achieving these common goals. We can therefore examine which of the two diverging ways is more likely to lead to those goals.

What, then, would be the objection to interpreting Interchapter VII as a story of Mars and Venus brought down in the muck, or to seeing Marcher as an inverted Ulysses among the leisured class? Note that Levin's arguments against thematic leaping do not have the same force when applied to Scholes's method, because that method does not claim that the text is really only about the themes of the general cultural code: it insists instead on accounting for the particulars of the text as a unique version of a pattern found in the general cultural code. Note further that the distortions Levin finds inevitable with thematizing are not readily apparent here. Scholes's approach does not restrict him to finding only a "central theme," and the various token-type fits between the individual story or character and the general cultural codes are plausible, if not invariably compelling. Without issuing a critical interdiction on interpreting texts in light of such cultural codes, on what grounds can one object?

The ground I choose is that provided by the consequences of reading for progression. Most generally, my objection is that readings that follow Scholes's principles typically lose precision and comprehensiveness as they gain generality. This loss results from both the method itself and its purpose of relating the text to the most general cultural codes. Let us look at the methodological issues first. To assume that the path to interpretation is to be found by dividing the text's forest of particulars into pairs of oppositions is to assume that the second-order understanding is not closely related to the first—or in other words, it is to assume that the experience of reading, of following the progression, has little to do with interpretation. Consequently, the dynamics resulting from the temporal process of reading do not figure in interpretation, and in that way the method fails to be comprehensive: though one cannot point to them in the same way one can point to say, a character's name, the dynamics of a text's movement are as much a part of it as the binary oppositions Scholes makes central. Both are elements that must be inferred from the literal surface of the text.

The second and third methodological problems of Scholes's system are also related to its neglect of progression as an influence on interpretation. His system precludes the possibility that there can be connections between paired textual elements other than the oppositional or repetitive; and it invites the equation of textual elements that are not given equal weight in the text. All three problems are evident in his interpretation of Interchapter VII of *In Our Time*. We have already seen that Scholes works by finding oppositions in the text—trench against Villa Rossa; Jesus against the girl—and then connecting these oppositions to such large cultural types as Mars and Venus. More particularly, Scholes says that he would keep a class discussion of the interchapter going until "some of the following features emerged: that the story takes place in two locations, trench and Villa Rossa; that the soldier in the trench promises Jesus, in prayer, that he will tell about him, and that he breaks that promise first at the Villa Rossa and then for ever after" (p. 33). Furthermore, the thematic oppositions in the story are built upon the basic opposition between trench and Villa. In each place, we are told or can infer that the soldier "lay very flat and sweated." In each place, we are told or can infer that he speaks in "intimate, personal terms" to someone—Jesus first and then the girl (p. 33). From here, as we have seen, Scholes connects the oppositions to broader cultural codes about love and war, Mars and Venus, sacred and profane love.

If, however, we look at the progression of the interchapter, the text does not divide so neatly into two equal and oppositional halves according to the difference in the setting. The first sentence describing the bombardment and the soldier's anxiety introduces the major instability. "While the bombardment was knocking the trench to pieces at Fossalta, he lay very flat and sweated and prayed oh jesus christ get me out of here." His making the promise to Jesus adds a new instability because the promise under such pressure raises a question about its fulfillment. Then, immediately after this complication, the first instability is removed: "I believe in you and I'll tell every one in the world that you are the only one that matters. Please please dear jesus. The shelling moved up the line." We are left then with the instability of the promise.

So far this analysis is not incompatible with anything that Scholes has said. From this point, however, the analyses diverge significantly. Concerned with opposition rather than progression, Scholes breaks the story sharply in two, concludes that the soldier "breaks the promise first at the Villa Rossa," and in effect assigns no function to the sentence describing the day between the shelling and the trip to the Villa Rossa ("We went to work on the trench and in the morning the sun came up and the day was hot and muggy and cheerful and quiet"). His only comment about it is that the shift to the "we" is a significant alteration of the point of view that may move one from reading to interpretation. In reading for progression, this shift and the whole sentence are very significant because together they signal the beginning of the resolution. Since the soldier has promised to tell "everyone," since he spends the next day in the trench not alone but as part of a "we," and since the day is "hot and muggy and cheerful and *quiet*," the sentence not only emphasizes the absence of the shelling but also reveals that the soldier fails to fufill his promise. Thus, the promise and the breaking of the promise both occur in the trench; the neatness of the oppositions that Scholes's interpretation is built upon comes at the expense of the textual details. Furthermore, the adjective "cheerful" emphasizes the soldier's radically different psychological state; the day is hot and muggy but he is not lying down and sweating and praying with all the anxiety of someone who is in fear of losing his life. Yesterday's experience does not touch today's mood, just as yesterday's promise does not affect today's behavior.

Once we understand this last description of the soldier in the trench as the beginning of the resolution, we are better able to understand the relation between trench and Villa Rossa. It is not, as

Scholes's reading would have it, that the soldier goes there and breaks his promise; instead he goes there because he has already broken his promise. Indeed, the very speed with which he has forgotten the promise causes us to reflect back on the fear that induced it and recognize it to be as prominent as the promise itself. The shift of setting from trench to Villa Rossa works as a very powerful way to signal how far (both physically and spiritually) and how quickly ("the next night") the soldier has traveled since experiencing that fear and responding with his prayer-promise. Thus, the villa is not put in direct opposition to the trench but is made to function as a very telling marker of the soldier's distance from the events of two days ago. Once the instability has been resolved to this extent, the last sentence can effectively provide both completeness and closure; the authorial audience is very willing to believe "he never told anybody."

I want to stress here that although I am reading for progression while Scholes reads for oppositions, and thus use different categories of analysis, both of us claim to base the validity of our findings on their ability to account for the whole text. Consequently, Scholes himself would have to acknowledge that his neglect of the sentence about the day after the shelling seriously damages his case. The problem is not just that he does not account for it, but also that he cannot account for it without disrupting the neatness of the oppositions upon which his whole interpretation is based.

The fourth problem with Scholes's system arises less from its methodological procedures than from its purpose of getting at the general cultural code. This problem, in other words, has less to do with his neglect of progression and more to do with his treatment of character. Because Scholes wants to get to those cultural codes and because he assumes that interpretation proper is thematizing, the model privileges the propositional elements of the narrative and subordinates or ignores the emotional, affective element. Regarding the soldier as Mars, the traitless prostitute as Venus ("Venus is a hooker, and Mars is a boy blubbering at the bottom of a trench" [p. 34]), Marcher as an inverted Ulysses, May as Penelope-becoming-Ulysses, and so on is a kind of thematizing that foregrounds the synthetic component at the expense of the mimetic for the purpose of making the greatest claims for the thematic. In a sense, this thematizing makes all narrative aspire to the condition of allegory.

Again part of the difficulty with this procedure is that it creates too wide a gulf between reading and interpretation. Just as the system denies the importance of the temporal dynamics of the text, so too it denies the importance of the mimetic involvement many texts offer us. And again to interpret mimetically developed characters through the lenses of the general cultural codes that Scholes so favors is to fail to do justice to their complexity. The token will correspond to the type but not in every respect. When we regard Marcher as an inverted Ulysses, for example, we do not account for his repeated failed attempts to combat his own self-centeredness in his relations with May. When we regard the soldier as Mars blubbering at the bottom of a trench, we lose sight of the understated portrayal of his quick shift from fear to callousness that is the main source of the story's effect.

My point here is not that the soldier has no thematic function. On the contrary, the very broad strokes of his characterization indicate that he is a representative rather than individualized figure. Hemingway uses his representativeness to offer a study in the psychology of the infantryman, a study which invites thematic generalizing but also restricts the degree and kind of that generalizing. Hemingway's typical understated style means that much of the effect is carried by the inferences we are required to make as we register, first, the soldier's fear and his flight to religion, then his apparent indifference to those very intense feelings. The nuances of the progression indicate that the thematic point is neither "there are no atheists in foxholes," nor "foxhole conversions don't take," but something more like "war in the trenches alternately induces both extreme fear and extreme callousness toward the person you were while you were afraid."

More generally, the point here is that the mimetic function of characters will act as a kind of weight which resists the high-flying generalizing that Scholes prizes so greatly. The question of where to stop in the generalization of the thematic function is answered for every narrative by the way in which the progression guides the interaction of the mimetic and the thematic functions of character. There are of course narratives that restrict the mimetic function in order to develop the thematic and to invite broad generalization (we call many of these narratives allegories). Frequently, however, the progression will develop mimetic and thematic functions simultaneously, and if I am right about "The Beast in the Jungle," it may occasionally even fuse them, but to the extent that it asks us to take the mimetic function seriously, the progression will work against the allegorizing implicit in Scholes's system. We can see Marcher as equally mimetic and thematic, but it is hard to take him seriously as a mimetic character when we are told that he is really a version of Ulysses.

This position does not mean that Scholes's interpretations are worthless or unhelpful. It does, however, mean that they are more limited than Scholes thinks. It also means that the link through character to the general cultural codes ought to be considered as an extrapolation of the thematic function proceeding by analogy rather than as an interpretation uncovering the basic codes of the text. If the text were working by those codes in the way that Scholes claims, the fit between type and token would be tighter, and the mimetic function would not have any significant force. Marcher may be like an inverted Ulysses, but to delete the preposition is to delete that part of the progression that insists he is a possible person. The analogies between the thematic functions of the characters and the general cultural types and codes they resemble can be highly illuminating, as I think they are in Scholes's discussion of Interchapter VII, but such illumination should not blind us to their status as analogies rather than identities.

II   Incorporating the Synthetic
Function: Reexamining
Audiences and Progression

3   The Functions of Character and
          the Relations of Audiences in
          The French Lieutenant's Woman

I

The two chapters of Part I have presented a case for the importance
of thematizing character and knowing where to stop in that thematizing (where the progression tells one to). At the same time, its specific
analyses of *1984*, *Pride and Prejudice*, and "The Beast in the Jungle"
have uncovered three different relationships between the mimetic
and thematic functions of character: subordination of one to the
other, equality along parallel tracks of interest, and fusion. This
chapter will attempt to complete the investigation into the mimetic-
thematic relationship and to move the inquiry into its consideration
of the interactions among the three components of character by focusing on the mimetic-thematic relationship in a narrative where the
synthetic component is at least an occasionally foregrounded feature
of the text. In other words, my question here is what kind of mimetic-
thematic relationships will develop when the synthetic component of
character moves out of the background of the narrative. Although this
one case may not be representative of all, John Fowles's *The French
Lieutenant's Woman* raises this question more provocatively than any
other narrative I can think of. Furthermore, Fowles's manner of incorporating the synthetic component into his narrative will require a
closer examination of the concepts of—and the relations between—
the authorial and narrative audiences than I have yet undertaken.

II

The most striking feature of Fowles's treatment of his characters is his
failure—or better, refusal—to give Sarah Woodruff, whom the narrator once ironically refers to as the "protagonist," a fully developed
mimetic function.[1] This refusal is striking not only because of Sarah's
importance in the narrative but also because Fowles takes pains to

83

develop the mimetic functions of the other major characters, especially Charles Smithson. Fowles's refusal is itself complexly incorporated into the progression of the narrative through the narrator's statement of principles in the famous Chapter 13. Because the narrator claims to respect the autonomy of his characters and because Sarah would reject a chapter devoted to revealing her thoughts, Fowles himself seems to escape the obligation to give us an inside view of her, an escape that allows him eventually to write his double ending.[2] But before we examine the crucial role of Chapter 13 in the progression and in the development of the functions of character, it will be helpful to sketch the general movement of the whole narrative, and then to look more closely at its initiating moments in the first two chapters.

The general trajectory of the narrative follows a path that results from the conflicting forces of Ernestina, Sarah, and Sam interacting with the conflicting values and beliefs of Charles. This path is finally one of growth and development for Charles—but that is not the whole story of the narrative. The major instabilities of the narrative center on Charles, but Fowles's narrative manner gives rise to some significant tensions that juxtapose the authorial audience's interest in Charles with other issues about the status of the narrative itself. Let us look at the instabilities first. When the action begins Charles is engaged to Ernestina, who is only slightly different from the conventional Victorian woman he has avoided marrying for much of his adult life. His encounters with Sarah emphasize his dissatisfaction with his situation and complicate the instabilities surrounding his engagement—and indeed, those surrounding the future course of his life as a young adult who has been born and bred a gentleman but now finds the social order changing. Fowles presents his attraction to Sarah as a function of his vague unease about his engagement to Ernestina and of Sarah herself, who through her appeals to his sympathy, her unconventional behavior, and indeed, her profound mystery, eventually leads him to reject the general judgment of her as a madwoman and to envision sharing his life with her. In ways that I will discuss later, Charles's choice for Sarah over Ernestina becomes thematized as a choice for the modern age over the Victorian, a choice for freedom over duty, and a choice that Fowles asks his audience to endorse.

Once Charles makes that choice most of the significant instabilities of the narrative are resolved. Nevertheless, the resolution is different for the authorial audience than it is for our protagonist. In a typical pattern for him, Charles misjudges the relation between his choosing and his getting what he chooses. Concerned with his own problems, he does not pay sufficient attention to the aspirations of Sam, who does not deliver the written proposal, since its acceptance would mean the end of his hopes for funds to open his own clothing store. Furthermore, it is not clear that Sarah would have accepted Charles's proposal anyway. Charles lives with the consequences of his choice for Sarah over Ernestina without looking back, although he never abandons hope that he will find her again—and again his constancy about his choice is a sign of his growth. When Charles does find Sarah through the intercession of Sam at the very end of the narrative, Fowles offers two versions of Sarah's response to his renewed proposal. In both she puts him through a difficult interview; in the first, she eventually accepts him and in the second she does not. The doubleness of the ending is one sign that Charles's growth is not the whole story of the narrative, and Chapter 13 is another. To see how Chapter 13 develops a potentiality in the initial narrative situation and, thus, adds a significant new tension to the narrative, let us consider how Fowles leads up to it.

The narrative begins at a leisurely pace as the first chapter does not introduce any instability until its last paragraph, when it also complicates the mild tension established by the opening paragraphs. Fowles begins by using the narrator to describe the setting—the Cobb at Lyme Regis—and an unnamed couple walking upon the Cobb. This initial narration also implicitly defines the narrator's temporal relation to the scene he is describing and thereby establishes the tension; consider, for example, this commentary on the Cobb:

> Primitive yet clean, elephantine but delicate; as full of subtle curves and volumes as a Henry Moore or a Michelangelo; and pure, clean, salt, a paragon of mass. I exaggerate? Perhaps, but I can be put to the test, for the Cobb has changed very little since the year of which I write; though the town of Lyme has, and the test is not fair if you look back towards land.[3]

At the end of the next paragraph, the narrator again refers to the temporal distance between the time of the action and the time of the narration: "No house lay visibly then or, beyond a brief misery of beach huts, lies today in that direction" (p. 10). The reference to Henry Moore indicates his twentieth-century perspective, and then the reference to "today," without any marking of a difference between the time of narration and the time of publication (1969), indicates that Fowles is placing the time of narration as the late 1960s, roughly one hundred years later than the March 1867 date given in the first paragraph as the time of the action.[4] Establishing this temporal distance influences the audience to align itself with the narrator as "we" all look back at the characters. In addition, establishing this distance predisposes us to direct our attention to their thematic components: aware of the distance between ourselves and the characters, we look for the ways in which they represent their age. When, as I shall discuss below, the narrator describes the couple walking on the Cobb according to how their appearance identifies them as people of their age, our predisposition toward the thematic becomes an active disposition.

At the same time, the whole manner of narration here establishes a slight tension between Fowles and the authorial audience. This audience, which knows the conventions of both nineteenth- and twentieth-century narration, recognizes the twentieth-century novelist adopting the nineteenth-century conventions and wonders why. As the narrator directs attention to the scene before him, this tension does not drive the narrative the way that, say, the tension between Lardner's Whitey and the authorial audience does; instead it remains in the background, something that needs to be resolved eventually, something that could be drawn upon later, but nothing that needs to be resolved—or even complicated—immediately.

Other elements of the narrator's treatment in Chapter 1 reinforce the authorial audience's interest in the representative status of the characters. The narrator takes up a distant spatial location and describes the couple from the perspective of a "local spy" with a telescope (p. 10). Looking through that lens, the authorial and narrative audiences focus primarily on the clothes and hair style of the couple. The woman is dressed in the latest fashion of the day, "while the taller man, impeccably dressed in a light gray, with his top hat held in his free hand, had severely reduced his dundrearies, which the arbiters of the best English male fashion had declared a shade vulgar—that is, risible to the foreigner—a year or two previously" (p. 11). These details of the character's appearance identify him as a member of a certain class—the conventionally fashionable well-to-do. At the same time, the reference to dundrearies reinforces the point that he is a citizen—and a decidedly British one—of another age, because it indicates an attention to an element of male appearance that in our age we all but ignore.

The impression of the man as conventionally fashionable is reinforced by the immediately preceding description of his companion: she is part of the incipient "revolt against the crinoline and the large bonnet," wearing "a magenta skirt of almost daring narrowness—and shortness" as well as a "'pork-pie' hat with a delicate tuft of egret plumes at the side—a millinery style that the resident ladies of Lyme would not dare to wear for another year" (p. 11). Again the details

indicate that the wearer is a member of the upper class. The elaboration of the last detail also identifies the woman—and by extension,
the man as well—as noteworthy because she is unusual—more daring, more advanced than the other residents of Lyme. (A subsidiary
effect of the detail is to provide a retrospective "justification" of the
narrator's adopting the perspective of the local spy.)

Although the perspective keeps us at a distance from the characters, we now see them as set off from their surroundings and begin
to wonder what they are doing in Lyme. But Fowles immediately complicates this reaction by introducing another character who is not only
set off from the surroundings but is also defined as unfathomable:

> But where the telescopist would have been at sea himself was
> with the other figure on that somber, curving mole. It stood right
> at the seawardmost end, apparently leaning against an old cannon
> barrel upended as a bollard. Its clothes were black. The wind
> moved them, but the figure stood motionless, staring, staring out
> to sea, more like a living memorial to the drowned, a figure from
> myth, than any proper fragment of the petty provincial day. (P. 11)

The nuances of the description highlight the mystery of the figure.
The pronominal reference does not allow us to tell whether this character is male or female, but "it" is defined in implicit opposition to
both members of the well-to-do couple. They are walking; "it" is mo-
tionless. They are together; it is alone. The woman's clothes are
marked by the brilliant, strident quality of their colors; its are black.
The couple represent a city fashion in a country environment; it is a
figure from myth set down in the provinces.

The introduction of this character is also a simultaneous complication of the tension and an introduction of an instability. When the
telescopist is hypothetically put at sea, so too are we, and we read
on in part to return to terra firma. Given the nature of the complication here, we wonder to what extent the initial tension surrounding
Fowles's adoption of the techniques of nineteenth-century narration
is connected to his handling of this mysterious figure. Moreover,
when the figure is juxtaposed to the couple, who in turn are juxtaposed to the residents of Lyme, we sense a rupture in the leisurely
presentation of the narrative; and we wonder what the presence of
the mysterious figure will mean for the couple in particular and Lyme
in general.

This initial movement is given a strong push by the events of the
next chapter, in which the narrator assumes a spatial location just
over the shoulder of the couple, and reports their conversation. This
dialogue introduces many of the major issues of the narrative—we

learn that Charles and Ernestina are engaged, that Charles is a gentleman by birth, Ernestina the daughter of a rich merchant; that Charles
believes in Darwin's theory of evolution, that his future father-in-law
does not. We also see that their talk is characterized by a kind of
formal banter, in which they play conventional roles. Despite Ernestina's attempts to protest against what Charles says or to undercut it
with her wit, he is clearly the superior partner. Like their clothes,
their talk appears to be conventionally fashionable, a Victorian version of what we would today call "cutesy." By giving us this closer
look at the couple, by letting them speak in their own voices, however
conventional, Fowles is also beginning to bring the mimetic component of the narrative more into the foreground. This movement is
accelerated with the interaction between Charles and the figure.

   After Charles finally notices the figure, his questions to Ernestina
produce the first version of her story: she is known as "Tragedy" or
the French Lieutenant's Woman, because she gave herself to the
French Lieutenant and then was abandoned. Now she haunts the
Cobb, waiting for his return. Because Ernestina, a conventional out-
sider who speaks about Sarah reluctantly, tells this tale, it does not
carry much authority. As a result, the tension aroused by the last
paragraph of Chapter 1 is partly alleviated, but not eliminated, and in
fact, our interest in "Tragedy" and her story increases. This effect is
reinforced by the further complication of the instability that occurs
when Charles, exercising his sense of his superiority to both Ernestina and the now identified figure, steps forward to her and expresses
concern.

> She turned to look at him—or, as it seemed to Charles, through
> him. It was not so much what was positively in that face which
> remained with him after that first meeting, but all that was not
> expected; for theirs was an age when the favored feminine look
> was the demure, the obedient, the shy. Charles felt immediately as
> if he had trespassed; as if the Cobb belonged to that face, and not
> to the Ancient Borough of Lyme. It was not a pretty face, like
> Ernestina's. It was certainly not a beautiful face, by any period's
> standard or taste. But it was an unforgettable face, and a tragic
> face. . . .
> Again and again, afterwards, Charles thought of that look as a
> lance; and to think so is of course not merely to describe an object
> but the effect it has. He felt himself in that brief instant an unjust
> enemy; both pierced and deservedly diminished.(Pp. 16–17)

Sarah's look not only upsets Charles's easy assumptions about his
superiority to her but also reverses the implicit power relationship he
had assumed to be in force. The description of the look emphasizes the

way in which it indicates that Sarah is not a woman of her age. In this respect, the look defines Sarah both mimetically and thematically—she has this power and it signifies her status as the anti-Victorian woman. Thus, even as Charles feels diminished by the look, even as the egocentrism implicit in his assumption of superiority is dealt a blow, he also comes for the first time face to face with an alternative to the conventional life he is drifting toward by being engaged to Ernestina. The effect of the lance on his relationship with Ernestina is immediately felt, because Charles does not tell Ernestina anything about the look, but covers up: "I wish you hadn't told me the sordid facts. That's the trouble with provincial life. Everyone knows everyone and there is no mystery. No romance." The words become ironic in retrospect but even immediately they emphasize the instabilities between Charles and Ernestina.

Between Chapters 2 and 13, the progression establishes Charles as the protagonist, as it defines instabilities in his relationships with himself, Ernestina, Sam, and Sarah. The following passage from the beginning of Chapter 3 is a good example of Fowles's method.

> His thoughts were too vague to be described. But they comprehended mysterious elements; a sentiment of obscure defeat not in any way related to the incident on the Cobb, but to certain trivial things he had said at Aunt Tranter's lunch, to certain characteristic evasions he had made; to whether his interest in paleontology was a sufficient use for his natural abilities; *to whether Ernestina would ever really understand him as well as he understood her*; to a general sentiment of dislocated purpose originating perhaps in no more—as he finally concluded—than the threat of a long and now wet afternoon. (P. 18, emphasis mine)

The vision here is Charles's while the voice is the narrator's, a technique that allows Fowles to let the audience see more about Charles than he sees about himself. We see that his obscure sense of defeat is connected with Sarah's look, though the same egocentrism that leads him to his invidious comparison between his understanding of Ernestina and hers of him will not yet allow him to admit it. At the same time, the nontrivial "trivial things" he had said also point to that sentiment of defeat. Charles is a man who is not at home with himself, a man who is especially vulnerable to the apparent alternative Sarah seems to offer.

As the progression develops, Charles's representative status is defined more clearly, even as his mimetic portrait is sketched more fully. He is a Victorian gentleman of a particular generation, one poised between the High Victorian era and the beginning of the modern age.

On the one hand, for example, Charles has beliefs and assumptions that indicate his unthinking allegiance to his class and its privileges. He has an almost instinctive belief in his own superiority. He assumes that a man in his position would naturally have a servant like Sam, and he believes that getting one's income in trade is inferior to getting one's income through an inheritance. On the other hand, he is also partly what he thinks he is: a forward-looking man who is not bound by old beliefs and assumptions. We see this side of him, for example, in his agnosticism, in his rejection of the Tories, and in his enthusiastic acceptance of Darwin's theory of evolution. His fondness for paleontology, his desire to hunt for fossils, nicely captures the contradictions of his character, which in turn are the contradictions that come with living on the cusp of a historical transition. On the one hand, paleontology is his modern substitute for his uncle's riding to hounds, and it is consistent with his interest in Darwin. On the other hand, his dilettantish pursuit of fossils ties him fruitlessly to the past even as it feeds his own self-satisfied sense of himself and his class as the surviving fittest.

Fowles gives us no comparable portrait of Sarah, though she has many mimetic dimensions, most of which define her according to her difference from Ernestina—and indeed, from Charles as well. Part of that difference is a difference in class; a victim of the divisions still very much in force in Victorian England, Sarah had been educated beyond her own lower class but had not been able to escape it. More particularly, Sarah has a firm, deep voice, she combines understanding with emotion, she has imagination and intelligence as well as the unconventional self-confidence to value her own intellect as the equal of Charles's. Furthermore, she has the ability to see through people and judge them accurately—she was born, the narrator says, "with a computer in her heart" (p. 61). But above all, she has a deep commitment, as we and Charles slowly learn, to her independence, to her freedom from the constricting codes of Victorian culture. On the thematic level most of these traits combine to make her represent a New Woman, but on the mimetic level she never ceases to be an enigma for Charles and the authorial audience: the tension established at the end of the first chapter is never wholly resolved.

The authorial audience enters Chapter 13, then, mimetically involved in Charles's situation—his vague dissatisfaction in his entanglement with Ernestina, his growing interest in Sarah—even as we typically view that mimetic situation through thematic lenses, view it, that is, as the playing out of some representative shift in Victorian society. In addition to the devices already mentioned that encourage this view, the narrator tells us at the end of Chapter 10, after Charles's first, inadvertent meeting with Sarah in the Undercliff that "in those brief poised seconds above the waiting sea, in that luminous evening silence broken only by the waves' quiet wash, the whole Victorian Age was lost" (p. 81).

Chapter 13 receives an even greater emphasis in the progression because Fowles appears to be setting it up to resolve some tension by revealing Sarah's inner life, by completing her mimetic portrait, and thus perhaps to shed more light, albeit indirectly, on the narrator's claim at the end of Chapter 10. The sequence of the narration until 13 has been following a rough pattern in which Fowles presents the characters in action and then a bit later gives background information along with an inside view of those characters. He follows the pattern for Charles, Ernestina, Sam, and Mrs. Poulteney. This strategy is largely responsible for the way in which the authorial audience moves easily from mimetic involvement to thematic understanding. When Fowles ends Chapter 12 with the questions, "Who is Sarah? Out of what shadows does she come?" he is poised to follow the pattern for her.

Instead he finally builds on the initial mild tension established by the discrepancy between his situation as a twentieth-century novelist and his adoption of the conventions of nineteenth-century narration. In a sense, this complication is also partly a resolution because Chapter 13 moves the whole narrative manner from the nineteenth-century mode into the self-reflexive modern mode. The resolution is not complete, however, because at this stage the authorial audience cannot discern the reasons for the shifts in narrative mode. Furthermore, the step toward resolution between author and authorial audience is accompanied by a new tension between the narrator and the authorial audience. In order to understand how this tension is developed, we need to combine a look at Fowles's moves in the chapter with some reflections on the concepts of narrative and authorial audiences.

III

When Rabinowitz makes his case that in order to participate in the rhetorical transactions offered by narratives the flesh-and-blood audience must enter two other audiences, the authorial and the narrative, he focuses primarily on the different knowledge that members of each audience are presumed to have.[5] As we have already seen, one major difference between the narrative and authorial audiences for all the texts we have examined so far is that the narrative audience remains unaware of the synthetic component of character while the authorial audience always has that awareness. We have also seen how

Orwell establishes some initial tension by assuming from the outset that the narrative audience is already familiar with the world of Oceania ("It was a bright cold day in April, and the clocks were striking thirteen"), and how James occasionally assumes that his narrative audience knows things that the authorial audience does not. What Fowles does in Chapter 13 is, in a sense, to exploit some fundamental differences among the *assumptions* of the two audiences, a strategy that leads to considerable distance between them—and that also brings the synthetic component of his characters into the foreground of the narrative. His strategy here is distinctive because the assumptions he draws upon are not assumptions about what the respective audiences know of the world he is depicting, but rather are assumptions about what each knows of reading.

Fowles's specific moves are to foil the expectations established by his previous pattern and to break the mimetic illusion which he has been developing so far, by having the narrator confess that he is not writing biography or history but fiction: "I do not know. This story I am writing is all imagination. These characters I create never existed outside my own mind" (p. 104). At first glance Fowles may seem to be speaking directly to the authorial audience; the passage appears to be one in which he is taking his audience into his confidence and explaining his craft. The confessional mode continues later as the narrating voice tells the audience that all novelists write because

> we wish to create worlds as real as, but other than, the world that is. Or was. This is why we cannot plan. We know a world is an organism, not a machine. We also know that a genuinely created world must be independent of its creator. . . .
> To be free myself, I must give [Charles], and Tina, and Sarah, even the abominable Mrs. Poulteney, their freedoms as well. There is only one good definition of God: the freedom that allows other freedoms to exist. And I must conform to that definition. (Pp. 105–6)

Thus, despite his intention to devote Chapter 13 to the "unfolding of Sarah's true state of mind," "I find myself suddenly like a man in the sharp spring night, watching from the lawn beneath that dim upper window of Marlborough House. I know in the context of my book's reality that Sarah would never have brushed away her tears and leaned down and delivered a chapter of revelation. She would instantly have turned, had she seen me there just as the old moon rose, and disappeared into the interior shadows" (p. 105).

Upon further reflection, however, the initial appearance of these passages as confessions from Fowles to the authorial audience cannot be sustained. Since the authorial audience takes as a first principle of its reading the idea that the whole narrative is itself a synthetic construction, it comes to regard this chapter as just one move in that larger construction. And it comes to recognize that, rather than being spontaneously confessional, the chapter is carefully calculated. Whether Fowles actually rejected his original plan for the chapter is a moot point; what matters to the authorial audience is that he does not reject the current plan to have the narrator tell us that he has rejected an earlier one. In other words, the authorial audience views this "confession" by the narrator as a move in the author's construction of the whole. Thus, we can identify the voice of the chapter as belonging to the narrator, not Fowles, and we can recognize a significant distance between those two figures that also corresponds to the distance between the narrative and authorial audiences. Reading without the first principle that everything is constructed, the narrative audience takes the narrator at his word, and therefore reads on in the expectation that the narrative will continue to develop in this unplanned, organic way. The authorial audience, meanwhile, will seek to uncover what synthetic purposes the signs of the allegedly unplanned development are actually serving.

In this respect, the chapter begins to take advantage of the peculiar narrative manner Fowles has adopted. The narrative audience continues to read as if it is in the company of a reliable nineteenth-century narrator, albeit one who is forthcoming about the limits of his omniscience, while the authorial audience recognizes that the communication from Fowles behind this narrator's back is precisely what makes the narration characteristic of the modern age. Another way of describing the relationships here is to say that the chapter establishes a significant tension between the narrator and the authorial audience but no new tensions between author and authorial audience or between narrator and narrative audience. The presence of the tension along the authorial audience-narrator axis and the lack of such tension along the narrative audience-narrator axis is a sign of the distance between the two audiences.

One of the behind-the-back passes of Chapter 13 is Fowles's maintenance of the mystery of Sarah, and thus the maintenance of the old tension between author and authorial audience. The narrator's extended commentary on the necessity of respecting his characters' autonomy is a smoke screen behind which Fowles escapes the task of completing her mimetic development. The full consequences of this artful dodge are not yet apparent to the authorial audience but it is clearly a significant part of the progression. A move with a more immediate effect is the way in which the narrator's discussion foregrounds the synthetic component of the characters.

> When Charles left Sarah on her cliff edge, I ordered him to walk straight back to Lyme Regis. But he did not; he gratuitously turned and went down to the Dairy.
>
> Oh, but you say, come on—what I really mean is that the idea crossed my mind as I wrote that it might be more clever to have him stop and drink milk . . . and meet Sarah again. That is certainly one explanation of what happened; but I can only report— and I am the most reliable witness—that the idea seemed to me to come clearly from Charles, not myself. It is not only that he has begun to gain an autonomy; I must respect it, and disrespect all my quasi-divine plans for him, if I wish him to be real. (Pp. 105–6)

This whole discussion calls attention to the novelist's role in constructing his characters and their actions. Fowles's apparent denial of his own power is of course an exertion of that power, one that only barely masks its own display. The logic that governs the other confessional passages is at work here: Charles may (or may not) have suggested his own action, but Fowles, not Charles, is responsible for this discussion of Charles as character. The result is that the narrator's claim about the autonomy of the characters functions as a signal from the author that those characters are constructs.

This signal functions to emphasize further that despite the genuine mimetic interests of the progression, this narrative is finally more concerned with the thematic sphere. By reminding us that the characters are constructed, the passage impels us to look for the reasons of their construction in their representativeness. Those reasons are still not entirely clear. In the last part of Chapter 13, the tension between narrator and authorial audience drops away as the narrative resumes ("I report only the outward facts") and Fowles and the narrator move closer together, but the tension generated here remains available for further exploitation. In Chapters 14 through 55, the progression keeps a consistent focus on the instabilities, on the unfolding of Charles's slow evolution toward his choice for Sarah. Indeed, the authorial audience's mimetic interest is developed to the greatest extent in this long section of the book. Then in Chapter 55, Fowles once again draws upon the tension of Chapter 13. Having taken both audiences through Charles's choice for Sarah and his discovery of her flight, the narrator addresses himself to the question of the ending.

> Now the question I am asking, as I stare at Charles, is . . . what the devil am I going to do with you? . . . the conventions of Vic-

torian fiction allow, allowed no place for the open, the inconclusive ending; and I preached earlier of the freedom characters must be given. My problem is simple—what Charles wants is clear? It is indeed. But what the protagonist wants is not so clear; and I am not at all sure where she is at the moment. Of course if these two were fragments of real life, instead of figments of my imagination, the issue to the dilemma is obvious: the one want combats the other want, and fails or succeeds, as the actuality may be. Fiction usually pretends to conform to the reality: the writer puts the conflicting wants into the ring and then describes the fight—but in fact fixes the fight, letting that want he himself favors win. And we judge writers of fiction both by the skill they show in fixing the fights (in other words, in persuading us that they were not fixed) and by the kind of fighter they fix in favor of: the good one, the tragic one, the evil one, the funny one and so on. (P. 417)

In his case, the narrator maintains, fixing the fight one way or the other is beside the point: the argument for fight-fixing is that it lets the reader know what the writer thinks of the world around him, but since he is now dealing with a world that is a century in the past, the argument does not apply. Therefore, he will take both sides in the fight and determine which side to present as the final one by flipping a coin.

The only significant difference between Chapters 13 and 55 in the relations among author, narrator, and their respective audiences is that in 55 the narrator's presence on the train with Charles more clearly emphasizes his own status as an authorial construct. The narrative audience again takes the narrator at his word, while the authorial audience recognizes that Fowles is fixing the fight by having the narrator claim that he cannot fix it. (Fowles acts like Browning's Duke here: "to fix the fight would be some stooping and I choose never to stoop.") He is, however, fixing it so that it will have two outcomes. The argument over which ending is better fails to see how Fowles has fixed the fight. The question is not whether one ending is better, but rather how Fowles has constructed the narrative so that completeness can be achieved only by his offering a choice of closures (even if as members of the narrative audience we are inclined to follow the narrator's injunction to choose one over the other). Why, in other words, would this narrative have closure but not completeness if Fowles gave the authorial audience only one ending?[6]

In order to answer that question we need to reflect more on the consequences of Chapters 13 and 55 for the rest of the narrative. Like 13, 55 refuses the task of revealing Sarah's character more fully—indeed, Fowles flaunts the narrator's inability to tell us more about her—and like 13, its foregrounding of the synthetic status of the whole narrative displaces some of our mimetic interest onto the thematic functions of the characters. In addition to seeking the reasons why he would want these effects, we need to ask why he should try to accomplish them in these ways. We can best answer the first question about reasons, I think, by noting its connection with one of the striking features of the crucial event of the progression—and one of the mimetic high points of the narrative: Charles's and Sarah's lovemaking.

> Their mouths met with a wild violence that shocked both; made her avert her lips. He covered her cheeks, her eyes, with kisses. His hand at last touched that hair, caressed it, felt the small head through its softness, as the thin-clad body was felt against his arms and breast. Suddenly he buried his face in her neck.
> "We must not . . . we must not . . . this is madness."
> But her arms came round him and pressed his head closer. He did not move. He felt borne on wings of fire, hurtling, but in such tender air, like a child at last let free from school, a prisoner in a green field, a hawk rising. He raised his head and looked at her: an almost savage fierceness. Then they kissed again. . . . He strained that body into his, straining his mouth upon hers, with all the hunger of a long frustration—not merely sexual, for a whole ungovernable torrent of things banned, romance, adventure, sin, madness, animality, all these coursed wildly through him. (Pp. 359–60)

The scene ends with the narrator's revealing remark about the intensity of Charles's desire: "Precisely ninety seconds had passed since he had left her to look into the bedroom" (p. 361). What is striking about the scene is that Charles's passion for Sarah is far out of proportion to his knowledge of her. This fact is soon brought home to him as he notices the blood on his shirt, and realizes that she had lied to him about giving herself to the French Lieutenant. Charles's intense passion, we realize, has less to do with Sarah herself than with what she represents; he loves his idea of Sarah even more than he loves Sarah herself. And his idea of her is very much like ours: although he would not call her a New Woman, he sees her as a contrast to Ernestina, duty, and a constricted way of life; her mystery is such that he is not entirely sure what kind of alternative she represents, but the mystery too is very much a part of her attraction. The language of the scene itself emphasizes Charles's sense of freedom in possessing Sarah, and the passion he exhibits is in large measure a passion for that freedom: "he felt borne on wings of fire, hurtling, but in such tender air, like a child at last let free from school, a prisoner in a green field, a hawk rising. . . . He strained that body into his . . . with all the hunger of a long frustration—not merely sexual, for a whole ungovernable torrent of things banned, romance, adventure, sin, madness, animality."

Had Fowles given us a full mimetic portrait of Sarah, we would be even more disturbed by Charles's behavior here—despite his feeling of being borne in tender air, and despite Sarah's willingness to give herself, we would more painfully register the violence of those ninety seconds. At the same time, the very surprise of the revelation that Sarah is a virgin, that she has more to her history than she has let Charles know undercuts the sense of possession that his sexual act otherwise implies. Because of this reassertion of Sarah's superiority and because we have been consistently turned away from the full mimetic view of Sarah, we focus less on her than on Charles and his reactions and we see him in part in his representativeness.[7] Thus, as the narrative technique gives us Charles's vision in the scene, we adopt it as Fowles's as well and reposition the strong mimetic force of the scene within its symbolic, thematic importance.

Fowles's pattern of engaging us mimetically and then directing that engagement to thematic issues is continued in his representation of Charles's debate with himself in the chapel. Charles's intense personal crisis is resolved very clearly in thematic terms: he chooses the freedom that Sarah values and represents over the duty that Ernestina represents. The choice becomes plain in his dialogue with himself: "You know your choice. You stay in prison, what your time calls duty, honor, self-respect, and you are comfortably safe. Or you are free and crucified" (p. 373). And then shortly after, while Charles stares at the crucifix, the choice is transformed further: Sarah "seemed there beside him, as it were awaiting the marriage service; yet with another end in view. For a moment he could not seize it—and then it came. To uncrucify!" (p. 374). Freedom, life with Sarah, represents a possibility of escaping the constricting hold of the past and opening oneself to the opportunities of the present and future. Charles's emancipation from the past is not complete here: his final thoughts are of having Sarah on his arm as he tours Europe. Nevertheless, in this sequence of scenes at Exeter, Fowles conclusively establishes Charles's choice for Sarah as a choice for the modern age over the Victorian. The rest of the narrative shows Charles living with the consequences of that choice, learning that "escape is not one act" (p. 373) and in the final scenes with Sarah learning more about what freedom for both of them means.

IV

This analysis of these scenes has important implications for our understanding of the relation between character and progression in the whole narrative, as well as for the relation between the mimetic and thematic functions of character. Although the mimetic portrait of Charles is a crucial means for engaging our emotions in the narrative, Fowles is ultimately less concerned with the mimetic functions of his characters than any of the authors we have seen so far, including Orwell. His narrative is neither an action of the kind we examined in *Pride and Prejudice* nor a thesis novel of the kind we examined in *1984*, but is rather an *explanation* of a historical shift that works by showing how individuals participated in—or were caught by—that shift from the Victorian age to the modern. He takes three characters on the cusp of the shift—Charles, Ernestina, and Sarah—indicates that the two women represent very different degrees and kinds of change—Ernestina is the emblem of the new middle class, while Sarah is a twentieth-century liberated woman—and puts the representative Victorian gentleman in the position of having to choose between them. He slowly works out the steps by which the choice is made and then shows that the new age is not to be created by a single choice. The narrator enunciates the principle behind the narrative explanation by quoting Marx on the book's last page: life is "*the actions of men* (and women) *in pursuit of their ends*" (p. 480). Fowles focuses on representative men and women pursuing their ends and shows how they participated in—and helped contribute to—a major historical and cultural shift.

In this kind of narrative, the thematic functions of the characters are developed differently from the way they are in *1984*, the other example we have seen where the thematic component is most important. The progression does not build from individual attributes to multiple thematic functions but rather takes the attributes in the aggregate and emphasizes the representative quality of that collectivity. Charles's belief in his natural superiority to others, for example, does not participate in any developing statement against that attitude but rather signifies one of the ways in which he is representative of his class. One of the things he learns after he makes his choice is to give up this assumption. Furthermore, because the work is a *narrative* explanation, the thematic functions are best seen after the narrative is complete. In *1984*, Winston's concern for the past gets converted into a thematic function as early as Book One when we see how the Party wants to control the past. In *The French Lieutenant's Woman* we are, as I have repeatedly noted, consistently repositioning our mimetic engagement into a broader thematic context, and the full meaning of the thematic sphere is not developed until the end of the narrative: it is only when the instabilities and tensions of the progression have been resolved that we can adequately understand the representative story being told.

Before I turn to the questions of why Fowles accomplishes the effects of chapters 13 and 55 through the narrator's self-conscious commentary and of how they prepare the way for the double ending as the appropriate resolution, it will be useful to indicate how this hypothesis accounts for other elements of the narrative. Much of the existing criticism on the book focuses on the narrative's concern with Darwin's theory of evolution and with Fowles's characteristic concern with existentialism.[8] This hypothesis locates both of those elements within the larger structure of the progression. The concern with Darwin's theory is incorporated in part to signal Fowles's belief in the significance of the shift—a new development in the human species occurred in the move from the Victorian age to the modern—and thus also as a way of understanding that shift. Sarah and Ernestina are both "mutations" of the conventional Victorian lady, but Sarah represents a far greater advance; Charles shows signs of making a successful adaptation to new conditions, and thus becomes a forerunner of what the modern successful man will be. Fowles's concern with existential freedom is incorporated into the value structure of the narrative, as the chapel scene makes the essence of Charles's adaptation his choice for this value. In addition, the hypothesis would account for Sam's role in the narrative as representing another way in which Charles is on the cusp of the shift, but a way which makes Charles's situation more difficult and qualifies the extent of his vision in the chapel, the extent of his adaptation. Charles fails to recognize how his own desire for change has its counterpart in Sam's and so must face the consequences of that failure when he discovers Sam's betrayal. The chapters after Sarah's flight and before the final encounter show that Charles is able to do so.

If this account of the progression and its consequences for character is accurate, then it points to a larger rationale for Fowles's handling of the narration, including the intrusions of Chapters 13 and 55 and the use of the double ending. With the exception of these two chapters and Chapter 61, which sets up the second ending, Fowles has the narrator both adopt the conventions of nineteenth-century omniscience and frequently remind his audience of his temporal location in the late 1960s. Clearly Fowles adopts the conventions of omniscience in order to make his depiction of the Victorian age more powerful, more in keeping with the age itself. If, however, he were to adopt those conventions wholesale, he would unselfconsciously give his audience full access to the thoughts of the major characters and he would conclude the narrative by fixing those characters in a single fate. To do that would be to belie in his method what he affirms in the narrative: the freedom that he prizes as the sign of the modern age would be lost for both the characters and the audience; our guide to both ages would not himself seem to be a creature of the modern age that he continually locates himself within. The solution to this dilemma provided by the narrator's intrusions in Chapters 13 and 55 and by the double ending has consequences for our further understanding of the functions of character in *The French Lieutenant's Woman*.

The solution is not of course one that genuinely allows the characters or the audience freedom; once Fowles commits himself to writing a narrative explanation, he commits himself to "controlling" his characters and persuading his audience. Instead the solution depends on his exploiting the distance between the narrative and authorial audiences in Chapters 13 and 55. As noted above, when we read these chapters, we accept the narrator's statements as members of the narrative audience and reject them as members of the authorial. We need to take one further step as members of the authorial audience and incorporate our acceptance on the narrative level into our understanding of the whole communication from Fowles. That step is to recognize the narrative statements of Chapters 13 and 55 as part of a challenge that Fowles sets himself, a challenge to create and sustain for the narrative audience two related illusions. The first illusion is that his narrative is in fact following the principles of freedom that it recommends; the second is that by creating the first he is transforming his apparent nineteenth-century narrative method into a decidedly modern one. As members of the authorial audience, we need to recognize the illusion, the steps by which it is sustained, and the transformation of method that ensues. If we judge that those steps are artfully concealed from the narrative audience even as they alter our own fuller perception of the narrative, then Fowles will have met his challenge. In other words, if we take this extra step, the tension between the authorial audience and the narrator can be "resolved," though not in the usual sense of bringing one's beliefs into line with the other's. It can be resolved by the authorial audience's growing awareness of how Fowles is using this narrator to help the narrative conform to the ideas it is endorsing.

The key step in creating the illusion is the artful dodge of Chapter 13, where the narrator's endorsement of freedom for characters acts as a screen behind which Fowles escapes the task of giving Sarah full mimetic life. As the narrative audience endorses many of its own pre-existing beliefs, it endorses the narrative's refusal to give an account of Sarah's motives. At the same time, it foregrounds for the authorial audience the synthetic nature of Sarah's character and by extension of all the characters. Both the narrative audience's endorsement and the authorial audience's awareness in turn make possible the non-fixed fixed ending. The narrative audience can accept both Sarah's rejection and Sarah's acceptance of Charles because she has not been, given enough of a mimetic function to make us certain that she would act one way rather than the other (though many of us may have our own convictions on this point). The authorial audience can accept the double ending because it grows out of the prior insistence on the synthetic nature of the characters—once we accept them as constructs then we can very readily accept them doing many things at the bidding of their maker, including of course agreeing to marry or to part forever.

With these considerations in mind, we can also see that the tension of unequal knowledge between author and authorial audience about Sarah's mimetic function ought not be resolved. In effect, this tension gets subsumed under the issue of whether Fowles can sustain the illusion of freedom for the narrative audience. Since it can only be sustained if Sarah remains mimetically incomplete, then the authorial audience is willing to let her remain that way. These considerations also explain why the completeness of the narrative requires a choice between closures: the status of the narrative itself as a product of the new age it is announcing requires such a completion.

At the same time, we need to be aware that Fowles's handling of Charles also makes both endings possible. After his choice in the chapel, Charles does learn that escape is not one act, but the extent of his own growth is not entirely clear. Just as he leaves the chapel with an image of freedom ("Sarah on his arm in the Uffizi" [p. 377]) that emphasizes he has not thrown off all the shackles of his age, so he exhibits other signs of those shackles throughout the later parts of the narrative. The most dramatic evidence of these is his shock at thinking of Sarah living among the Pre-Raphaelites. Consequently, just as both audiences do not know for sure whether Sarah would choose him, both can readily imagine each possible ending for Charles.

Yet these doubts and possibilities do not touch much that is determinately resolved in both endings. By choosing Sarah in the chapel and then not looking back, Charles resolves the major instability of his own life, as he comes to terms both with the past and his future. Furthermore, since his idea of Sarah has been as important—or even

more important—than Sarah herself and since he has grown by following his impulse toward that idea, the difference between the two
endings, though real, is not all that significant. It is not, for example,
equal to the difference between two endings of *Pride and Prejudice* in
one of which Elizabeth and Darcy are united and in the other of
which they are not. Thus, Fowles has erected another smoke screen
with Chapter 55: the fight-fixing that goes on in the double ending is
far less crucial than the fight-fixing that has already gone on in the
chapel scene. In this way, Fowles works a characteristically twentieth-
century narrative subterfuge on his audiences.

Nevertheless, as members of the authorial audience we need to see
that the order of the two endings is not as arbitrary as the narrator's
coin-flip would have the narrative audience believe. In the second
ending, Charles takes another step along the path to the modern age
because he finds some strength after the rejection, something upon
which to build as he faces the now uncertain future with the certainty
that Sarah will never share it with him. Once we have seen Charles
take such a step, we could not go back to an ending in which he stops
short of it. In this respect, given the emphases of the narrative on the
shift toward the modern age, the second ending not only must be
second, but it will also probably be preferred by most readers. But
there is nothing in the narrative that *requires* Charles to take this last
step or renders Sarah's acceptance of his proposal in the first ending,
an acceptance which she makes in her characteristically enigmatic
way through Lalage, inconsistent with what has gone before.

The double ending, finally, is also appropriate for the narrative because it removes us once again from our mimetic involvement with
the characters and focuses some of our attention on the twentieth-
century method of narration. It also reminds us of the synthetic elements of the characters and thereby reinforces for the last time their
importance as representative figures. Consequently, the final emphasis of the narrative is not on the individual characters but on the history in which they participate.

V

All this analysis raises one final question about the relation between
the narrative and authorial audiences. This account of the two audiences maintains that there is a considerable distance between them in
Chapters 13, 55, 60, and 61, and much less distance during the other
chapters. The narrative audience accepts the illusion of the spontaneously developing, unfixed narrative and so remains focused on the
mimetic components of the characters throughout (for the narrative

audience the issue of Sarah's motivation remains an unresolved problem in the narrative). The authorial audience, on the other hand, sometimes accepts the illusion and sometimes—in 13, 55, 60, and 61—sees behind it to the synthetic component of the characters and the narrative as a whole. Can Fowles really have it both ways? Can the authorial audience be asked both to develop the emotional responses to characters that go along with the development of the mimetic component and then move away from those responses when the foregrounding of the synthetic increases our distance from the mimesis?

In one sense, these questions boil down to another one: how flexible is the authorial audience? Or, to put it another way, how able is the authorial audience to move from reading mimetically to reading thematically-synthetically? I do think that there are limits on the jerks and jolts an author can legitimately put his audience through, but I do not think that Fowles violates those limits here. If at the end of "Haircut," Whitey started reflecting on his own role as Lardner's narrator, or if at the end of *Pride and Prejudice* Austen's narrator announced that she was not going to tell us about the aftermath of Elizabeth and Darcy's engagement because it was time to admit that these characters were really only her puppets, then the implicit rhetorical contracts of these narratives would be violated. The authorial audience would have been asked to invest a kind of commitment and feeling for the greater part of the narrative that was then undermined or even mocked by the ending.

Fowles takes several steps to avoid that kind of jarring effect on his audience. First, establishing the initial tension through the narrative manner of the opening chapter puts the authorial audience on notice to begin thinking about the synthetic construction of the whole narrative. Second, the emphasis on the representative quality of the characters even as the authorial audience develops expectations and desires about their fates keeps the thematic import—and implicitly the synthetic component—of the characters as an important element of the narrative. Third, the foregrounding of the synthetic in Chapter 13 occurs early enough for the authorial audience to incorporate the tensions it produces into their developing response to the narrative. It complicates the authorial audience's reactions on the mimetic level and to some extent qualifies our subsequent mimetic involvement. Fowles's challenge, in part, is to reengage the authorial audience on the mimetic level sufficiently to make us care about Charles's choice not only for what it means thematically but also for Charles himself. The novel's popular success is indirect but eloquent testimony to his ability to meet that challenge. From this perspective, we can also see Chapter 55 as a necessary intrusion after the point of greatest mimetic intensity—the events at Exeter and their consequences in Charles's last trip to Lyme to break his engagement—to move the authorial audience back to the importance of the thematic issues of the novel—and the way they are reflected in the synthetic.

If this analysis has merit, then it suggests that authorial audiences can be veritable Olympic gymnasts in their flexibility at shifting levels of reading, provided that the author's program is orchestrated skillfully enough to make those shifts function coherently within the narrative as a whole. The alternative hypothesis, that Fowles is asking too much of his audience in requiring us to change our commitments from the mimetic to the synthetic (and then to the thematic) spheres, has the advantage of emphasizing the way in which the authorial and narrative audiences do merge for long stretches of Fowles's book, but it has the greater disadvantage of straitjacketing the authorial audience by presuming that it does not pay attention to the initial tension and that the only way it can resume reading mimetically after Chapter 13 is to forget the effects of that chapter. Its great disadvantage, in short, is to presume that the authorial audience cannot simultaneously be aware of the three components of the characters and of the narrative as a whole. My claim is that developing such an awareness is essentially what it means to be in Fowles's audience here, and that Fowles provides the mechanisms for that awareness to develop.

VI

The issues raised in these opening three chapters about thematizing in interpretation and about the different ways characters can function thematically will remain with us as we broaden our focus in the next two chapters and look harder at the synthetic component of character and its relation to the mimetic and thematic components. To some extent, however, these issues will move to the background as others become more pressing. Consequently, it will be helpful to emphasize some of the conclusions of the study to this point.

1. Although thematizing is a fundamental part of interpretation, it is only a part. To pay attention only to the thematic ends of any of the narratives we have looked at, including *1984* and *The French Lieutenant's Woman*, would be to do a partial analysis at best and would likely lead to significant distortions as well.

2. Different narratives require different kinds of thematizing. The clearest difference here is that between the way the thematic functions of the protagonists work in *Pride and Prejudice* and *The French Lieutenant's Woman*. In Austen's narrative individual attributes are con-

verted by the progression into different thematic functions, whereas in Fowles's the progression works on the representative quality of the aggregate of attributes.

3. The progression, and especially the way it makes use of the mimetic function, determines the point at which the generalizing move of thematism should stop. In this respect, the lack of a full mimetic function for Sarah actually invites broader thematic generalizations about her than the mimetic function of, say, Marcher, invites about him, and I believe that the narrative leaves some room for such generalizations—for example, we can take quite seriously the narrator's reference to her as the Sphinx. At the same time, the progression's dominant concern with the shift from the Victorian age to the modern requires us to treat the reference as a metaphorical rather than literal one.

4. The foregrounding of the synthetic component of character frequently introduces a significant difference between the narrative and authorial audiences. This difference typically means that the progression will be complicated by some tension between the narrator and the authorial audience, and the author may use that tension to displace our interest from the mimetic to the thematic component of character.

5. There are no hard-and-fast rules about the way that progressions may develop. Instabilities can be introduced immediately as in *Pride and Prejudice* or more leisurely as in *The French Lieutenant's Woman*. Progression may be generated for a time by the arousal and resolution of tension as in *1984* and then switch to movement by instability. Atlernatively, progression may intermittently be complicated, as it is in *The French Lieutenant's Woman*, by the development of tensions. The corollary of this finding is that there are no hard-and-fast rules about how or when mimetic and thematic dimensions of a character will be converted into functions. All such questions deserve the answer, it depends on the particular progression.

6. What all these previous conclusions suggest is that the development of this rhetorical theory is not so much the development of conclusions about the necessary connections among the components of character as it is the establishment and illustration of categories and principles that allow us to discover the functions of character within any one work. This point is clearly one that I must return to before the progression of this argument can be complete.

In addition to working toward these conclusions, I have implicitly been arguing for the importance of conceiving progression as I do, and of course in the previous chapter I have argued that this conception has a greater explanatory power than Scholes's method of reading by oppositions. As I turn in the next chapter to take up the interaction among the mimetic, thematic, and synthetic roles of a secondary character, I shall also take up an alternative model for analyzing progression: the psychoanalytically based one offered by Peter Brooks in *Reading for the Plot*. Just as this chapter has required me to expand on the concepts of audience I have been employing so far, a consideration of Brooks's model will require me to expand on the concept of progression I have been using. The specific focus of my discussion will be Dickens's Wemmick in *Great Expectations*, a narrative that Brooks himself discusses at length.

4 Progression and the Synthetic Secondary Character: The Case of John Wemmick

I

As noted in the introduction, my approach to the analyis of narrative progression claims to be an advance over other discussions of plot and structure because it pays attention to the temporal dynamics of the authorial audience's experience of narrative. In the discussions of thematizing so far, I have been illustrating that conception of progression, and as particular occasions such as the discussion of Scholes have allowed, I have been taking small steps to substantiate the introductory claim. I turn now to focus explicitly on the concept of progression and its explanatory power. I will compare the ideas about progression, both implicit and explicit, that I have drawn upon to this point, with the ideas about "reading for the plot" advanced by Peter Brooks in his attempt to account for the dynamics of narrative.[1] Brooks's model provides a good test of my own not only because it is the most powerful model recently advanced but also because, like mine, it wants to consider how the reader's experience is directed by the text.[2] Rather than being a rhetorically based theory, however, it is a psychoanalytically based one.

I will compare the models for analyzing narrative dynamics in connection with Dickens's *Great Expectations*, a narrative that Brooks also analyzes and that raises questions about the synthetic component of character—especially through Dickens's use of Wemmick. Indeed, Wemmick provides us with an occasion to consider the potentially problematic relationships among the three functions of character, because his outlandish mimesis foregrounds his synthetic status and has consequences for both our sense of Dickens's thematic intentions and our own understanding of Pip's mimetic function. Moreover, the variety of Wemmick's functions also illustrates some important general principles of progression that are highlighted by the comparison with Brooks's model.

107

Brooks offers an initial definition of plot that coincides with much of my own definition of progression, especially in its twin emphases on the temporality and centrality of plot: "Plot . . . is not a matter of typology or of fixed structures, but rather a structuring operation peculiar to those messages that are developed through temporal succession, the instrumental logic of a specific mode of human understanding. Plot . . . is the logic and dynamic of narrative, and narrative itself is a form of understanding and explanation" (p. 10). From this definition, Brooks sets out to develop a model for discussing the experiential dynamics of reading for the plot, a model that he labels an "erotics of art" (p. 36). As I examine that model and its application to Dickens's novel, I shall argue that despite Brooks's success in moving beyond the essentially static conceptions of structure proposed by other narratologists, he nevertheless fails to offer an adequate theory of reading for the plot.

As noted briefly above, Brooks departs from much previous psychoanalytic criticism by focusing not on the unconscious of the author, reader, or characters, but rather on the psychodynamics of the text: he wants, in his words, to "superimpose psychic functioning on textual functioning" in order to discover "something about how textual dynamics work and something about their psychic equivalences" (p. 90). His method privileges psychoanalysis as the way to explain how texts operate, but the method also respects textual functioning: in reading Brooks, one typically feels that narrative structure is being illuminated rather than made to lie on a bed fashioned by Procrustes for Freud.

Brooks begins with narrative, not psychoanalysis, and comments on the paradox of endings. The end always acts in some influential way on everything that precedes it, since the ending is what the beginning and the middle are preparing us for. Furthermore, "it is at the end—for Barthes as for Aristotle—that recognition brings illumination, which then can shed its retrospective light" (p. 92). Thus,

> if in the beginning stands desire, and this shows itself ultimately to be desire for the end, between beginning and end stands a middle that we feel to be necessary . . . but whose processes, of transformation and working-through, remain obscure. Here it is that Freud's most ambitious investigation of ends in relation to beginnings may be of help, and may contribute to a properly dynamic model of plot. (P. 96)

That most ambitious investigation is *Beyond the Pleasure Principle*, and Brooks focuses first on what help it might be in thinking about repetition in narrative. "Narrative always makes the implicit claim to be in a state of repetition, as a going over again of a ground already covered: a *sjužet* repeating a *fabula*, as the detective retraces the tracks of the criminal" (p. 97). In addition, repetition is the stock in trade of literary discourse: "rhyme, alliteration, assonance, meter, refrain, all the mnemonic elements of literature and indeed most of its tropes are in some manner repetitions that take us back in the text, that allow the ear, the eye, the mind to make connections, conscious or unconscious, between different textual moments, to see past and present as related and as establishing a future that will be noticeable as some variation in the pattern" (p. 99). In Freud's text, repetition is first introduced as a compulsion directed toward the assertion of mastery, as in the *fort-da* game, and then it becomes a compulsion directed at "binding" the instinctual drive for immediate gratification. Thus, Freud views repetition as making possible both the attainment of mastery and the postponement of gratification.

Similarly, Brooks argues, repetition in narrative functions as a "binding of textual energies that allows them to be mastered by putting them into serviceable form, usable 'bundles,' within the energetic economy of the narrative;" "repetition, repeat, recall, symmetry, all these journeys back in the text, returns to and returns of . . . allow us to bind one textual moment to another in terms of similarity or substitution rather than mere contiguity" (p. 101). In this respect, repetition is a key to our mastery over—and hence, pleasure in—the text; at the same time it will frequently involve postponement of that pleasure. "As the word 'binding' itself suggests, these formalizations [i.e., elements of the text that cause us to recognize sameness in difference] and the recognitions they provoke may in some sense be painful: they create a delay, a postponement in the discharge of energy, a turning back from immediate pleasure, to ensure that the ultimate pleasurable discharge will be more complete" (pp. 101–2).

Brooks next follows Freud through his examination of the relation between the repetition compulsion and the instinctual drives, and his conclusion that instincts are not drives toward change but toward stability, or indeed, toward the restoration of an earlier state of things. This conclusion in turn leads to the concept of the death instinct, a concept that stresses not just an organism's drive toward death but also its drive to follow the path to death in its own way. Brooks summarizes the point this way: "'the organism wishes to die only in its own fashion,'" and therefore, it will "struggle against events (dangers) that would help it to achieve its goal too rapidly—by a kind of short circuit" (p. 102). Repetition in narrative, then, says Brooks, works first to allow the operation of the death instinct, the drive toward the end as it is manifest in the text's attempt to return to an earlier state. But repetition also works to "retard the pleasure princi-ple's search for the gratification of discharge" which will occur when the end is reached. Thus, if we begin in an initiation of tension that seeks its own release and generates a desire for the end, the middle must be the place where the narrative seeks that end in the appropri-ate way, avoiding short-circuit even as it inexorably moves toward a return to the quiescent state before the beginning. The middle is a kind of detour between two states of quiescence at either end of the narrative.

Brooks offers the following succinct summary of his model.

[Plot] structures ends (death, quiescence, nonnarratability) against beginnings (Eros, stimulation into tension, the desire of narrative) in a manner that necessitates the middle as detour, as struggle to-ward the end under the compulsion of imposed delay, as ara-besque in the dilatory space of the text. The model proposes that we live in order to die, hence that the intentionality of plot lies in its orientation toward the end even while the end must be achieved only through detour. This re-establishes the necessary distance be-tween beginning and end, maintained through the play of those drives that connect them yet prevent the one collapsing back into the other. . . . Crucial to the space of this play are the repeti-tions serving to bind the energy of the text so as to make its final discharge more effective. In fictional plots, these bindings are a system of repetitions which are returns to and returns of, con-founding the movement forward to the end with a movement back to origins, reversing meaning within forward-moving time, serv-ing to formalize the system of textual energies, offering the plea-surable possibility (or illusion) of "meaning" wrested from "life." (Pp. 107–8)

Brooks's model is, I think, very attractive. It not only focuses on the temporal, experiential dimension of reading, but also offers strong accounts of beginnings, middles, and ends. It offers a sensible account of the beginning as the introduction of some tension which produces desire for resolution; a suggestive analysis of the paradoxi-cal drives of the middle, toward both continuation and closure; and a powerful account of the end as the dominant position of the narra-tive, one which exercises control over both the beginning and the middle. As in his definition of plot, there is considerable overlap here with my discussions of the introduction of instabilities and tensions, their complication in the middle, and their resolution at the end. At the same time, his discussion indicates that there are significant dis-agreements between us.

II

First, my conception of progression does not give so much dominance to the ending. Where Brooks sees the beginning and the middle as determined by the end, I see the three parts as more mutually determinative. When we read for the progression, we experience the ending as determined by the beginning and the middle, even as it has the potential, in providing both completeness and closure, to transform the experience of reading the beginning and the middle. This difference about the relation between the three stages of narrative is related to a larger difference based on a principle that I have been working with only implicitly to this point. This principle begins to emerge when we ask if there is anything beyond beginning, middle, and end that determines all three, or perhaps better, determines the way in which they are mutually determinative of each other. Can we extend our rhetorical (as distinct from our biographical or sociohistorical) analysis and explain why a particular beginning is chosen or why one out of many possible paths through the middle of the narrative is taken or why a particular kind of resolution might be better than another one? Answering these questions depends on our developing some working hypothesis of an overall design, some principle of a whole that is greater than the sum of the parts.

Austen's choice to begin *Pride and Prejudice* with the conversation between the Bennets not only has significant consequences for the middle and the end but is itself a consequence of a larger design, the development of a comic action that incorporates the narrator's norms and judgments about the marriage market as part of the comic satisfaction to be associated with the ending. Perhaps even more telling are Austen's choices in the middle. To have Darcy's first proposal occur at Rosings, a setting permeated by the values of Lady Catherine, Collins, and to a lesser extent of Charlotte; to have Elizabeth drawn to Darcy first through the intersection of his letter and her own sense of justice, then through what she sees and hears at Pemberly, and then finally through her own gratitude for his intercession in the Lydia-Wickham affair; to have the second proposal come about in part through the meddling of Lady Catherine: all these turns of the progression, which could have been managed in other ways, are in some nontrivial sense determined by the overall design. All these turns not only work to complicate and resolve the instabilities along the track established in the first half of the narrative but they also develop the nuances of the narrator's norms and thus significantly define the kind of satisfaction offered by the final resolution.

Similarly, although Fowles might have ended *The French Lieuten-ant's Woman* in many ways—Charles and Sarah might have been re-united and sent to an uncertain future in America—the ending is determined not just by what the beginning and middle allow but also by what the principle of design revealed in those parts allows. Given that design of explaining the shift from the Victorian Age to the mod-ern, his ending, with its choice of closures, is more appropriate than the one suggested above. The reasoning may appear circular here but the circularity is more apparent than real. The notion of the whole is, to be sure, developed from reading the parts, but since developing that notion is always part of reading for the progression—since our sense of the whole is itself always in motion—it is also always corri-gible. When we read the first chapter of *Pride and Prejudice*, we make inferences about the whole of which it is a part, and our sense of that whole does influence our reading of new parts. But as the analyses of the ending of "Haircut" and of Chapter 13 of *The French Lieutenant's Woman* indicate, the new parts are also capable of radically reshaping our sense of the whole.[3]

Perhaps the most useful way to illustrate the differences between Brooks's model and mine is to consider the different ways they would deal with the relations between beginning, middle, and end in works with flawed endings. Within Brooks's system there are two ways an ending can go wrong: it can come too soon, and thus short-circuit the working out of the desires aroused by the beginning and the mid-dle; or it can unbind textual material that has been bound by the pattern of repetitions and thus fail to leave the reader in a state of quiescence.

In my terms, the first kind of flaw would be the production of an arbitrary resolution, one in which an author substitutes the impera-tive to provide a resolution for the greater imperative to work out the possibilities for resolution inherent in the introduction and compli-cation of instabilities and tensions. The second kind would be the reintroduction of—or the failure to resolve—instabilities of the begin-ning or middle. Although I would be more concerned than Brooks with relating these flaws to some conception of a developing whole for each specific case, the differences between the models at this point are as much terminological as they are conceptual. A close look at the problems raised by a case such as the Phelps farm episode at the end of *Huckleberry Finn* will indicate that Brooks's two explanations of how endings can go wrong are insufficient. This conclusion in turn sug-gests that his model does not do full justice to the ways that endings can relate to beginnings and middles.

The trouble with the Phelps farm episode is certainly not one of short-circuit; the whole business is unduly protracted. In part, however, the trouble may be that as Twain tries to bind some early textual material through the return of Tom Sawyer, he unbinds some material about Huck's relation to Jim that has been apparently bound for good in Huck's decision to go to hell: The intuitive sense of Jim's humanity that resides behind Huck's decision does not lead him to resist some of Tom Sawyer's inhumane plans for Jim in the Evasion. Yet the whole problem with the ending is more complicated than that, as a look at the tasks Twain sets for himself in the narrative makes clear.

In brief, Twain's narrative progresses by intertwining the two logically independent stories of Jim's quest for freedom and Huck's more intuitive, reactive attempt to find his niche in the world (calling Huck's efforts a "quest" would overstate his sense of direction) by working out his relationship to his society. The dominant focus, of course, is on Huck, and we see him in the beginning unable to enter fully into the world of Miss Watson and the Widow Douglas, or that of Tom Sawyer and his romantic fancies, or that of his Pap. Life on the raft with Jim presents a refuge from the larger world and its problems, but that life is itself provisional and unstable as both the steamboat and the King and the Duke dramatically prove. Twain nevertheless gives his audience enough of their undisrupted life to show the developing bond between the white boy and the black man. He then uses the shore episodes both to portray Huck's intuitive education in the hypocrisy and corruption of "sivilization" and to make his audience even more aware of those features. That development in turn makes the decision to go to hell a kind of resolution to Huck's hitherto unstable situation: he decides he must live outside the professed morality of his society, even if it means suffering the worst consequences the society predicts for such outsiders. What Twain needs at this point is not so much a device of completeness for Huck but a device of closure: a major part of the developing whole, the story of the moral implications of Huck's attempts to define his relation to his society, is essentially complete. If Twain could find a way to have Huck decide to light out for the territory at this point, he would be well on his way to a satisfactory ending.

The problem he faces, however, is how to end Jim's quest. Having intertwined Huck's story with Jim's, Twain cannot conclude Huck's until he also concludes Jim's. And the options he has open are not many: Jim is now in the Deep South where he will be regarded as the rightful property of some one or other of the white folks. The most logical thing to do is have Jim be set free by his owner, but given the way Miss Watson has already been portrayed, to do that would be to create a deus ex machina effect. So, falling back on his skills as a humorist, satirist, and scene writer, Twain gives us the Evasion, his way of trying to hide the deus ex machina behind a cloud of Tom Sawyer's romantic dust. But creating the cloud causes more problems than unbinding the material about Huck's relation to Jim. It introduces material that is largely extraneous to the instabilities that have moved the plot until this point and it develops that material at great length. Although the scenes of the Evasion are funny in themselves, their irrelevance to what has gone before makes them as annoying as they are humorous.

The more general point here is that the beginning and the middle of *Huckleberry Finn* get developed in such a way that Twain has an unsolvable problem on his hands: given that beginning and middle, he cannot write a satisfactory ending. The ending in this case is not determinative of the beginning and the middle, and I would suggest that no ending could be. Furthermore, the ways the ending goes wrong exceed the ways predicted by Brooks's theory. One could perhaps say that had Twain initially chosen a better ending, he could have made it determinative of the beginning and the middle. But such a move would have required him to write a different beginning and middle, and who would want to give up the beginning and middle that Twain has created?

The corollary of this point about Brooks's overemphasis on the power of the ending is that he underestimates the power of the middle. Although he attributes to middles the important role of appropriately guiding the desires aroused by the beginning, the middle remains a means subordinated to the end of reaching resolution. It is a place of detour, of deflected direction, of arabesques. As *Huckleberry Finn* and *Pride and Prejudice* show, it is all those things—but can be much more as well. In Twain's novel, the middle creates the impossibility of satisfactory ending, while in Austen's it is the place where many of the thematic functions of Elizabeth's character—especially those surrounding her own pride—are realized.

A second significant difference between Brooks's model and my own is what each one implies about the reader's activity—and thus, ultimately what each implies about the nature of the narrative text. Brooks's discussion of the dynamics of reading becomes finally a description of a sequence of drives and reactions—the beginning establishes an initial tension that produces desire for ending, the middle produces the detour or arabesque leading eventually toward the end, and the end produces the discharge of pleasure with the release of the tension. This account is very consistent with Brooks's announced intention of imposing "psychic functioning on textual functioning." The problem is not with its consistency but with its adequacy as a description of the reader's activity. In Brooks's account, the dynamics of the plot itself merge with the dynamics of reading that plot. To give an account of reading for the plot is to give an account of the structure of the plot. In this respect, Brooks is working with a model of a single-layered text.

By contrast, the model of the text implied in my account of progression is double-layered. On this account, the text contains not just the patterns of instabilities, tensions, and resolutions but also the authorial audience's responses to those patterns.[4] In other words, the concept of progression assumes that the narrative text needs to be regarded as the fusion of two structures: (1) the narrative structure per se—essentially the structure that Brooks describes in his model, or what I call the pattern of instabilities and tensions; and (2) the sequence of responses to that structure that the text calls forth from the authorial audience.[5] In still other words, we might say that progression involves not only the developing pattern of instabilities and tensions but also the accompanying sequence of *attitudes* that the authorial audience is asked to take toward that pattern. This conception has been operating throughout my analysis so far, perhaps most obviously in the discussion of Scholes's model and my arguments about the importance of the authorial audience's involvement with the mimetic component of character. The pattern of judgments, fears, hopes, desires, expectations, and so on that typically but not exclusively cluster around the mimetic component is as much a part of the dynamics of reading as the sequence of actions in which the character participates. I will return to this point shortly because it has consequences for a third difference between Brooks's model and mine, but there is another side to this present difference that needs to be illuminated.

In the discussion of "Haircut" in the introduction, I noted that the final sentences help resolve the instabilities by contributing to the completion of the narrative through the alteration of the authorial audience's understanding of the resolution that has already been narrated. In the discussion of *Pride and Prejudice*, I claimed that although Charlotte Lucas's marriage to Collins does not complicate the instabilities of the main narrative line it nevertheless had a significant influence on the authorial audience's understanding of that line, and indeed, played an important role in Austen's development of the thematic function associated with Elizabeth's attribute of independence from the marriage market. Such conclusions about the dynamics of reading these narratives are, I think, simply not available if one is operating within Brooks's system. When the dynamics of reading are merged with the dynamics of plot structure, the reader's role is implicitly limited to responding to the movement of the instabilities.

Both consequences of this second difference between Brooks's model and my own are related to the third difference. Because Brooks conflates the dynamics of reading and the dynamics of plot, he must find the key to reading for the plot not in the reader's affective experience of the text but in formal features of the text, and as we have seen, his psychoanalytical framework leads him to repetition as the identifiable key. In order, however, to account for the significance of repetition within the limits of his way of talking about the reader's experience, he must resort to talking about the thematic importance of the repetitions. The problem again is not so much that this is wrong, but that it is inadequate. When repetition gets linked to theme, then reading for the plot becomes reading for the themes in motion.

III

These last two differences between the models should become clearer as we examine Brooks's analysis of *Great Expectations*, a novel that he chooses in part because it "gives in the highest degree the impression that its central meanings depend on the workings-out of its plot" (p. 114). Furthermore, the novel is "concerned with finding a plot and losing it, with the precipitation of the sense of plottedness around its hero, and his eventual 'cure' from plot. The novel imagines in its structure the kind of structuring operation of reading that plot is" (p. 114). Note here that in the very act of setting up his analysis Brooks implicitly makes reading for the plot reading about plot. Brooks's model is already committing him to read about themes in motion, but that model leads him away from such standard themes as the individual and society toward this more reflexive one.

Brooks begins his account with an analysis of the novel's famous opening paragraphs, where Pip discusses his acquisition of his name and his "first most vivid and broad impression of the identity of things." This impression occurs on the day in the churchyard when he became fully conscious of his environment and his own place in it as an orphan, a consciousness that in turn leads to his tears that are then interrupted by a "terrible voice," crying out "Hold your noise!"[6] Brooks has many insightful things to say about this passage, some of which I shall return to, but his main conclusion stresses what the passage suggests about the role of plot in the novel. "This beginning establishes Pip as an existence without a plot, at the very moment of occurrence of that event which will prove to be decisive for the plotting of his existence, as he will discover only two-thirds of the way through the novel" (p. 117). In the first part of the novel, Brooks argues, Pip is in search of a plot and the novel recounts how a plot seems to gather around him. In fact, Brooks identifies four lines of plot moving around Pip before the declaration of his expectations:

1. Communion with the convict/criminal deviance.
2. Naterally wicious/bringing up by hand.
3. The dream of Satis House/the fairy tale.
4. The nightmare of Satis House/the witch tale. (P. 117)

Brooks argues further that the four plots are paired as follows: 2/1 = 3/4. "That is, there is in each case an 'official' and censoring plot standing over a 'repressed' plot" (p. 117). Pip himself favors plot 3, and when Jaggers comes with the news of Pip's Expectations, it appears that reality is conforming to his desire, and that the question of plot is now taken care of. But of course the Expectations "in fact only mask further the problem of the repressed plots" (p. 117).

The relation between the official and the repressed plots is perhaps best illustrated by the relation between the official, public events of Pip's life and both the continual return of "the convict material" and the repetitive features of Pip's experience in Satis House. After Pip is "bound" as an apprentice to Joe, the plot is all but suspended as the narrative recounts what Brooks calls a "purely iterative existence" in which the romance of life appears to be shut out. After the announcement of the expectations, Pip thinks that he need only wait for the next turn of the plot that is now happily controlling his life. Yet for the reader neither binding is sufficient to contain the energy discharged by the initial graveyard scene and the initial visits to Satis House. Moreover, the reappearance of the convict's leg-iron, and of Joe's file, as well as the "compulsive reproductive repetition that characterizes every detail of Satis House" (p. 123), including the trips by Pip and Miss Havisham around the bridal cake, signal the important presence of the repressed plots.

The middle of the narrative is, according to Brooks, "notably characterized by the return," specifically Pip's returns from London to his hometown, ostensibly to see and make reparation to Joe Gargery, and perhaps to find out something of Miss Havisham's intentions for him, but deflected always to a reminder of the nightmare of Satis House and his association with the convict. "Each return suggests that Pip's official plots, which seem to speak of progress, ascent, and the satisfaction of desire, are in fact subject to a process of repetition of the yet unmastered past, the true determinant of his life's direction" (p. 125).

Pip comes face to face with this determinant in the novel's recognition scene, which Brooks sees operating "for Pip as a painful forcing through of layers of repression, an analogue of analytic work, compelling Pip to recognize that what he calls 'that chance encounter of long ago' is no chance, and cannot be assigned to the buried past but must be repeated, reenacted, worked through in the present" (p. 128). Pip's "education and training in gentility turn out to be merely an agency in the repression of the determinative convict plot. Likewise, the daydream/fairy tale of Satis House stands revealed as a repression, or perhaps a 'secondary revision' of the nightmare" (p. 130). The "return of the repressed shows that the story Pip would tell about himself has all along been undermined and rewritten by the more complex history of unconscious desire, unavailable to the conscious subject but at work in the text. Pip has in fact misread the plot of his life" (p. 130).

The resolution of the plot for Pip occurs after he comes to accept Magwitch, which also means accepting his past as both "determinative and *past.*" Once Pip is able, through the repetitions of the aborted escape, to work through the material from his past, he is in effect able to escape from plot. In this respect, Dickens's original ending to the narrative is superior to the amended ending in which Pip's reunion with Estella may undercut the extent of his escape. Brooks offers the following summary of his conclusions:

> *Great Expectations* is exemplary in demonstrating both the need for plot and its status as deviance, both the need for narration and the necessity to be cured from it. The deviance and error of plot may necessarily result from the the interplay of desire in its history with the narrative insistence on explanatory form: the desire to wrest beginnings and ends from the uninterrupted flow of middles, from temporality itself; the search for that significant closure that would illuminate the sense of an existence, the meaning of life. The desire for meaning is ultimately the reader's who must mime Pip's acts of reading but do them better. Both using and subverting the systems of meaning discovered or postulated by its hero, *Great Expectations* exposes for its reader the very reading process itself: the way the reader goes about finding meaning in the narrative text, and the limits of that meaning as the limits of narrative. (P. 140)

As even this somewhat truncated summary of Brooks's reading indicates, he is an impressive reader, one who uses his model with appropriate flexibility to produce an interpretation that is in many ways both compelling and original. My quarrel is less with the particulars of that reading than with its adequacy as an account of the experiential dynamics of *Great Expectations.* Brooks's theoretical conflation of plot structure and the reader's experience has its corresponding practical conflation here. The affective component of reading for the plot is nowhere present in Brooks's analysis. The reader's activity is exclusively cognitive: "The desire for meaning is ultimately the reader's who must mime Pip's acts of reading but do them better." Brook's reading in effect collapses the question of the experiential dynamics of the narrative with the question of how Pip's narrative can itself be seen as about plot. If one wants to know an answer to this second question, then Brooks is the man to see, but if one wants to know the answer to the first question, one better look somewhere else. In short, Brooks's conflation of the question of experiential dynamics with a question about a theme in motion fails to do justice to the complexity of the response built into Dickens's narrative. I shall now try to substantiate these brave words by offering a contrasting analysis of the progression. In order to build the contrast with Brooks's reading, I shall focus first on material he does discuss—the opening chapters—and then on material he does not discuss—the functions of Wemmick. Considering Wemmick will also add to the general movement of this part of the book, because he is a good example of how a character with a foregrounded synthetic component can affect both the mimetic and thematic levels of our reading.

IV

If we are not asking how *Great Expectations* is itself about plot, then we will respond more directly to the literal level of the opening paragraphs, and thus can recuperate some of Brooks's shrewd, specific insights. Rather than noting that these paragraphs characterize Pip as an existence without a plot, we note instead that they establish a specific instability that becomes the generating moment for the whole narrative. With Pip's description of his "first fancies" about his parents on the basis of the shapes of the letters on their tombstones, the narrative introduces the important idea that at this stage Pip is not the best reader of signs.[7] Thus, later when Pip concludes that Miss Havisham is the agent behind his Expectations, we have cause to recognize that the tension of unequal knowledge between Dickens and the authorial audience is nevertheless maintained. More germane to the opening itself, the way in which Pip is wrong—imagining appearances from the shapes of the letters on tombstones—emphasizes the force of the initial instability, as it emphasizes his distance from and ignorance of his parents.

In the passage recounting his "first most vivid and broad impression of the identity of things," Pip tells us, as Brooks points out, how in effect he has become certain of his own difference from and aloneness among everything else. He concludes his litany of what he knows ("this was the churchyard, there were the graves of my dead parents and brothers, that was the marshes, that over there was the river, and beyond that was the sea") with his conclusions that "the small bundle of shivers growing afraid of it all and beginning to cry, was Pip." Because Pip's acquisition of self-consciousness is accompanied by his fear and grief, the narrative identifies the initial instability as one involving Pip's own identity and place in the world. In this respect, the omission of Pip's situation as the adopted son of Joe and Mrs. Joe is significant: that situation is less a part of his identity than his awareness of himself as orphan. Furthermore, the information of the first paragraph—Pip's account of how he got his name—now functions to emphasize his aloneness: he has not only lost his parents and brothers but also the name he shared with them.[8] The narrative, then, gets its initial movement from the problem of whether and how this orphan will achieve an identity that will enable him to overcome his fear and anxiety. This question gets modified in different ways as the narrative progresses (when Pip the narrator speaks from the time of narration we worry less about whether and more about how) and redefines and resituates Pip's fear and anxiety, but it remains a significant issue until the very end of the narrative.

Again if we are not asking about how Dickens's novel is itself about plot, but rather what its temporal dynamics are, then we will redescribe Brooks's four plot lines in the opening chapters as three, because there are three distinguishable tracks along which the instabilities operate, all three of which are related to the initial instability of Pip's anxiety about identity. These three are what we might call the convict plot, the home plot, and the Satis House plot. In addition, the initiating moments of the convict plot and the Satis House plot establish some significant tensions that suggest an expansion of the scope of the narrative beyond Pip's struggle; the early moments of the convict plot establish a tension about the relationship between Pip's convict and his hated counterpart, and the introduction of Miss Havisham immediately introduces a tension about her past as well as about the presence of Estella in her house. Although the resolutions of these tensions, like the development of the instabilities along three different tracks, does place Pip's story in a much broader thematic context, those resolutions are more striking for the way in which Dickens skillfully links them to the pattern of instabilities surrounding Pip. But that is getting ahead of our ourselves.

As we move into the middle of the narrative we see that the chief (though by no means only) source of the complication of the instabilities is Pip's resistance to the identity offered by his home: he can be an honest blacksmith like Joe. At the same time, we recognize that the way in which Dickens has intertwined the plots makes Pip's acceptance of that identity virtually impossible. He begins with the convict plot, immediately interlaces it with the home plot, and then further entwines them both with the Satis House plot, first covertly, then overtly. More specifically, Pip's association with the convict not only complicates his life with Mrs. Joe by making him steal from her, but for him it also increases his tendency to internalize her treatment of him as "naterally wicious." With this sense of his identity firmly established by the time he goes to Satis House, he is of course easily stung by being regarded as "common" and his desire to escape the scenes of his identity as criminal is understandably strong. At the same time, however, the home plot shows us that another side of his identity, the one that develops in his relationship with Joe, has made him unfit for the role he tries to play when the Expectations arrive. He goes on miserably caught between these two sides of his identity until Magwitch makes himself known, a resolution of a tension that sets in motion a major shift in the development of the instabilities. In short, Magwitch's return sets in motion a chain of events in which Pip works through his anxiety and fear about his identity by working back through the instabilities of the now fully interconnected plots and coming finally to accept and appreciate first Magwitch, then Joe, and finally himself.

In the course of these events the main tensions of the Satis House plot and the convict plot are also resolved in a way that signals the success of Pip's working through. Magwitch gives Pip part of the story about Compeyson, Herbert gives him part of the story about Miss Havisham, and he—and the authorial audience—learn of the connection between Miss Havisham and Magwitch through Compeyson. Jaggers and Wemmick give Pip part of the story about Molly, he makes the connection between Molly and Estella, Magwitch tells Herbert about the woman in his past, and Pip puts all the pieces together, even going so far as to startle Jaggers with his conclusions. When Pip is able to tell Magwitch on his deathbed that his daughter is alive and that he, Pip, loves her, the working through is essentially complete. It then remains for Pip to reestablish his relation with home first, through his reunion with Joe in London when Joe comes to nurse him through his illness and then through his being appropriately chastened for his dream of marrying Biddy by arriving home on the day of her wedding to Joe.

This sketch of the progression overlaps to some extent with Brooks's account of the plot but from this overlap our analyses move in two different directions—his toward the way in which the narrative is itself about plot, mine toward the affective structure of the progression, including the way it defines the relations among the mimetic, thematic, and synthetic components of character.[9] Let us return then to the first chapter.

Even as the first chapter identifies the initial major instability of the narrative and sets in motion the convict plot, it also induces the authorial audience to adopt a set of attitudes that are crucial to our experience of the whole narrative. Dickens handles the style of the first-person narration to convey Pip's discovery of his own misery with a combination of wit and matter-of-factness that results in our responding to the discovery with full and deep sympathy rather than seeing in it a sign of Pip the narrator's own unattractive self-pity. In fact, the humor of Pip's misreading of his parents' tombstones and of the "five little stone lozenges" (p. 1) marking the resting places of his brothers all but deflects our overt attention from Pip's situation as an orphan. As we have already seen, when Pip declares his own discovery of self-consciousness, it comes both matter-of-factly and wittily at the end of a series of discoveries (this place was the churchyard, etc. down to "the small bundle of shivers growing afraid of it all and beginning to cry, was Pip" [p.2]). With this arrangement and the shift to the third person, we register the narrator's own distance from the scene and so give our sympathy without reservation. Because Dickens establishes this initial sympathy at the time he establishes the initial instability, he has almost irrevocably established the authorial audience's positive attitude toward Pip. He then takes advantage of this firm foundation of sympathy later in the narrative when he shows how egregiously Pip wrongs Joe. At these points our foundational sympathy—as well as Dickens's recourse to letting the mature Pip comment on his former self—moves us to be pained not just for Joe but also—and perhaps even more—for Pip. The importance of this element of the dynamics will become clearer when I turn to discuss the functions of Wemmick; for now I want to emphasize that initially at least this pattern of judgments is developed in a context where the mimetic function of Pip is given more emphasis than any other. Indeed, the very presence of so many psychoanalytic readings of Pip's character is itself a sign of the strong mimetic signals being sent by the text.[10]

Following hard upon the initial instability, the arrival of the convict (whom Pip describes as a man "in coarse grey, with a great iron on his leg") plays a crucial role in the development of Pip's identity. Through Dickens's alternation between Pip on the marshes with the convict and Pip at home with Joe and Mrs. Joe in the first four chapters, he establishes the interpenetration of the convict plot with the home plot. Forced to act to aid the convict, and being told in countless ways by Mrs. Joe that he was no better than a convict, Pip identifies

very deeply with him, an identification that propels much of his behavior in the novel until the very end. At the same time, Dickens shows
us that Pip also identifies with Joe, though not nearly as deeply. Indeed, the way the convict plot intertwines with Mrs. Joe's reminders
of Pip's "nateral wiciousness" itself hinders the full identification: Pip
thinks of Joe as an innocent child, himself as a wicked offender. Yet
again Dickens's narrative technique complicates the audience's understanding of Pip's identification with the convict. In the second part of
Chapter 1, Dickens restricts us to Pip's vision at the time of the action,
and the overt comments focus, as we might expect given what we've
just read about Pip's anxiety, on his growing terror. Yet what comes
through the vision is Pip's intuitive sense of the convict's own misery:

> A fearful man, all in coarse grey, with a great iron on his leg. A
> man with no hat, and with broken shoes, and with an old rag tied
> round his head. A man who had been soaked in water, and smoth-
> ered in mud, and lamed by stones, and cut by flints, and stung by
> nettles, and torn by briars; who limped, and shivered, and glared,
> and growled; and whose teeth chattered in his head as he seized
> me by the chin. (P. 2)

> At the same time, he hugged his shivering body in both his arms—
> clasping himself, as if to hold himself together—and limped to-
> wards the low church wall. As I saw him go, picking his way
> among the nettles, and among the brambles that bound the green
> mounds, he looked in my young eyes as if he were eluding the
> hands of the dead people, stretching up cautiously out of their
> graves, to get a twist upon his ankle and pull him in. (P.4)

First and most obviously, such passages (there are similar ones in
Chapter 3) generate our own sympathy for Magwitch, and thus give
us a vision of him that is considerably softer than Pip's conscious one,
a vision later confirmed and expanded on by his "confession" of having stolen from the blacksmith's. Second, these passages lead us to
recognize a subtler motive in Pip's own desire to carry out his promise
to the convict: not only will he do it to avoid the terrible young man
but also to give the convict some relief. This subtler motive becomes
more obvious in Pip's extra effort to take along the pork pie that his
sister had tucked away in the corner of the pantry. Despite his emphasizing that "I had no time for verification, no time for selection,
no time for anything" (p. 13), he takes extra time for the pie. "I was
nearly going away without the pie, but I was tempted to mount upon
a shelf, to look what it was that was put away so carefully in a covered
earthenware dish in the corner, and I found it was the pie, and I took
it" (p. 13).

The motive is further reinforced as it is essentially echoed in Joe's response to the convict's apology for having eaten the pie, which in turn reminds us of the essential similarity of Pip and Joe: "We don't know what you have done, but we wouldn't have you starved to death for it, poor miserable fellow-creatur.—Would us, Pip?" The force of all these effects is of course felt later in the narrative when Dickens returns to the convict plot and Magwitch is revealed to be Pip's benefactor. Pip's initial revulsion at that point seems not only unjust to Magwitch, but also untrue to his own earlier self, and thus a further sign of how his expectations have hindered rather than helped him.

But even at this early juncture of the narrative, the effects have their force. Although Pip feels that his behavior justifies his sister's many references to him as guilty and deserving of punishment,[11] passages such as these enable us to recognize both the strength of Pip's feelings and the great error he is making—in this sense we have a much broader view of Pip than he does of himself. As we see Pip moving further and further away from Joe, a movement that begins in this opening section and gets accelerated once the Satis House plot begins, we also see him moving further and further away from the best and truest part of his own developing identity.

But of course that is not all that is accomplished by these opening chapters. More than anything else, they establish the depth and strength of Pip's identification with the convict and thus his conviction of his own guilt. In recognizing the strength of his feelings, we also recognize the important beginnings of what I might call the psychoanalytical side of the narrative: the set of associations that is set up here between Pip and Magwitch as father and son; the cluster of devices of setting—the wet, cold, misty weather in the early evening— that always recalls by association this first meeting, and Pip's subsequent guilt, e.g., when he first learns of his sister's being injured, and when Magwitch himself makes his return.[12] Pip's identity, we feel, is not of his own making. When that identity is further confused by his visits to Satis House, we see him more and more in the grip of forces beyond his control. This background then enables Dickens to develop the home plot in such a way that Pip continually seeks to deny that home, even as he is never able to kill entirely his attachment to it. And as Dickens undertakes that development, he takes Pip to a very low point in that plot without seriously threatening our fundamental sympathy with the character.

Now while all that is going on in the mimetic sphere, the progression is creating multiple developments in the thematic sphere. Although the narrative itself is complicated with many more turns than

Pride and Prejudice, the principles governing thematization are essentially the same in the two works: we have multiple characters with multiple attributes, many of which are converted by the turns of the progression into thematic functions, without there being a single dominant function acting as the central point of the progression. We can nevertheless identify an especially significant group developed from the actions of the main characters: both Magwitch and Miss Havisham function in part to exemplify the dangers of making others conform to our own images of what they should be; Joe functions as the exemplification of simple, honest dignity, while Estella exemplifies the absence of feeling. Pip, like Elizabeth Bennet, has multiple thematic functions. His responses to his expectations exemplify the consequences of a false pride. His responses to Estella offer a picture of irrational love. His susceptibility to the convict, Mrs. Joe, and Satis House all exemplify the difficulty of forging a strong identity in the world of this novel. This list is neither exhaustive nor impressive for the subtlety of its inferences about thematic functions. But lack of subtlety in the thematic sphere is, I think, a characteristic feature of Dickens's work. It is in the ingenious working out of those thematic elements in both the mimetic and synthetic spheres that his strength and distinctiveness are to be found.

Indeed, we are often led to pay attention to the thematic sphere of his works not only by the turns of the progression but also by his occasional foregrounding of the synthetic sphere. As a result, the reading of a Dickens novel typically involves a more fluid movement by the authorial audience among the spheres of meaning than occurs in the reading of a narrative by, say, Austen or James where the synthetic remains covert. One of the features of *Great Expectations* that contributes to this fluidity of movement—and to the ingenious working out of thematic material—is Dickens's handling of Wemmick.

V

After even a quick consideration of Wemmick's function in the narrative, we ought not be surprised that Brooks does not discuss his character at any length. Not only does Wemmick not fit into the pattern of repetition and return that Brooks identifies as the central part of the narrative's middle, but he also plays no main role in the working out of the resolution. If he were not in the novel, Dickens would have to find another means to accomplish such tasks as informing Pip about the best time to make his escape, but I daresay that none of us would feel that there was a big hole in the narrative, that Dickens just ought to have invented a virtually schizophrenic character whose life was as sharply divided between home and office as Wemmick's. Our first question then is whether Wemmick actually makes a contribution to the progression that is consonant with the attention that the narrative gives to his character, and if so, what precisely the nature of that contribution is. Our second question will be about the relation of the components of his character and the influence of that relation on the progression as a whole.

I shall begin with the relation between Wemmick's peculiar mimetic status and the variety of synthetic functions that he performs in the novel. Wemmick is a character with multiple mimetic dimensions and a doubtful mimetic function. This mid-fortyish man has two distinct personalities—Walworth Wemmick and Little Britain Wemmick. The first is a gentle, caring, sensitive soul who takes devoted and patient care of his Aged Parent and who dotes on Miss Skiffins. He also exercises his imagination, as we see in the way he has done up Walworth like a fort. The fort motif is of course symbolic: his private self is hidden behind that fort—so much so in fact that even when he ventures outside of it in his private mode he hides his intentions, as we see in the appearance of serendipity he tries to put upon his marriage to Miss Skiffins. As a rule, once Wemmick moves to the Little Britain side of the "moat," his character gradually hardens until he becomes the man with a mouth like the slit in a post office box, and with dints instead of dimples in his chin. His values undergo a corresponding change: he is almost as hard as Jaggers himself and his raison d'être becomes the acquisition of portable property.[13]

In the Wemmick of Little Britain, Dickens gives us a character who is part of the convict plot, and he takes advantage of the character's mimetic dimensions to accomplish certain synthetic functions. Wemmick shows Pip the importance of portable property in their tour through Newgate and at other times keeps Pip in contact with the "soiling consciousness" of his own identification with the convict, a contact that encourages his repression of the connection between Estella and Molly until after he has worked through his own relation to Magwitch, and that also contributes to his neglect of Joe.[14] In Walworth Wemmick, Dickens gives us a character who invites reflection on the instabilities of the home plot. Wemmick performs the synthetic function there of providing a contrast between his treatment of his Aged P. and Pip's treatment of Joe. To that extent, the synthetic function reinforces the authorial audience's and the mature Pip's own judgments about Pip's treatment of Joe.

Yet the predominant effect of Wemmick's presence on the affective structure of the text is quite different from the function of either the Little Britain or the Walworth Wemmick alone. The very facts that foreground Wemmick's synthetic component—the sharp division and exaggeration of his two sides—give him a thematic function that in turn has consequences for our response to the mimetic function of Pip. Wemmick's extreme self-division exemplifies the difficulty of living satisfactorily in two different spheres, among two very different sets of people. Consequently, Wemmick's very presence in the novel works to generalize Pip's difficulty in honoring his own lower-class background as he embarks upon his expectations. The problems we see Pip face are not just ones of his own reactions but ones endemic to living in a society where social mobility is becoming more common and where the separation between public and private spheres is becoming more and more pronounced. At the same time, Wemmick's situation indicates one kind of solution to that difficulty. Although Wemmick is more succesful than Pip in living in both spheres, the very division of his personality indicates that his solution is less than ideal. Despite the charm of the Walworth Wemmick, Dickens's point is clear: Pip needs to work through to an integration of his different spheres that Wemmick never attains.

In these ways, then, Dickens uses Wemmick to complicate our judgments about the instabilities of the home plot, especially Pip's relation to Joe. Even as the mature Pip is appropriately severe in his judgments of his earlier self's treatment of Joe, Dickens's elaboration of Wemmick's character puts his behavior in a broader context, which allows a greater understanding of Pip's problem and a softer judgment of his failures to solve it until so late in the narrative. Dickens also uses Wemmick to complicate our judgments in the convict plot, which of course is tightly wound together with the other plots in the latter stages of the narrative. Wemmick's self-division functions to deepen our sense of what it is that Pip must overcome as he slowly comes to accept Magwitch. If Wemmick shuts out his private self from his public life, if Pip experiences a difficulty acknowledging Joe once he comes into his expectations, then how much more difficult is his task of acknowledging and accepting the fact that the source of those expectations is the convict. Consequently, Wemmick's presence substantially increases our sense of what Pip eventually achieves in working through to that acceptance. Thus, despite being "compartmentalized" in both Little Britain and Walworth, Wemmick functions to influence significantly the authorial audience's responses to the main narrative line. At the same time, the way in which his foregrounded synthetic component leads to an emphasis on his thematic function, which in turn influences our response to the mimetic sphere of Pip's story, illustrates my earlier claim about the fluidity of movement among the three spheres of meaning in Dickens. When

Pip and Wemmick interact, the authorial audience has an overt awareness of all three components of their characters. In one sense, this simultaneous overt awareness makes *Great Expectations* less strictly realistic than, say, "The Beast in the Jungle," but it does not lead either to a rejection or even a subordination of the mimetic level of reading.

There is more to the story of Dickens's handling of Wemmick, but it is worth pausing here to reflect on the nature of the claims just made. In effect, I am arguing that Wemmick functions the way Charlotte Lucas does in *Pride and Prejudice*, only on a larger scale. Just as Charlotte's marriage to Collins influences the authorial audience's affective response to (and thematic understanding of) Elizabeth's rejection of Darcy's first proposal, so too does Wemmick's presence influence the authorial audience's affective response to and thematic understanding of many of Pip's actions. The question the analysis raises is one of limits: if the connection between the main and the secondary characters is to be found in the thematic sphere, can't one always find a thematic connection—if only by making a thematic leap of the kind that Levin has justly criticized?

The answer is that the thematic connection is not itself sufficient to justify the relevance or explain the contribution of the secondary character. (If it were, all narratives could be elaborated endlessly.) The connection in the thematic sphere needs to be tied not only to an affective result but also to the specific narrative means for achieving that effect. In *Pride and Prejudice*, Austen largely restricts herself to Elizabeth's point of view and commits herself to a mode of presentation that limits her own role as commentator and thus leaves much to her readers' inferences. By rendering Charlotte's decision within this largely dramatic mode of presentation, Austen gives the thematic point a force that would be impossible through the narrator's overt commentary on the pressures of the marriage market. In *Great Expectations*, Dickens's use of Wemmick works wonderfully well with his decision to have the mature Pip tell his own story. Dickens can then guide his audience's judgment by having Pip judge his treatment of Joe in the harshest possible terms, while also directing that audience to see the difficulty of Pip's position in relation to both Joe and Magwitch through the presentation of Wemmick. In that sense, Dickens's handling of Wemmick can be seen as the consequence of his decision to write the novel as a retrospective first-person account.

Another aspect of this same general point concerns some of the specific actions that Pip performs in his association with Wemmick. When Pip stays with the Aged P. and not only takes care of him but enjoys taking care of him, we see that side of his own character that has only intermittently appeared since the bestowal of his expectations. Because we see Pip still able to act from the better side of his character, that side associated with Joe, we remain sympathetic to him and indeed strengthen our desires that he will correctly resolve the instabilities about his own identity, especially as these relate to Joe and Magwitch. Dickens's treatment of Wemmick is, in short, very well integrated with the progression of the whole narrative.

Consider, by contrast, Dickens's handling of Pip's visits to Matthew Pocket's household. This material, which emphasizes the way in which the Pocket children "were not growing up or being brought up, but were tumbling up" (p. 178), can be seen as thematically related to Pip's own experience of being brought up by hand. Significantly, however, that thematic connection is not sufficient to give it any significant role in the progression. As far as I can see, it does not materially alter our understanding or judgment of Pip or his actions. It does indicate some of the difficulties and ironies of his situation—with his great expectations comes this environment—and it does increase Pip's desire to help Herbert, but the extended focus on the family is much less a functioning part of the progression than the material on Wemmick, if in fact it is not altogether extraneous. Dickens's depiction of the Pocket family is funny in the way that Dickens is often funny, but the humor lacks the punch accompanying his depiction of Wemmick because the depiction itself is finally digressive.

Let us return then to Wemmick and Dickens's development of his mimetic dimensions into a function or at least a quasi-function. In effect, what Dickens does here is elaborate a mini-plot about Wemmick, one based on the tensions about the relations between his two selves, and complicated by the resolution of that tension in such a way that we can posit him as having at least a quasi-mimetic function, which makes possible a kind of satisfaction for the authorial audience in the last event of this mini-plot, his so odd ("Halloa! Here's a church!" "Halloa! Here's Miss Skiffins!" Halloa! Here's a ring!") but so characteristic wedding. For a time our awareness of Wemmick's synthetic function is heightened by our uncertainty about how aware Wemmick himself is of the difference between the two sides of his personality. Then, after he refers to the difference, we remain unsure whether one side or the other is in effect the "real" Wemmick. This question does not get resolved until after Pip himself has come to accept Magwitch, has worked out the solution to the mystery of Estella's parentage, and desires confirmation from Jaggers at his office in Little Britain. When Jaggers initially tries to put him off, Pip successfully appeals to the Walworth Wemmick, and thus we know for certain that it is that side of his personality that is the real Wemmick:

the Little Britain twin is a creation of the Walworth character, a creation that has become a second nature, but a creation nonetheless. It is striking, I think, that it is only after this event that Dickens shows us Wemmick's marriage to Miss Skiffins, as if this alteration in Wemmick's situation could not occur until the question of the relation between the two sides of his character were settled.

At this point in the progression, the effects of Wemmick upon Pip's story that I described above have already occurred. Wemmick's marriage adds one small additional effect, even as it predominantly makes a different contribution to the whole. As the Walworth Wemmick functions to offer an alternative reading of the home plot, his marriage to Miss Skiffins raises questions about Pip's own eventual marrying. At first, the event may seem to suggest that Pip ought to marry Biddy. But a little reflection shows that Wemmick's marriage is working by contrast. Wemmick has a claim, while Pip has none. More importantly, however, the marriage itself adds another positive note to the ending of the book. It occurs right after Magwitch's trial and right before his death. We take a kind of pleasure in Wemmick's marriage that carries over and lightens the potentially dolorous emotions associated with Magwitch's death. This chain of effects could not have been possible without Dickens's gradual movement of Wemmick toward the mimetic. Again, Dickens proves to be a master of using the secondary characters to influence the affective structure of the progression, even as that use depends on the rather fluid movement among spheres of meaning.

Wemmick's marriage to Miss Skiffins also, I think, has the effect of making Dickens's revised ending, in which Pip sees no shadow of a further parting from Estella, less problematic. There is certainly no necessity for such an ending: the major instabilities of the narrative are resolved—Pip has worked through the issues of his identity, his relation to his own home, to his expectations, and to his past—in both the first and the second endings. Furthermore, unlike the situation in *The French Lieutenant's Woman*, the completeness of this narrative does not require two closures. To have closure Dickens does need to bring Pip into contact with Estella one last time, but since completeness has already been achieved, he has some latitude in choosing the outcome of the final meeting. In any representation, he must show that Estella is as altered as Pip or else Pip's feelings for her won't be in keeping with his present state; that stricture in turn means that any indication of their facing the future together must itself be muted, accompanied as it will be by their mutual knowledge of the unhappy past. Thus, regardless of the details of the closure, its emotional quality is already determined by the progression to this point. The ending can be hopeful, indeed, it should be hopeful, but it cannot signal a fulfillment: too much painful education has preceded it; to make the ending triumphant would be to deny the validity of the middle. Within those limitations, Dickens can choose to unite Pip and Estella or to have them meet and pass on.[15]

My own preference is for the original ending because I prefer the idea of Pip living independently now that he has achieved his peace with himself and his acceptance of who he is. Nevertheless, Wemmick's recent marriage is a reminder that the narrative has been concerned from the very beginning with questions of identity as they relate to family and, to some extent, to marriage. Consequently, the impulse to see Pip with his newly forged identity end, like Herbert and like his older allies Wemmick and Joe at slightly earlier stages, in a relationship that will lead to marriage and family is rather strong. It is that impulse that Wemmick's marriage strengthens and that Dickens's revised ending is responding to.

VI

A final note about the relation between Brooks's model and my own. In emphasizing the differences between the two models, I have shied away from any claim that the trouble with Brooks's model is its commitment to psychoanalysis. I locate that trouble rather in Brooks's limited conception of the nature of the narrative text, a limit that stems more from the heritage of the New Criticism (reading for the plot must be reading the structure of the plot) and the whole Anglo-American critical habit of equating interpretation with thematizing. One consequence of this approach to Brooks is that he—or more likely another theorist committed to psychoanalysis—could come along and recast my whole rhetorical approach to progression in a psychoanalytical frame. That is, such a theorist could situate my interests in the sequential and affective structure of narrative in a psychoanalytical framework, one that would among other things psychoanalyze the responses of the authorial audience. I would have no great objection to such a procedure provided that no strong claims were being made about that recasting being a superior (rather than an alternative) form of explanation.

The reason I would object to any claim for superiority is connected to the one way in which I would fault Brooks for his turn to psychoanalysis. Such a move presupposes that to explain the surface structure of texts, to explain the experience of reading, we need to move away from that surface and propose a model of its deep structure. The trouble with that assumption is that it immediately causes one to work at some distance from the details of texts, as one tries to find a model that will be applicable to all texts. In Brooks's case, we see him going to psychoanalysis, which gives him the concept of the death instinct, which in turn gives him the idea of the dominance of endings, which in turn causes him to underrate the importance of beginnings and middles.

The moral I draw at this point is that we need to do more work with the details of the surface structures before we are ready to consider different models of deep structures. My concept of progression commits its user to very little in the way of conclusions about the nature of any narrative to be read and interpreted. Instead, it seeks to posit categories and principles of analysis that correspond to the experience of reading, categories and principles that are specific enough to lead to detailed insights into individual narratives but flexible enough to be useful across the wide variety of surface structures that narratives offer us. As an additional test of my categories and principles, I turn in the next chapter to take an extended look at a self-reflexive, metafictional text in which the synthetic component of the protagonist is foregrounded throughout the whole narrative: Italo Calvino's *If on a winter's night a traveler*.

5   Foregrounding the Synthetic: Calvino's "Reader" and the Audiences of Narrative

I

The previous analyses of both *The French Lieutenant's Woman* and *Great Expectations* have given some indications of the effects created when the mimetic illusion is broken and the authorial audience's usual covert awareness that character is an artificial construct becomes overt. In those narratives, however, the synthetic foregrounding of character is only an occasional feature of the text, and one not much applied to the protagonist. What happens when the synthetic component of the protagonist's character becomes the dominant one? Italo Calvino's *If on a winter's night a traveler* raises this question with a kind of playful vengeance, as its foregrounding of the synthetic leads Calvino's audience to a wonderfully complicated self-consciousness about its own reading activity. Indeed, in a sense, Calvino's narrative also functions as a critical text: by inducing so much reflexiveness into the activity of its own reading, it investigates—or better, puts under a metafictional microscope—the concepts of character, progression, and audience. Thus, even as *If on a winter's night a traveler* presents a new and challenging example of a narrative where the synthetic component is dominant, its reflexiveness requires a more comprehensive view of the concept of audience than we have yet developed. Furthermore, it can initially be seen to challenge the conclusions of the last chapter about the importance of the affective structure of the narrative text and about the connection between that affective structure and the mimetic component of character. In short, Calvino's narrative will require me both to extend my account of the relation between character and progression and to reflect upon—and revise—some of the theoretical foundations and conclusions of the study so far.

The main issue of the whole narrative is rather disarmingly raised in its first sentence: "You are about to begin reading Italo Calvino's new novel, *If on a winter's night a traveler*."[1] The issue is what it means to read this narrative, and the sentence itself introduces subtle but significant tensions between author and authorial audience. The use of the second-person, the present tense, and the content of the sentence suggest that it is a kind of "Before the Curtain" address to the flesh-and-blood reader—me and you in all our commonality and idiosyncracy. But other elements of the sentence work against that inference. First, the use of the adjective "new" locates the address—and thus its audience—in time. The "you" of the sentence is not the me rereading this novel in 1987, or the you reading it after it is no longer new.[2] Second, the address is actually after the curtain, part of the novel proper. The addressed "you" is *about* to begin reading the novel, while we are *already* reading it. In this way, Calvino's very first sentence asks the authorial audience to take its first step toward self-reflexiveness, and that step seems to reinforce the distinction between authorial and narrative audiences. We (the authorial audience) are reading about a reader (whom, following our usual practice, we'll label the narrative audience, addressed as "you") who is about to begin reading a novel by the same author and with the same title as the one we are reading.

Once we take that step, however, other questions arise. Is the narrative audience's *If on a winter's night a traveler* the same as the authorial audience's? Is Italo Calvino the same for both audiences? The tensions implicit in these questions generate the initial movement of the narrative, as it continues with its location of "you" in a particular reading situation, flashes back to an account of the purchase of the book, begins telling the tale proper in the chapter entitled "If on a winter's night a traveler," and then breaks off when "you" discovers that the book has one sixteen-page signature repeated several times. This discovery, which, as we shall see, is a crucial point in the progression, leads the "you" back to the bookstore and to his initial meeting with the Other Reader.

At this stage of the narrative, the initial tensions appear to be resolved as new ones take their place (why disrupt the narrative in this way?) and as new instabilities develop (will "you" and we ever hear the end of the story? what will happen between "you" and the Other Reader?). Furthermore, at first glance the resolutions of the initial tensions appear to reinforce further the distinction between authorial and narrative audiences. The narrative audience's *If on a winter's night a traveler* is clearly different from the authorial audience's: "you"'s is only that repeated sixteen-page signature, ours contains the story of "you"'s response to that limit. By the same logic, "Calvino" is different for each audience: he speaks to the narrative audience only in that sixteen-page signature, but he speaks to the authorial audience in every sentence of the whole book. Continuing with this logic, we can also see that Calvino has playfully inverted the author-narrator relationship for the narrative audience. In Chapters 1 and 2, indeed in all the numbered chapters, "you" is addressed by a narrator figure who is distinct from the Italo Calvino named in the book's first sentence and subsequently identified as just the author of the first titled chapter—or so it seems until chapter 12, when Calvino ends the narrative with another twist on the author-narrator-audience relationships, a twist we shall later examine in detail.

This logic, essentially the same as that employed in the discussion of Chapters 13 and 55 of *The French Lieutenant's Woman*, helps explain the complicated author-narrator-audience relationships Calvino is establishing in the opening three chapters, but it does not go quite far enough. The logic would be adequate if Calvino had employed either the first or third person. "He is about to begin reading Italo Calvino's new novel, *If on a winter's night a traveler*." (Notice that one consequence of using the second person is that Calvino can include both sexes in his address.) "I am about to begin reading Italo Calvino's new novel, *If on a winter's night a traveler*." In each case the narrative voice would evoke the double audience—one implicitly addressed within the fiction, one implicitly addressed outside it—and each audience would recognize the "I" or the "He" as a character distinct from itself. The reading activities of the character and the audiences might coincide (as in the titled chapters) but the distinction between character and audience would always be clear. By using the second person, however, Calvino makes the "you" both character and audience, a situation that in Chapter 2 leads to the eventual separation of "you" not just from the authorial but also from the narrative audience. In other words, by using the second person in combination with the present tense, Calvino in effect makes "you" the addressed party of the discourse without making "you" equivalent to the narrative audience. If I am right about this separation, then Calvino's narrative strategy suggests that we need to recognize an additional possible audience in narrative discourse, what I will call the *characterized* audience.[3]

The differences between Calvino's strategies and those of first- and third-person narration help explain how his addressed audience, "you," is not identical to the narrative audience. First- and third-person narration presuppose a narrative audience that will be taken in by the narrative, "held round the fire," in James's words, by their insistent desire to see how the instabilities and tensions will be complicated and resolved, by their desire to reach narrative's end. In Calvino's narrative, there is also such an audience implied, although its separation from the characterized audience is not accomplished until the beginning of Chapter 2. It is this audience that gets caught up in "you"'s double quest—as character—for the continuation of all the narratives he begins and for a union with the Other Reader. In this respect, the narrative audience is as distinct from "you" as it would be if the protagonist were an unnamed "I" or a "he" named, say, Jack Dereader. Yet the use of the second person allows Calvino to begin by merging the narrative and characterized audiences, to separate them later, and then occasionally to merge them again. I shall undertake a detailed consideration of these strategies and their consequences for character and progression in *If on a winter's night a traveler* after I explain further this concept of a characterized audience.

I

Most simply, a characterized audience is created whenever a narrator, using direct address, ascribes attributes to his or her audience. From the perspective of the narrative audience, the characterized audience may be either real or hypothetical—that is, it may be an actual character such as Shreve McCanlin in *Absalom, Absalom!* or any number of figures in epistolary novels, or it may be a construction of the narrator such as the various Sirs and Madams invented by Tristram Shandy. The actual functions of characterized audiences are various, but as we might imagine, the most significant of them involve their role as a screen between the narrator and the narrative audience. Behind those screens author and authorial audience frequently engage in some complex kinds of communication. In cases where the characterized audience is "real," the possible effects are similar to those created by any dialogue: the narrative audience's relation to the narrator's address will depend heavily on what it knows about and how it judges the addressee. When, for example, Conrad has Marlow tell the final part of Lord Jim's story to the one previous listener who was most interested, Marlow addresses him thus:

> I remember well you would not admit he had mastered his fate. You prophesied for him the disaster of weariness and of disgust with acquired honour, with the self-appointed task, with the love sprung from pity and youth. You had said you knew so well "that kind of thing," its illusory satisfaction, its unavoidable deception. You said also—I call to mind—that "giving your life up to them" (them meaning all of mankind with skins brown, yellow, or black in colour) was "like selling your soul to a brute." You contended that "that kind of thing" was only endurable and enduring when based on a firm conviction in the truth of ideas racially our own, in

whose name are established the order, the morality of an ethical progress. "We want its strength at our backs," you had said. "We want a belief in its necessity and its justice, to make a worthy and conscious sacrifice of our lives. Without it the sacrifice is only forgetfulness, the way of offering is no better than the way to perdition." In other words, you maintained that we must fight in the ranks or our lives can't count. Possibly! You ought to know—be it said without malice—you who have rushed into one or two places single-handed and came out cleverly, without singeing your wings. The point, however, is that of all mankind Jim had no dealings but with himself, and the question is whether at the last he had not confessed to a faith mightier than the laws of order and progress.[4]

Given Conrad's effort to transform the material basis of Jim's story—his jump from the *Patna*, his failure in Patusan—into a narrative that insists on the significance of his life despite the ambiguous meaning of his actions, we can see that this use of a characterized audience functions to foreclose some judgments of Jim that the authorial audience might otherwise make. Marlow, whom both the authorial and narrative audiences view as reliable, declares some of those judgments to be less than pertinent: "The point . . . is that Jim . . . had no dealings but with himself." Furthermore, Conrad implicitly asks the authorial audience to reject the characterized audience's judgments as too easy, based as they are on the suspect attitudes about the superiority of the white race that underlay British colonialism. During this part of Marlow's address to the characterized audience the screen between him and the narrative audience is very thick and significant; when Marlow goes on to tell him the final events of Jim's life, the screen all but disappears.

Some different effects are frequently created when the characterized audience is constructed by the narrator himself. Listen for a moment to a famous eighteenth-century gentleman-narrator:

My uncle TOBY SHANDY, Madam, was a gentleman, who with the virtues which usually constitute the character of a man of honour and rectitude,———possessed one in a very eminent degree, which is seldom or never put into the catalogue; and that was a most extream and unparallel'd modesty of nature;———tho' I correct the word nature for this reason, that I may not prejudge a point which must shortly come to a hearing; and that is, Whether this modesty of his was natural or acquir'd.———Which ever way my uncle Toby came by it, 'twas nevertheless modesty in the truest sense of it: and that is, Madam, not in regard to words, for he was so unhappy as to have very little choice in them,———but to things;———and this kind of modesty so possess'd him, and it arose to such a height in him, as almost to equal, if such a thing could be, even the modesty of a woman: That female nicety, Madam, and inward cleanliness of mind and fancy, in your sex, which makes you so much the awe of ours.[5]

Tristram's characterization of his audience here is minimal: the relevant attributes of "Madam" are only her sex and its allegedly accompanying modesty—indeed, Tristram's discourse works in large part on the principle that "Modesty, thy name is woman." In the first part of the address (down to "modesty in the truest sense of it"), the screen erected between Tristram and the narrative audience by Sterne's use of the characterized audience is thin and transparent: the information is reliable and Tristram's manner of delivering it is not significantly altered by the presence of the characterized audience. In the latter part of the discourse, however, the screen becomes thicker and more opaque. Indeed, the narrative audience comes to recognize Tristram's address as part of his own narrative performance, another indication of those narrative abilities that, along with his foibles as both person and narrator, provide a major center of interest in the narrative. The screen in turn allows Sterne to incorporate different degrees of irony into his communication to the authorial audience: he is least ironic about Toby's modesty, more ironic about the modesty of women, and most ironic about the relation between the sexes.

Now compare Tristram to the narrator of *Vanity Fair*:

We say (and with perfect truth) I wish I had Miss MacWhirter's signature to a cheque for five thousand pounds. She wouldn't miss it, says your wife. She is my aunt, say you, in an easy careless way, when your friend asks if Miss MacWhirter is any relative? Your wife is perpetually sending her little testimonies of affection, your little girls work endless worsted baskets, cushions, and foot-stools for her. What a good fire there is in her room when she comes to pay you a visit, although your wife laces her stays without one! The house during her stay assumes a festive, neat, warm, jovial, snug appearance not visible at other seasons. You yourself, dear sir, forget to go to sleep after dinner, and find yourself all of a sudden (though you invariably lose) very fond of a rubber. What good dinners you have—game every day, Malmsey-Madeira, and no end of fish from London. Even the servants in the kitchen share the general prosperity; and, somehow, during the stay of Miss MacWhirter's fat coachman, the beer is grown much stronger, and the consumption of tea and sugar in the nursery (where her maid takes her meals) is not regarded in the least. Is it so, or is it not so?[6]

Here the screen between narrator and narrative audience is erected by the end of the second sentence and maintained throughout the passage. Although the characterized audience is more particularized than Tristram's "Madam," the screen does not provide as much distance between audiences as in Tristram's discourse. Despite the particularization, the characterized audience is still a representative figure: he is a middle-class Englishman with a wife and daughters, a house and servants, and above all a desire to increase his worldly possessions. Partly because of that representativeness and partly because of the tight connection between the point of this passage and the narrative's central thematic message about the vanity of human actions, the narrative audience recognizes that the narrator intends them to apply the passage to themselves. At the same time, the narrative audience registers the witty creation of the screen as another performance by the Showman of Vanity Fair. The authorial audience, in turn, makes the corresponding inferences about Thackeray. As a consequence of his performance in creating this characterized audience, Thackeray induces his authorial audience to recognize the necessary application of the passage—it's not just Becky, Amelia, and Dobbin, I'm talking about, but you too—without having us feel directly attacked by the narrator.[7]

As the analysis of these three passages indicates, isolating the characterized audience for critical attention is worthwhile to the extent that that audience acts as a screen or buffer between the narrator and the narrative audience. In narratives such as "Haircut" or *Lolita* a characterized audience is coextensive with the narrative audience, and the buffer effect does not exist. In fact, in these works the distinction between the two audiences has no analytical payoff, except to the extent that it is helpful to remind ourselves that in Lardner's tale we need to imagine ourselves in Whitey's barber chair and in Nabokov's narrative in the jury box as one of the "ladies and gentlemen" Humbert Humbert so impassionedly addresses. Similarly, such addresses as Jane Eyre's famous "Reader, I married him," or the *Middlemarch* narrator's various comments to a generalized "you" explicitly acknowledge the importance of the narrator's relationship to a narrative audience without creating a characterized audience of any significance.

The concept of characterized audience can perhaps be further clarified by considering its relation to Prince's notion of the narratee and to Rabinowitz's notion of the ideal narrative audience. Any characterized audience would also be a narratee in Prince's sense of the term. The difference between the concepts is not so much in their definition but in our respective understandings of the consequences of the concepts. For Prince, the creation of the category of "narratee" means that he does not need a category analogous to narrative audience, whereas for me the importance of the characterized audience arises out of its difference from and relation to the narrative audience. Our differences become clear in Prince's argument in his essay "The Narratee Revisited."[8] Prince claims that the notion of a metanarratee is untenable. "Just as in 'I ate a hamburger for lunch,' the character-I is the one who ate and the narrator-I the one telling about the eating, in 'You ate a hamburger for lunch,' the character-you is the one who ate and the narratee-you the one told about the eating" (p. 301). Thus, just as the use of "I" allows the double function of acting and narrating, so too the use of "You" allows the double function of acting and receiving the narration. The example supports Prince's conclusion, but it is not sufficiently representative of the range of narrative communication. As soon as we complicate the example, a metanarratee emerges: "You, who so well know the nature of your stomach, ate a hamburger for lunch and now must face the consequences." Because the "character-you" is distinct from the authorial audience, that audience adopts a triple perspective: receiving the narration as if it were the "you" addressed (i.e., adopting the position of narratee/characterized audience); receiving the narration while knowing it is not "you," but nevertheless participating in the illusion that "you" is real and therefore interested in following "character-you's" story (i.e, adopting the position of narrative audience); recognizing these two previous perspectives as part of the indirect manner of communication between the creator of "you" and itself. Or, to take a better example: in the passage from *Tristram Shandy*, the effect of Sterne's irony depends not only on his use of a characterized audience but on the characterized audience's relation to two others: first, one that believes in Tristram as an autonomous narrator and sees the address to Madam as part of his performance; and second, one that sees both of those audiences as devices for a complex communication from Sterne as orchestrator of the whole discourse. My point, in short, is that what Prince calls a narrateee and I call a characterized audience will sometimes be distinguished from a narrative audience, and when that happens the narrative audience will function as a metanarratee. At the same time, Prince is right to resist the notion that all second-person addresses result in the creation of a metanarratee; sometimes the characterized and narrative audiences will, for all intents and purposes, merge.

More generally, I think it is worth noting a key difference between structuralist models of audience like Prince's and rhetorical models like Rabinowitz's or Wayne Booth's slightly modified version of it. The structuralist account remains anchored to the idea that the discourse of the narrative will define the features of the audience, whereas the rhetorical approach considers the presuppositions and beliefs that operate for the different audiences that are always present in the apprehension of narrative. Perhaps the easiest way to illustrate the difference is to note that the structuralist notion of a narratee is not easily transferable to the audiences of drama (the discourse of drama is addressed to other characters) while the rhetorical notion of a narrative audience can be thus transferred (the audience that believes that it is watching Hamlet rather than an actor playing Hamlet). In any case, my general claim is that we can better understand the way communication operates in narrative discourse by considering the narrative and characterized audiences as two separate entities whose relations with each other may vary from narrative to narrative and indeed within the same narrative. Furthermore, I follow Rabinowitz rather than Prince in finding the narrative audience similar to the authorial audience except to the extent that the narrative indicates otherwise.[9]

At the same time, my concept of the characterized audience is different from Rabinowitz's concept of an ideal narrative audience, which he defines as the narrator's equivalent of the authorial audience, i.e., the audience who is always on the narrator's wavelength, who shares his values, beliefs, opinions, and so on.[10] First, not all ideal narrative audiences will be characterized audiences, and not all characterized audiences will be ideal. Second, the presence of the ideal narrative audience does not genuinely place the narrative audience in a position of the metanarratee. In fact, I have not discussed the ideal narrative audience in this book (which is otherwise so fond of making distinctions) because all its operations are subsumed by the narrative audience. We can say that when Huck Finn tells us about his disdain for Moses ("I don't take no stock in dead people"), he expects his (ideal) audience to share his view though the narrative audience, being like the authorial, actually does not, and that the humor arises in part from the gap between the audiences. But we can also say, without any loss of analytical capacity, that the narrative audience sees Huck's mistake and laughs. In sum, although the ideal narrative audience is a logical category of analysis, it has insufficient analytical payoff for me to want to invoke it.[11]

III

Calvino, I think, has discovered new uses for the characterized audience, uses that are crucial to the workings of character and progression in his book. Some of those uses and their consequences emerge in the opening paragraphs of chapter 2, where the progression of the narrative takes its first major turn with the first clear separation of the narrative and characterized audiences:

You have now read thirty pages and you're becoming caught up in the story. At a certain point you remark: "This sentence sounds somehow familiar. In fact, this whole passage reads like something I've read before." Of course: there are themes that recur, the text is interwoven with reprises, which serve to express the fluctuation of time. You are the sort of reader who is sensitive to such refinements; you are quick to catch the author's intentions and nothing escapes you. But, at the same time, you also feel a certain dismay; *just when you were beginning to grow truly interested, at this very point the author feels called upon to display one of those virtuoso tricks so customary in modern writing,* repeating a paragraph word for word. Did you say paragraph? Why it's a whole page; you make the comparison, he hasn't changed even a comma. And as you continue, what develops? Nothing: the narration is repeated, identical to the pages you have read!

Wait a minute! Look at the page number. Damn! From page 32 you've gone back to page 17! What you thought was a stylistic subtlety on the author's part is simply a printers' mistake: they have inserted the same pages twice. (P. 25; emphasis mine)

To appreciate the consequences of this development in the narrative, it will be useful to consider the objection that positing a characterized audience in a second-person narrative may be counterintuitive, especially since the first sentence here supports that view. All four audiences I have posited—the flesh-and-blood, the authorial, the narrative, and the characterized—have been reading the chapter entitled "If on a winter's night a traveler." Certainly at least the last three of these are "becoming caught up in the story." Why then make the distinction? Alternatively, if we make it, how does it help us analyze what is happening in that first sentence? We need to make the distinction, I think, because of what happens in the rest of the passage. The characterized audience becomes a character, whose actions the other audiences read about: "you" compares pages, while neither the authorial nor narrative audiences join him. Just as Elizabeth Bennet does not know—as we do—that she is a character in a novel by Jane Austen, "you" does not know—as we now clearly do—that he is a character in a novel by Italo Calvino (though not necessarily the "new novel, *If on a winter's night a traveler*" referred to in the book's first sentence).

The distinction is useful for even the first sentence of this passage because it helps us understand how Calvino guides the authorial audience to reflect on the activity of its own reading. Calvino's strategy is to vary the thickness of the screen between the narrator and the narrative audience erected by the use of the characterized audience, and then to take advantage of the second-person narration to make the authorial audience reflect on the nature and significance of that variation. As we move from the thin, transparent screen in the first sentence to the thick, opaque screen in the second paragraph, we pass through the clauses emphasized in my quotation: "just when you were beginning to grow truly interested, at this very point the author feels called upon to display one of those virtuoso tricks so customary in modern writing, repeating a paragraph word for word." In these transitional clauses overtly addressed to the characterized audience, Calvino covertly but directly addresses the authorial audience. Just as "you" thinks he is witnessing a "virtuoso trick" on the part of his Calvino, the authorial audience becomes aware that it is witnessing such a trick on the part of our Calvino. The virtuoso trick is the introduction of the device of the repeated signatures, which alters the course of the progression by effecting the separation of the characterized audience from the others. The instability of the narrative now has less to do with the situation of the spy whose adventures we were following in the titled chapter than it does with the experience of "you"'s reading.

The corresponding tension of the narrative now centers on the relationship between Calvino and the authorial audience: why has the author displaced our interest in the titled chapter with this interest in "you"'s experience of reading? Even more significant is a further tension that arises as a result of the previous sentence. There all three audiences are told that "You are the sort of reader who is sensitive to such refinements; you are quick to catch the author's intentions and nothing escapes you." Acting upon the implied message here, and attempting to catch the intention of the refinement introduced by the dual communication about virtuoso tricks, the authorial audience begins to reflect on the complexity of its own reading about reading, without yet reaching any firm conclusions about that activity. At this point, the affective structure of the book is not being destroyed but rather redefined. Rather than the characters and our interest in them carrying our affective interest in the whole narrative, the characters will act as a vehicle for a more direct kind of interplay between author and audience: the affective component of the structure comes from Calvino's setting various challenges for himself to meet and for the audience to decipher—and reflect upon.

The significance of this separation among audiences at the beginning of Chapter 2 can be more fully appreciated by understanding the "retrospective patterning" it produces.[12] Again it will be helpful to look at specific passages of narrative discourse from Chapter 1 and the first *incipit*:

In the shop window you have promptly identified the cover with the title you were looking for. Following this visual trail, you have forced your way through the shop past the thick barricade of

Books You Haven't Read, which were frowning at you from the tables and shelves, trying to cow you. But you know you must never allow yourself to be awed, that among them there extend for acres and acres the Books You Needn't Read, the Books Made for Purposes Other Than Reading, Books Read Even Before You Open Them Since They Belong To The Category Of Books Read Before Being Written. And thus you pass the outer girdle of ramparts, but then you are attacked by the infantry of the Books That If You Had More Than One Life You Would Certainly Also Read But Unfortunately Your Days Are Numbered. With a rapid maneuver you by-pass them and move into the phalanxes of the Books You Mean To Read But There Are Others You Must Read First, the Books Too Expensive Now And You'll Wait Till They're Remaindered, the Books ditto When They Come Out In Paperback, Books You Can Borrow From Somebody, Books That Everybody's Read So It's As If You Had Read Them, Too. (Pp. 4–5)

The great fun of this passage (which continues for another three paragraphs) the first time we come upon it depends upon the merging of the characterized and narrative audiences, both of which are also very close to the authorial audience. (In addition, we may speculate that each of these audiences will be close to virtually any flesh-and-blood reader likely to pick up a book like *If on a winter's night a traveler*.) As we join the narrative audience, we are asked not just to witness this trip through the bookstore but to imagine ourselves having actually taken it. Moreover, because the authorial audience is so close to the narrative audience here, it endorses the witty accuracy of this description of the trip. In general the description functions as part of the authorial and narrative audiences' charming introduction to the whole narrative. After we get to Chapter 2, however, and discover the separation of the narrative and characterized audiences, the passage—and indeed, the whole chapter—takes on a quite different import. The "you" addressed is not just the narrative audience but the characterized one as well, and so the authorial audience once again has to be conscious of how the discourse of the first chapter has a double application: it is being introduced not just to the situation of the narrative audience but also to the first events of the Reader's story, his trip to the bookstore and his preparations before reading his copy of *If on a winter's night a traveler*. These opening events take on greater importance as the Reader's story continues, but before I pursue them, let us look at some samples of the narrative discourse in the first *incipit*.

This chapter, like "Outside the town of Malbork," is different from the other eight titled chapters because of the degree to which it incorporates reflections on its own reading.[13] It opens this way:

The novel begins in a railway station, a locomotive huffs, steam from a piston covers the opening of the chapter, a cloud of smoke hides part of the first paragraph. In the odor of the station there is a passing whiff of station cafe odor. There is someone looking through befogged glass, he opens the glass door of the bar, everything is misty, inside, too, as if seen by nearsighted eyes, or eyes irritated by coal dust. The pages of the book are clouded like the windows of an old train, the cloud of smoke rests on the sentences. It is a rainy evening; the man enters the bar; he unbuttons his damp overcoat; a cloud of steam enfolds him; a whistle dies away along tracks that are glistening with rain, as far as the eye can see. (P. 10)

The blurring of audiences continues here: are we reading the actual first paragraph of "If on a winter's night a traveler" or a summary of its beginning? Is the "you" of the first chapter reading something different from what the narrative and authorial audiences of the whole narrative are reading here? Is this narrative itself to be one that induces reflection on its own reading? How are these questions related to the soon-to-be-introduced instabilities of the *incipit*, the man's possible relation with Madame Marne, and his failure to switch his suitcase with another just like it? Because the transition from the voice of these passages to the voice of the action is virtually seamless, the narrative audience is, I think, inclined to take the chapter as the full replication of the book that "you" is reading and thus to regard the references to the clouded pages and smoky sentences neither as summaries nor as metafictional maneuvers but as devices designed to contribute to the mood of mystery and intrigue that hangs over the narrative. In having this internal function, they are similar to such reflexive passages as the following:

I am not at all the sort of person who attracts attention, I am an anonymous presence against an even more anonymous background. If you, reader, couldn't help picking me out among the people getting off the train and continued following me in my to-and-froing between bar and telephone, this is simply because I am called "I" and this is the only thing you know about me, but this alone is reason enough for you to invest a part of yourself in the stranger "I." Just as the author, since he has no intention of telling about himself, decided to call the character "I" as if to conceal him, not having to name him or describe him, because any other name or attribute would define him more than this stark pronoun; still, by the very fact of writing "I" the author feels driven to put into this "I" a bit of himself, of what he feels or imagines he feels. Nothing could be easier for him than to identify himself with me; for the moment my external behavior is that of a traveler who has missed a connection, a situation that is part of everyone's experience. But a situation that takes place at the opening of a novel always refers you to something else that has happened or is about to happen, and it is this something else that makes it risky to identify with me, risky for you the reader and for him the author; and the more gray and ordinary and undistinguished and commonplace the beginning of this novel is, the more you and the author feel a hint of danger looming over the fraction of "I" that you have heedlessly invested in the "I" of a character whose inner history you know nothing about, as you know nothing about the contents of that suitcase he is so anxious to get rid of. (Pp. 14–15)

The internal function here is to increase both the mystery of the "I" and the suspense about the coming danger. When, however, we get to Chapter 2, the retrospective patterning gives both sorts of passages a double application. Their potential to function as comments on the act of reading in general is actualized. The first kind teases us into thought about the relation between style and atmosphere, as the sentences themselves produce the smoky effect they appear to be claiming for other sentences. This second passage functions as an invitation to the authorial audience to explore the analogy between the multiple roles of "I"—Calvino, the author of the whole book, "Calvino," the alleged author of this *If on a winter's night a traveler*, and the nameless narrator of this version—and the multiple roles of "You"—authorial, narrative, and characterized audiences. Other passages in the *incipit* offer different specific variations on Calvino's general technique of inducing the double application:

These remarks form a murmuring of indistinct voices from which a word or a phrase might emerge, decisive for what comes afterward. To read properly you must take in both the murmuring effect and the effect of the hidden intention, which you (and I, too) are as yet in no position to perceive. In reading, therefore, you must remain both oblivious and highly alert, as I am abstracted but prick up my ears, with my elbow on the counter of the bar and my cheek on my fist. (P. 18)

Here the authorial audience applies the narrator's directions about reading properly not just to the reading of the *incipit* but to the reading of the whole narrative—including the passage itself. The authorial audience thus becomes self-consciously aware of its warrant for reading self-consciously.

In summary, then, the opening paragraphs of Chapter 2 do not obliterate either the narrative audience's participation in the address of Chapter 1 or the mimetic reading experience of the first *incipit* but they do complicate those two acts of reading. As a result of the turn

taken in the progression with those paragraphs, the authorial audience needs in effect both to preserve and uplift those experiences, to
recognize each of them as part of the whole narrative's general concern with the nature of reading, including the nature of reading this
narrative itself. To see how the narrative further complicates and perhaps resolves this concern, we must consider how Calvino guides the
authorial audience's responses to the character of the Reader and to
the subsequent progression of his story.

IV

As we have already seen, much of Calvino's treatment of the Reader,
including of course giving him that name, works to foreground his
synthetic component. The narrator, moreover, deliberately refrains
from any detailed mimetic portrait: "Who you are, Reader, your age,
your status, profession, income: that would be indiscreet to ask. It's
your business, you're on your own" (p. 32). Nevertheless, the Reader
has several mimetic dimensions. In Chapter 1, the narrator tells us,

> You're the sort of person who, on principle, no longer expects any-
> thing of anything. . . . You know that the best you can expect is to
> avoid the worst. . . . What about books? Well, precisely because
> you have denied it in every other field, you believe you may still
> grant yourself legitimately this youthful pleasure of expectation
> in a carefully circumscribed area like the field of books, where
> you can be lucky or unlucky, but the risk of disappointment isn't
> serious. (P. 4)

This attribute contributes to the Reader's desire to find the continua-
tions of the various *incipits*: since reading is the last area of expectation he has, it is all the more important to him that he can
find out how the expectations generated by the narrative beginnings
he encounters are brought to some resolution. In Chapter 2, when
he meets Ludmilla, the Other Reader, another mimetic dimension
emerges. He acts like the proverbial boy in a boy-meets-girl narrative:
he wants to get the girl as much as he wants to get the continuation
of the narrative he began. In the later chapters we see that part of
being the proverbial boy is to be jealous of any possible rival for the
Other Reader's affections. This first encounter also reveals him to be
an ordinary Reader relative to the extraordinary Other Reader, who
has read many more novels than he, and who has much better recall
of what she has read. As we see later when he describes himself explicitly, he is in effect defined as the ordinary reader:

> "I like to read only what is written, and to connect the details with
> the whole, and to consider certain readings as definitive; and I like

to keep one book distinct from the other, each for what it has that is different and new; and I especially like books to be read from beginning to end." (Pp. 256–57)

At the end of Chapter 2, then, the main movement of the Reader's story is established: this ordinary man with the strong desire for the completion of his interrupted reading and a strong hope for the development of his relationship with the Other Reader sets out on his double quest to achieve both his desire and his hope. The narrator's summary of the situation at this point both sets the stage for the rest of the quest and reminds the authorial audience of its own reading activity:

> You are bearing with you two different expectations, and both promise days of pleasant hopes: the expectation contained in the book—of a reading experience you are impatient to resume—and the expectation contained in the telephone number—of hearing again the vibrations, at times treble and at times smoldering of that voice, when it will answer your first phone call in a short while, in fact tomorrow, with the fragile pretext of the book, to ask her if she likes it or not, to tell her how many pages you have read or not read, to suggest to her that you meet again . . .
> Who you are, Reader, your age, your status, profession, income: that would be indiscreet to ask. It's your business, you're on your own. What counts is the state of your spirit now, in the privacy of your home, as you try to re-establish perfect calm in order to sink again into the book. . . . But something has changed since yesterday. Your reading is no longer solitary: you think of the Other Reader, who, at this same moment, is also opening the book; and there, the novel to be read is superimposed by a possible novel to be lived, the continuation of your story with her, or better still, the beginning of a possible story. . . . Does this mean that the book has become an instrument, a channel of communication, a rendezvous? This does not mean its reading will grip you less: on the contrary, something has been added to its powers. (P. 32)

The double application here is more intermittent than in some of the passages we have just looked at, but its presence is equally significant. The authorial audience's expectations are not identical to the Reader's, but they do overlap: we are bearing with us the expectation of a reading experience contained in the book, one consisting of both further embedded narratives and of the developing relationship between the Reader and the Other Reader. Furthermore, although the authorial audience is not in precisely the same relation to this narrative and an Other Reader as the characterized audience, the pattern of reflexive reading already established—and reinforced by this passage—induces the members of the authorial audience to contemplate the effects of reading-relationships, the importance of reading as a social activity, the relation of each one's reading of this book to that of his or her fellow readers.

At this point, the authorial audience's understanding of Chapter 1 takes on a new layer: beneath the ingenuity of the description of the trip to the bookstore, beneath the wit of the merging of the audiences, there also exists the opening step in a story about reading and its conditions. That chapter has in effect presented the Reader one-on-one with the bookstore and with the book. Now the progression is moving us to consider a two-on-one situation, or better, given the reflexiveness already established and the existence of inner and outer narratives, it is inviting us to consider the relations between intertextuality and interreaderality.

The relation between character and progression here is typical of the relation between the two in the whole narrative: the minimal attributes of the character give the narrative movement a slight push, but the most important features of that movement revolve around Calvino's relationships with the narrative and authorial audiences. Consequently, the character fades back into the progression; it is not his drives and desires that we are most interested in following but rather how Calvino manipulates them as he keeps announcing and enacting his concerns with reading. This relationship between character and progression is strikingly different from anything we have seen so far. The other characters we have analyzed have all been given a clear identity, and the progression has affected the functions that those characters perform while preserving that identity. In this narrative, the Reader has a minimal identity, one that is sometimes merged with the generalized portraits of the narrative and authorial audiences. Furthermore, because that identity just is the identity of the ordinary reader, and because the analysis of the progression just is the analysis of the authorial audience's temporal reading, the progression here does not only affect the functions of the character, but it also absorbs or subsumes them.

This point is given further support when we consider the relation of the Reader's thematic component to his mimetic and synthetic ones. As the discussion of the first few chapters of the book indicate, Calvino presents us with the other side of James's coin: where James merges the thematic and the mimetic components of John Marcher, Calvino merges the thematic and synthetic components of the Reader. In *If on a winter's night a traveler*, the primary ideational concerns of the text are about the activity of its own reading. Since these concerns are both announced and enacted as part of the progression of the whole narrative, to discuss the synthetic component of character and of the narrative in general is to discuss the thematic component as well. Thus, to analyze the relation between the mimetic and synthetic components here is simultaneously to analyze the relation between the mimetic and thematic components. And again, since the mimetic component of the Reader's character is limited to a few traits necessary for a surface narrative underneath which the more significant narrative of our own reading about reading is developed, the detailed analysis of character here can best be done by folding it into the analysis of the progression.

These conclusions reinforce my earlier statements about the affective structure of the progression here. Accompanying the fusion of the synthetic and thematic components of character is our awareness of Calvino's relation to the authorial audience, and this relation becomes more and more playful as the narrative progresses. We ask questions like these: what twist will he give his construction next? Will I be able to follow it? What will that in turn set up? In general, can he meet his own challenges to write this self-reflexive work that induces reflection on its own reading and can we catch all the devices by which he tries? We progress through the narrative enjoying the challenge, wanting to be equal to it, but hoping also that we are not so equal to it that we feel somehow ahead of our playful guide. Whenever we do feel like we're catching up to Calvino, we have not only the satisfaction of meeting his challenge but also the payoff of learning something new—or articulating more clearly something we've already known—about our reading. The story of the Reader becomes the occasion for this serious play.

V

The pattern of the progression after Chapter 2 is in one sense fairly predictable and in another characteristically surprising. The Reader's two quests appear to proceed along parallel lines until Chapter 7. Every lead that the Reader follows to find the continuation of the previous narrative brings him only to the beginning of another new narrative, and the pattern of the opening chapters continues: numbered chapter addressed to characterized audience; titled chapter read in common by the Reader, the narrative audience, and the authorial audience; numbered chapter, and so on. Each lead the Reader follows takes him into a new situation of reading: reading aloud, reading in a university setting, reading followed by academic analysis of it, reading against the backdrop of its production in a publishing house. The result is that the authorial audience is led to reflect on the variety of situations and relationships that contextualize its own reading.

During this stage, two other sorts of readers are introduced, and these set off how even the ordinary reading of the Reader is defined by a specific set of interests and desires. First, Calvino introduces Ludmilla's sister, Lotaria, the Utilitarian Reader who wants only to know "the author's position with regard to Trends of Contemporary Thought and Problems That Demand a Solution" (p. 44). Second, he introduces Irnerio, the Non-Reader who has trained himself not even to read what appears before his eyes. Through the Reader's interactions with these two and with Ludmilla herself, Calvino maintains the instability surrounding the Reader's quest for her. During this stage, the Other Reader is far more interested in her reading than in him. In Chapter 7, however, a new stage of the progression begins as Calvino introduces one of his surprises and thereby intertwines the two major instabilities. Ludmilla matter-of-factly invites the Reader "to begin," and they engage in a reading of each other's bodies. The surprise here is that Calvino reverses the conventions of the boy-meets-girl, boy-wants-reluctant-girl, boy-eventually-gets-no-longer-reluctant-girl formula that he has been working with until this point. One important consequence of the move is to take the narrative even further away from the mimetic and into the realm of the synthetic: characters need not follow the minimal mimetic characterizations that they are initially given, but may act in new ways at the convenience of the author. At the same time, Calvino's use of the characterized audience and the metaphor of reading to describe their lovemaking allows the authorial audience to make a personal application of the description if it sees fit.

One effect of this surprise in the progression is of course to comment upon the conventions of the boy-meets-girl plot that Calvino is inverting here. The other is the way it intertwines the two instabilities:

> in the satisfaction you receive from her way of reading you, from the textual quotations of your physical objectivity, you begin to harbor a doubt: that she is not reading you, single and whole as you are, but using you, using fragments of you detached from the context to construct for herself a ghostly partner, known to her alone, in the penumbra of her semiconsciousness, and what she is deciphering is this apocryphal visitor, not you. (P. 156)

Since the jealous Reader suspects his rival to be either the translator who injects falsehoods into books, Ermes Marana, or the author who is said to "produce books the way a pumpkin vine produces pumpkins," Silas Flannery, the Reader is unable to be satisfied in his quest for the Other Reader until he satisfies his quest for—or at least gets to the bottom of the mystery about—the continuation of the interrupted narratives. Thus, Calvino continues the focus on the production, uses, and situations of books and their reading as the Reader goes first to visit Silas Flannery, and then to an imaginary country in South America, fruitlessly trying to unravel the "apocrypha conspiracy." Finally, he ends up in a library in his hometown, where the ten books he has begun are all catalogued but unattainable. Instead of getting the books themselves, he gets into a discussion on reading with seven other readers that eventually leads him to decide to marry Ludmilla. No sooner decided than done, and the narrative ends with one final twist that I shall examine below.

Meanwhile, the story of the Reader's quest continues to be punctuated by the beginnings of new narratives that always break off. Just as the numbered chapters explore different conditions of reading, these *incipits* explore different kinds of reading experiences, each one anticipated by a wish of Ludmilla's: before "Outside the town of Malbork," she says, "I prefer novels that bring me into a world where everything is precise, concrete, specific," and lo and behold that is just what the narrative is. Similarly, before "Looks down in the gathering shadow," the story of the man trying to get rid of the corpse of his rival, Jojo, she says "The novel I would most like to read at this moment should have as its driving force only the desire to narrate, to pile stories upon stories, without trying to impose a philosophy of life on you, simply allowing you to observe its own growth, like a tree, an entangling as if of barbs and branches" and again that is just what we get (p. 92).

In sum, then, there are two main underlying principles of the progression: to explore reading and its multifaceted relationships and to offer a variety of distinct reading experiences. As compared, say, to the principles of progression in *Pride and Prejudice*, these allow their author considerable freedom. Once Austen establishes the particular instabilities of her narrative, she then must carefully select—and situate—those incidents that will contribute to the authorial audience's greatest satisfaction in the eventual resolution of the instabilities accomplished by the engagement of Elizabeth and Darcy. Calvino, on the other hand, is relatively free to employ his narrative ingenuity to use the surface movement of the progression in his exploration of reading and its situations. Both the particular way in which he induces self-reflexiveness on the part of the authorial audience and the particular issues that he chooses are only minimally constrained by the early strokes of the narrative. The constraints imposed by his general principles are only that he actually display the variety of reading and that he move the narrative further and further into its exploration of the synthetic component of narrative. The surprises I alluded to above satisfy those constraints, even as they exhibit Calvino's ingenuity and substantially affect the specific development of the progression. The surprise of Chapter 7 is soon followed by the deviation of Chapter 8, where the second-person address to the characterized audience gives way to the diary of Silas Flannery, written in the first person. Furthermore, the status of the diary within the whole narrative situation is not at all clear. At the end of chapter 7, the Reader resolves to visit Flannery, but the narrator never tells us that the Reader actually gets the diary in his possession. Indeed, toward the end of the chapter he appears as a figure in the diary seen now from Flannery's perspective, and the diary continues beyond the Reader's last visit. Thus, for the first time both the narrative and authorial audiences now have access to information about the characterized audience that the Reader himself does not have. Where previously the Reader's actions in effect controlled the narrative discourse—in Chapters 1 through 7 (and indeed, in 9 through 12) the narrator describes and sometimes reacts to or comments further upon the Reader's actions—the discourse in Chapter 8 is quite independent of him.[14] Since the narrator of the other chapters does not appear until the very end of Chapter 8 and does not account for the presentation of the diary, the authorial audience is inclined to take it as a gift from Calvino himself. This inference of course further supports the authorial audience's awareness of the synthetic nature of our reading experience here.

This drive further and further into the synthetic continues with the embedding of the idea of Calvino's own book within Flannery's diary. Characteristically, Calvino also gives a twist to this rather obvious narrative maneuver, and the twist leads to another of the progression's surprises.

> I have had the idea of writing a novel composed only of the beginnings of novels. The protagonist could be a Reader who is continually interrupted. The Reader buys the new novel A by the author Z. But it is a defective copy, he can't go beyond the beginning. . . . He returns to the bookshop to have the volume exchanged. . . .
>
> I could write it all in the second person: you, Reader. . . . I could also introduce a young lady, the Other Reader, and a counterfeiter-translator, and an old writer who keeps a diary like this diary. . . .
>
> But I wouldn't want the young lady Reader, in escaping the Counterfeiter, to end up in the arms of the Reader. I will see to it that the Reader sets out on the trail of the Counterfeiter, hiding in

some very distant country, so the Writer can remain alone with the young lady, the Other Reader.

To be sure, without a female character, the Reader's journey would lose liveliness: he must encounter some other woman on his way. Perhaps the Other Reader could have a sister. . . . (Pp. 197–8)

Since Flannery is the author-figure of the narrative, and since the first part of the description encapsulates Calvino's own narrative, the latter part establishes a tension between Calvino and the authorial audience: will this plan be carried out? The tension is resolved in Chapter 9 when the Reader has the following encounter with Lotaria, who has successively appeared under the names Corinna, Alfonsina, Ingrid, Gertrude, and Sheila.

> . . . Sheila-Alfonsina-Gertrude has thrown herself on you, torn off your prisoner's trousers; your naked limbs mingle under the closets of electronic memories.
>
> Reader, what are you doing? Aren't you going to resist? Aren't you going to escape? Ah, you are participating. . . . Ah, you fling yourself into it, too. . . . You're the absolute protagonist of this book, very well; but do you believe that gives you the right to have carnal relations with all the female characters? Like this, without any preparation. . . . Wasn't your story with Ludmilla enough to give the plot the warmth and grace of a love story? What need do you have to go also with her sister (or with somebody you identify with her sister), with this Lotaria-Corinna-Sheila, who, when you think about it, you've never even liked. . . . It's natural for you to want to get even, after you have followed events of pages and pages with passive resignation, but does this seem the right way to you? Or are you trying to say that even in this situation you find yourself involved, despite yourself? You know very well that this girl always acts with her head, what she thinks in theory she does in practice, to the ultimate consequences. . . . It was an ideological demonstration she wanted to give you, nothing else. . . . Why, this time, do you allow yourself to be convinced immediately by her arguments? Watch out, Reader: here everything is different from what it seems, everything is two-faced. . . . (P. 219)

The narrator's remarks to the Reader about the freedom that comes with his role as "absolute protagonist" are reminiscent of Fowles's narrator's remarks in Chapter 13 of *The French Lieutenant's Woman* about the autonomy of his characters, and here too those remarks actually emphasize the synthetic status of the protagonist. Because Calvino's narrator is addressing a characterized audience, however, he creates the effect in a somewhat different way. Although the question is about the character's rights to independent action, it presupposes that the Reader knows he is a character, a knowledge that he did not seem to have before this point.

This further foregrounding of the synthetic is effected by another use of the characterized audience: the double applications it invites do allow almost everything in the discourse to be two-faced—at least. Why does the Reader fling himself into it? His action violates the few mimetic dimensions that he has: as the narrator says, the Reader has never even liked Lotaria and what we have seen of his own jealousy leads us to infer that he would regard a sexual encounter with her as a kind of betrayal of his own feelings for Ludmilla. The answer to the narrator's question is that the Reader has no choice; the event appears to be dictated by the plan in Flannery's diary, which is itself of course dictated by a plan of Calvino's. Or to put it another way, the Reader is flung into it by Calvino, who wants his authorial audience to wonder about the levels of reality in the narrative: at this point, in addition to the frame story and the *incipits*, we have Flannery's diary embedded in the frame and then, in a sense, this episode growing out of that embedded diary: the inside has become the outside, making the former outside an inside—perhaps. The effect of this development is to induce the authorial audience to reflect upon the irreducibly synthetic and wonderfully complex nature of reading fiction, especially this one, a reflection that take us to the role of the author in controlling the synthesis, and the role of the reader in seeking to detect its "hidden intention."

As we see in this development of the progression, part of the intention here is to take a character with a prominent synthetic component and minimal mimetic dimensions and make that synthetic component increasingly prominent, even as some pretense about the mimetic consistency and/or autonomy is preserved. This part of the intention is given one of its most striking—and appropriate—twists in the final chapters, but before examining them, I would like to back up and consider the relation of the *incipits* to the progression of the outer story.

As noted above, one of the relations between these *incipits* and the outer story is that each of them (except the first) offers a reading experience that fulfills the wish of the Other Reader.[15] In this respect, their relation to the outer story parallels the relation of the Reader's encounter with Lotaria to Flannery's diary: the apparent autonomy of the later development is undercut because it is actually a consequence of an earlier moment in the narrative. (Furthermore, there are certain proper names carried over from one *incipit* to the other that also serve to undercut their apparent autonomy.) At the same time, because Ludmilla's desires are consistently fulfilled, her way of reading—her openness to a variety of experiences, her delight in reading for reading's sake, her excellent recall of what she has read—is presented as superior to the Reader's.

Of course, Ludmilla's desires are not so specific that they determine in advance the precise details and developments of the *incipits*. As a result, Calvino sets himself a very challenging narrative project. The challenge, in effect, is to emphasize the distance between the authorial and the narrative audiences and then get us to participate in the narrative audience in spite of ourselves. Although the stories range from following the conventions of realism to invoking the elements of the fantastic, the narrative audience in each is clearly invited to believe in the reality of the events, to get caught up in the developing plots. Of course, as the outer narrative emphasizes the synthetic more and more, the challenge becomes greater: the authorial audience, in effect, has to travel farther and farther to enter the narrative audience of each succeeding *incipit*. Moreover, after the first two or three titled chapters, we enter the next ones knowing that they too will break off before they reach resolution, a knowledge that also inhibits our entrance into the narrative audience. By inducing us to enter these different audiences in spite of these difficulties, Calvino not only displays his own narrative virtuosity, but also teaches something about the power of our own desires for the mimetic illusion. Thus, in a curious way, even the experience of participating in the narrative audience gets transformed by the whole narrative into something that ultimately reinforces the synthetic nature of the whole narrative.

Within this general account of the role of the *incipits*, some further distinctions need to be made. Because the first two are part of the whole narrative setup, introducing the authorial audience to the concern with reading and with the shifting planes of narrative action, they are set apart from the rest by their own use of second-person narration. I have argued above that in "If on a winter's night a traveler" the second-person address appears to be a part of the actual narrative. In "Outside the town of Malbork," the situation is more ambiguous. At first, the evidence suggests that the second-person discourse is a summary made by the narrator of the outer story:

> Here everything is very concrete, substantial, depicted with sure expertise; or at least the impression given to you, Reader, is one of expertise, though there are some foods you don't know, mentioned by name, which the translator has decided to leave in the original. . . . (P. 34)

Then, however, the voice will employ the first person as well as the second and will therefore appear to be a voice within this narrative only:

> Every moment you discover there is a new character, you don't know how many people there are in this immense kitchen of ours, it's no use counting, there were always many of us, at Kudgiwa, always coming and going. . . . (P. 35)

The ambiguity within "Outside the town" has its appropriate correspondence on the level of the narrative as a whole: even as we are entering the new narrative audience here, the ambiguity keeps us actively involved in the narrative audience of the frame story: we are again aware of our situation as readers reading about readers reading. Later on, however, when Calvino's problem is to get us to enter the narrative audience of the *incipits*, he drops this kind of ambiguity and offers more direct mimetic narration. Here, for example, is the beginning of the eighth *incipit*, "On the carpet of leaves illuminated by the moon:"

> The ginkgo leaves fell like fine rain from the boughs and dotted the lawn with yellow. I was walking with Mr. Okeda on the path of smooth stones. I said I would like to distinguish the sensation of each single ginkgo leaf from the sensation of all the others, but I was wondering if it would be possible. Mr. Okeda said it was possible. (P.199)

We could, at this stage, be reading Hemingway-among-the-ginkgos— or any one of a number of novelists committed to preserving the mimetic illusion.

Interestingly, although the *incipits* consistently explore themes of identity and of shifting realities and in that sense echo and reinforce the frame story, Calvino does not establish any direct correspondences between the action of any given *incipit* and the action of the outer story that follows. His interest rather seems to be in keeping the audiences stretching to move from one to the other.[16] One consequence of this strategy is that beyond the shift that occurs in the narrative discourse after "Outside the town of Malbork," Calvino is not especially tied down to the order of these fragments. If "On the carpet of leaves illuminated by the moon" preceded the third *incipit*, "Leaning from the steep slope," a story of a naive narrator who gets mixed up in a dangerous situation that he doesn't understand, there would be no significant consequences for the narrative. Similarly, there are no definite limits on the number of such fragments Calvino could incorporate into the narrative. If we had twelve or eight rather than ten, it would work much the same way. At the same time, there are some general limits. At the lower end, he needs to include a sufficient number to give his audiences a significant variety of reading experiences; only in that way can the whole narrative's exploration of the nature of reading be satisfactory. While eight might be enough, five would doubtless be too few. At the upper end, he faces the constraint imposed by his own return to the irreducibly synthetic nature of reading. He is, I think, able to meet his difficult challenge of inducing us to enter new narrative audiences in spite of ourselves for the ten *incipits* he gives us, but he could not do so indefinitely. He is skillful enough to win us over a few more times if he chose, but by the fourteenth or fifteenth time, the whole process would doubtless grow tedious.

Within the *incipits* themselves, Calvino faces another constraint. He needs to generate a progression that will in fact catch us up and he needs to break it off before any resolution is reached. Beyond that he also needs to provide a partial closure so that we do not end up simply frustrated that the fragments are never completed. In general, his strategy is to offer us some initial incident of a narrative, one that points toward further possible complications even as the incident itself is essentially completed. For example, in "In a network of lines that enlace," the story of the professor who, while out jogging, answers the phone in an empty house, the audience is taken through the whole process of his hesitation about answering the phone, his initial escape from it, his irresistible attraction to it, his answering it and receiving the message about Marjorie being tied up and in danger of death, his doubt about whether this could be any Marjorie he knows, his suspicion that this Marjorie is one of his students, his sudden decision, when learning from other students that she hasn't shown up for two days, to go to the address given in the message. Then we have the conclusion:

> I have already run off. I leave the campus. I take Grosvenor Avenue, then Cedar Street, then Maple Road. I am completely out of breath, I am running only because I cannot feel the ground beneath my feet, or my lungs in my chest. Here is Hillside Drive. Eleven, fifteen, twenty-seven, fifty-one; thank God the numbers go fast, skipping from one decade to the next. Here is 115. The door is open, I climb the stairs, I enter a room in semidarkness. There is Marjorie, tied on a sofa, gagged. I release her. She vomits. She looks at me with contempt.
> "You're a bastard," she says to me. (P. 139)

The conclusion resolves most of the tensions and the instabilities: his neurosis about answering the phone seems to have suited somebody's purpose; furthermore, his reaction has proven, at least in one sense, to be a sound one: we now know that the Marjorie of the message is the Marjorie he knows. In short, we have a full incident here. At the same time, other instabilities remain: Who called him? How much does the caller know? Why is Marjorie bound and gagged?

Why does Marjorie swear at him, when he has apparently rescued her? And of course, what will happen next? In short, having entered the narrative audience here, we are interested in hearing more, but our desires for resolution have been partially satisfied.

If this analysis of the progression of the *incipits* is correct, especially in its discussion of the number of such beginnings the narrative can incorporate, then it suggests that they cannot establish their own closure, either singly or as a group. Since the Reader's two quests become intertwined in Chapter 7, and since one of the few absolute certainties of the narrative is that the Reader cannot succeed in the quest to find the end of any of the *incipits*, Calvino cannot end the narrative by taking the usual route of resolving the major instabilities. However, if I am right in saying that after Chapter 7 the progression increasingly emphasizes the synthetic nature of the whole reading experience, then an appropriate ending ought at least to make some gesture toward resolving the instabilities as it also offers some final twist on the issues explored in the synthetic realm. By bringing the Reader back to his hometown library and having him decide to marry Ludmilla, Calvino solves his problem with characteristic ingenuity.

The Reader's discussion with the other readers in the library serves several important functions, but before looking at those, we should note that Calvino has gone so far away from the mimetic that he does not even trouble to explain how the Reader got out of his apparent difficulties in Ircania to return to his hometown. Calvino wants the Reader there, so he puts him there. In effect, the same thing happens with the marriage. He wants to get the Reader and Ludmilla married, so he declares them married—Ludmilla's desires, motivations, possible hesitations, etc. are simply not an issue at this point. The reason the authorial audience does not object to Calvino's doing these things is that they have come to regard the mimetic surface of the narrative as only an occasion for him to explore his concerns with the nature of reading. He can thus manipulate that surface as long as the manipulation pays off on the thematic-synthetic level.

The first function served by the discussion among the readers in the library is to complicate the authorial audience's reflections on reading by introducing each reader's explicit credo about reading. Because these readers discuss their experiences in reading both one book and many books, the authorial audience is led to reflect not just on its own reading of this book but also on the relation of that reading to its reading of other books. As Calvino presents the different kinds of readers here—the one who is so stimulated by reading that he can never read more than a few pages of any book, the one who cannot take his attention from what he is reading, another who continually rereads, discovering a new book each time, the one who sees all books as part of the same book, and so on—he does not favor one over the others, and he does not favor Ludmilla's over any of them. Consequently, the authorial audience, having been brought to a heightened awareness of the nature and variety of reading fictional narrative, must now reexamine its own typical habits of reading, and adopt the stance that any one habit may be too limiting. This step goes a long way toward completing Calvino's exploration of one of the main issues in the narrative.

The second function is to supply a twist on the Reader's search for the continuation of the *incipits*, a twist sufficient to help end the quest and thus provide closure. That twist comes through the sixth reader, the one who revels in the moment preceding reading. He takes the step of putting all the titles together:

> *"If on a winter's night a traveler, outside the town of Malbork, leaning from the steep slope without fear of wind or vertigo, looks down in the gathering shadow in a network of lines that enlace, in a network of lines that intersect, on the carpet of leaves illuminated by the moon around an empty grave—What story down there awaits its end?—he asks, anxious to hear the story."* (P. 258)

Although the Reader initially objects that this is not the first paragraph of a book, the authorial audience recognizes it as the final reflexive move of the *incipits*: here we have a new *incipit*, constructed out of the titles of the ten previous ones and the fragment from the *Arabian Nights* included in this chapter. Furthermore, the move sets up the comment by the seventh reader—the one concerned with endings—that leads the Reader to his decision to marry Ludmilla:

> "Do you believe that every story must have a beginning and an end? In ancient times a story could end only in two ways: having passed all the tests, the hero and heroine married, or else they died. The ultimate meaning to which all stories refer has two faces: the continuity of life, the inevitability of death." (P. 259)

Suddenly aware of his own developing story, the Reader chooses marriage and life, while the authorial audience acknowledges and admires Calvino's witty manner of bringing about the resolution of the surface instability. The final stroke of the narrative comes appropriately in its final line.

> Now you are man and wife, Reader and Reader. A great double bed receives your parallel readings.
> Ludmilla closes her book, turns off her light, puts her head back against the pillow, and says, "Turn off your light, too. Aren't you tired of reading?"

And you say, "Just a moment, I've almost finished *If on a winter's night a traveler* by Italo Calvino." (P. 260)

This last line of course brings the authorial audience back to the first—"You are about to begin reading the new novel by Italo Calvino, *If on a winter's night a traveler*"—and functions as a strong signal of closure in the same way that Whitey's "Comb it wet or dry?" signals closure in "Haircut:" it signals the end of the action or situation that makes the narrative possible. At the same time, the line contributes to the appropriate completeness of the narrative because it provides a final twist on the development of Calvino's relations to his audiences.

The similarities and differences between the first and last sentences are revealing of how far the authorial audience has traveled. Whereas the first sentence conceals the distinction between the narrative and characterized audience, the final one overtly plays with the distinction. It remains ambiguous in a way that the first one does not. Once the authorial audience reaches Chapter 2, it must disambiguate the first sentence by reading it as referring to the first *incipit*. That reading of the first line actually reinforces a secondary meaning—and thus, the ambiguity—of this last line: perhaps the Reader has finally obtained the full text of the narrative he began lo those many narratives ago and is finally about to reach its end. At the same time, of course, the primary reading of the line is one that interprets it as referring to the book that the authorial audience finishes reading when it finishes the line.

But to hold onto that reading, we must assume that the Reader has in a sense adopted our perspective on himself, i.e., has become the authorial audience for the narrative of his own life, including his final action of discussing his reading of that narrative. This authorial audience recognizes that such a narrative situation leads to an infinite regress of mirrors-reflecting-mirrors, readings-within-readings, but from Calvino's point of view that recognition is a contemplation devoutly to be wished. In this respect, the final line is the culmination of all the reflexive devices of the narrative.

In this reading of the line, we also see the screen erected by the use of the characterized audience expand and contract. By having the characterized audience speak in the narrative that the narrative audience is reading, Calvino is obviously communicating with the narrative audience behind a thick screen. When the characterized audience, however, utters a sentence that can more easily be applied to the narrative audience (the application doesn't require as many mirrors), the screen quickly becomes thinner. Nevertheless, it cannot become fully transparent—the characterized audience presumably has more to read after speaking, while the narrative audience finishes its reading with that utterance. Thus, Calvino appropriately leaves the authorial audience reflecting on the quickly shifting relationships between the two audiences, relationships that have been crucial to the experience of the entire narrative. In so doing, the line appropriately completes the affective structure of the narrative as well: Calvino's last move is appropriately among the strongest signs of his virtuosity, one that offers in a highly concentrated dose the serious pleasure that has marked the entire developing interchange of the progression.

As its title indicates, this second part of my study has been concerned with showing how different narratives have exploited the synthetic component of character for specific uses in their different progressions. The examples we have looked at in detail are not exhaustive but they certainly represent a broad range of functions for the synthetic component. *The French Lieutenant's Woman* shows how the occasional foregrounding of the synthetic can displace interest from the mimetic to the thematic sphere. *Great Expectations* is an example of how the foregrounded synthetic component of a supporting character can cause a ripple effect through the mimetic and thematic functions of a protagonist. *If on a winter's night a traveler* is above all an example of how the synthetic can subsume the other two functions—and in so doing, establish an admirably inventive kind of progression.

At this stage the principles of the interpretation of character and progression in narrative have been repeatedly exemplified and reexamined. In the next part, I turn to consider another, equally crucial side of the rhetorical transaction of reading narrative: resisting the understanding that these principles might lead one to. My focus will be the character of Catherine Barkley in Hemingway's *A Farewell to Arms*, but the actual analysis of her case will draw on most of the principles that have been developed so far. In another sense, though, my discussion of her character is an extension of the concerns of this part of the study: I will be looking at the interaction of the mimetic, thematic, and synthetic functions in this character where the synthetic component remains in the background.

III   Evaluating—and Resisting—
Character and Progression

6 Evaluation and Resistance: The Case of Catherine Barkley

To this point, my questions about character and progression have been contained within the fence erected by my concern with entering the authorial audience. Moreover, in specifying the way the components of character relate to each other and to the progression of the different narratives we have examined, I have also implicitly been accepting—even honoring—those works. Now I would like to turn my attention to the great wide world beyond the fence, or, to switch metaphors, to move from understanding to "overstanding"—that is, to some critical evaluation of what we have understood.[1] What happens when we enter the authorial audience only to find the author's hospitality lacking—or even offensive? On what rhetorical ground do we take our stand when we want not only to resist a narrative and its characters but also to claim that the resistance is more than personal or idiosyncratic? Or to phrase the question in the way most pertinent to this inquiry: what happens when a character performs thematic functions that clash with the values of a substantial number of flesh-and-blood readers?

The thematic functions of Catherine Barkley in Ernest Hemingway's *A Farewell to Arms* provide an instructive and challenging opportunity for exploring this side of our rhetorical exchange with authors. On the one hand, these thematic functions seem to invite negative responses from most modern readers—Catherine apparently reflects Hemingway's sexism—but on the other, their relations to her mimetic and especially her synthetic functions complicate the act of overstanding by making us reassess our understanding. Indeed, of the narratives we have examined so far, Hemingway's has probably received the greatest range of interpretation and evaluation. For some critics Frederic Henry is an estimable hero, for others a figure to be scorned or perhaps pitied; for some, the novel is an achievement of

the first rank, for others a sentimental or pernicious tale. Consequently, before our overstanding can proceed with any confidence we
will need to reconstruct carefully the narrative's progression and
Catherine's various functions within it. We will pay special attention
to her synthetic component, not because it is foregrounded like Wemmick's but because the uses to which Hemingway puts Catherine
have an especially intricate relation to her thematic functions. In order to provide the best context for this whole investigation, let us
begin with a look at a vigorous attack on the novel that includes a
strong indictment of Hemingway's characterization of Catherine: Judith Fetterley's feminist critique in *The Resisting Reader*.[2]

II

Fetterley's project is to "make palpable" the designs that American
fiction has on its female readers (p. xii), to uncover the covert story of
men's power over women that repeatedly appears in the canonized
works of male authors. In *A Farewell to Arms*

> the issue of power is thoroughly obscured by the mythology, lan-
> guage, and structure of romantic love and by the invocation of an
> abstract, though spiteful "they" whose goal is to break the good,
> the beautiful, and the brave. Yet the brave who is broken is
> Catherine; at the end of the novel Catherine is dead, Frederic is
> alive. . . . Frederic survives several years of war, massive injuries,
> the dangers of a desperate retreat, and the threat of execution by
> his own army; Catherine dies in her first pregnancy. Clearly, biol-
> ogy is destiny. Yet Catherine is [also] . . . a scapegoat. . . . For
> Frederic to survive, free of the intolerable burdens of marriage,
> family, and fatherhood, yet with his vision of himself as the heroic
> victim of cosmic antagonism intact, Catherine must die. Frederic's
> necessities determine Catherine's fate. He is, indeed, the agent of
> her death. (Pp. xv–xvi)

Fetterley divides her detailed reading of the novel into five sections. The first opens by claiming that the novel is a lie, whose surface
idealization of romantic love disguises Frederic's "true aims:" to evade
the fact that he must grow up and to eliminate Catherine because she
threatens to force adulthood upon him (p. 47). This surface idealization, then, disguises "a hostility whose full measure can be taken
from the fact that Catherine dies and dies because she is a woman"
(p. 49). From these claims, this section moves on to explore the way
in which the background of the whole love story, the culture of
war—reflected for the most part in Rinaldi's comments—"erases the
distinctions among women that normally keep male hostility under

some restraint and . . . legitimizes aggression against all women" (p. 49). The second section narrows its focus to Frederic Henry. Fetterley claims that despite his superficial apparent difference from his companions, Frederic embodies the attitudes of his culture toward women. He resents women such as Miss Van Campen who are in positions of authority and is contemptuous of women such as Mrs. Walker who are less than competent. More importantly, his ultimate attitude toward Catherine is hostility:

> If the violence of the novel's ending is striking, so too is its abstract nature, its reliance on a biological trap which is the agent of an impersonal "they" who break the brave and the beautiful. Yet surely this abstraction masks both Frederic's fear of Catherine and his hostility toward her. The image of strangulation, suggested by the comparison with Othello [Catherine has called Frederic "Othello with his occupation gone"], persists, leaving in us the nagging suspicion that Frederic Henry sees himself in the dead fetus which emerges from Catherine's womb and that her death, however much it may be shaped as biological accident, is in fact the fulfillment of his own unconscious wish, his need to kill her lest she kill him. (P. 53)

The third section seeks to demonstrate this charge more fully by examining the relation between Frederic and Catherine. The basis of that relationship is Frederic's desire to be served and Catherine's willingness to meet his needs.

> It is possible for Frederic to love Catherine because she provides him with the only kind of relationship he is capable of accepting: he does not have to act; he does not have to think about things because she thinks for him . . . ; he does not have to assume responsibility; and he does not have to make a final commitment because both her facile logic and her ultimate death give him a convenient out. (Pp. 59–60)

Furthermore, Frederic erects a phony moral basis for his refusal to accept responsibility in his "sense that he is a victim of betrayal" (p. 61). Catherine serves this sense by betraying him too. She "entangles him in a relationship with her, pretending that there will be no drawbacks, no demands, pressures, or responsibilities, only benefits; then she gets pregnant" (p.61). That pregnancy of course eventually leads to her death, which makes Frederic feel even more like a victim. So in serving his sense of betrayal, she also fails him. She can't win, but "her death is the logical consequence of the cumulative hostilities Frederic feels toward her, and the final expression of the connection between the themes of love and war" (p. 62).

In the fourth section, Fetterley seeks to demonstrate that the novel connects the womb and death. She notes the connection made in the first chapter's description of soldiers carrying their ammunition—"the cartridge boxes . . . bulged forward under the capes so that the men, passing on the road, marched as though they were six months gone with child"—and comments that the novel could hardly state more clearly "that pregnancy is death and the womb an agent of destruction" (p. 61). Fetterley then traces the contrasts the novel establishes between inner and outer space, arguing finally that the safe inner world of the womb becomes "a chamber of horrors filled with blood and death" (p. 65).

In the fifth and final section, Fetterley discusses the contradictions of Catherine's character—sometimes tough, sometimes gentle, sometimes romantic, sometimes businesslike, sometimes a partner who acts as Hemingway's version of the male buddy, sometimes a companion who is the essence of the feminine. Fetterley maintains that "Catherine's contradictions are *not* resolvable because her character is determined by forces outside of her; it is a reflection of male psychology and male fantasy life and is understandable only when seen as a series of responses to the male world that surrounds her" (p. 66). To read her character carefully, for Fetterley, is once again to discover the hostility toward women underlying the whole narrative. Catherine "defines herself in terms of men," and she adopts a negative self-image as a result: "in a world in which the ideal is an asexual priest and in which women are defined solely in sexual terms, it is no wonder Catherine hates herself and feels guilty for existing" (p. 69). And so she is always apologizing. Moreover, in a final expression of hostility, according to Fetterley, "the responsibility for both her death and the child's is implicitly placed on Catherine" (p. 70), while the male doctor's competence is never questioned. In summary,

> if we weep at the end of the book . . . , it is not for Catherine but for Frederic Henry. All our tears are ultimately for men, because in the world of *A Farewell to Arms* male life is what counts. And the message to women reading this classic love story and experiencing its image of the female ideal is clear and simple: the only good woman is a dead one, and even then there are questions. (P. 71)

The specifics of this powerful indictment, I think, are best assessed not one at a time but as part of a consideration of Fetterley's whole interpretive method. Her practical criticism, like that of Scholes and Brooks, raises some significant questions about methodology, though, unlike theirs, her project is not explicitly theoretical and so does not directly address those issues. The methodological question underlying her analysis is how one determines what a covert story is, or, more formally, what principles guide the operation of uncovering the covert story implied in a narrative. We can readily identify two: (1) The inferences about what is covert need to follow from a satisfactory explanation, tacit or expressed, of the overt story. If one mischaracterizes the overt story, then the inferences one draws about its covert message will be highly suspect—at best one could be right for the wrong reason; at worst, one could be resisting not the author's narrative but only some of the material out of which the narrative is built, or even a different narrative constructed by the critic out of the same materials as the author's. (2) Those inferences ought to follow from a pattern detectable in the overt story. Since any one character, incident, or narrative comment can easily be recontextualized and offered in support of countless covert messages (one could, for example, construct a hypothesis about Hemingway's covert negative message about Switzerland on the basis of Catherine's dying there or a positive one on the basis of its being like the priest's homeland, the Abruzzi), the plausibility of any one hypothesis will depend in large part on its being anchored in a recognizable pattern in the overt story.[3] In any one case, then, the successful execution of this second principle will depend on the successful execution of the first. One can only detect the patterns after the details of the whole have been arranged.

My claim here is that characterizing the whole is logically prior to detecting the pattern; it may or may not be temporally prior. Some critics may detect a pattern before they detect the configuration of the whole; the understanding of that pattern and its effects, however, must be confirmed or disconfirmed by the understanding of the whole.

Fetterley implicitly acknowledges the necessity of seeing the covert as tied to the overt in her characterization of the overt as based on the mythology of romantic love and in her attempts to show the various patterns of the novel's hostility toward women under that myth. But since she spends so much time on her claims about the patterns of hostility and so little on the way in which the overt narrative asks the reader to take those elements constituting the pattern, we must pause before fully accepting her indictment. Is Fetterley resisting Hemingway's narrative or some possible narrative she has implicitly constructed out of Hemingway's material? This question has greater force when we note that her handling of the textual evidence in making her case for the covert message rests on three significant methodological assumptions: (1) There is no significant progression in the book, except for its gradual revelation of male hostility toward women. Although Frederic's external circumstances change, his character remains largely unchanged. Thus, Frederic's attitudes toward Catherine early in the narrative can be taken as an accurate sign of his later attitude toward her. Imagery from one part of the narrative can be related directly to later parts; to take just one instance, Fetterley has no apparent qualms in building her case that *Catherine's* remark about Othello is a sufficient sign that Henry wants to kill Catherine before she kills him.[4] (2) The male characters can be seen as reliably reflecting Hemingway's beliefs. Thus, Rinaldi's views of women can be taken as Hemingway's views of women. Thus, Frederic's attitude toward Catherine early in the narrative reflects Hemingway's. (3) Efficient causes are actually final causes. Although Frederic sees the final cause of Catherine's death as the nature of the world, Fetterley never gives serious consideration to that explanation. For her, it is simply a mask behind which Frederic hides the real final cause, his—and Hemingway's—hostility toward her.

Now this third assumption is one that is clearly part of Fetterley's resistance. We can ask for a warrant for the assumption, but simply to point out that the narrative makes a distinction between the two kinds of causes is only to tell Fetterley what she already knows. The first two assumptions, however, have a different status. Fetterley does not claim that the overt story offers a progression that is covertly undermined, or that it offers an apparent distance between author and character that is covertly closed. Instead, she is working to uncover the attitudes hidden beneath the romantic surface of an overt story that exhibits progression of circumstance but no progression of attitudes and that establishes no significant difference between the author and his male characters.

As might be expected by anyone who has stayed with me this far, I think that the key assumption is the one about the progression. If Fetterley is justified there, then her indictment will be far more convincing than otherwise. If, for example, she is justified there, then she will in effect be giving a warrant for her third assumption: if the only significant progression is the gradual revelation of the hostility of men to women, then the covert message of Catherine's death would be that she died because she was a woman. If, however, her assumption about the progression does not hold up, then much of her case will be in jeopardy, because in effect the narrative that she is resisting will not be Hemingway's. Let us now turn to consider the progression of the overt story in some detail.

III

The central progression of the novel begins in the first chapter with the establishment of a tension between Frederic and the authorial audience. That tension is made possible by Hemingway's careful control of the first-person narration in the famous opening.

> In the late summer of that year we lived in a house in a village that looked across the river and the plain to the mountains. In the bed of the river there were pebbles and boulders, dry and white in the sun, and the water was clear and swiftly moving and blue in the channels. Troops went by the house and down the road and the dust they raised powdered the leaves of the trees. The trunks of the trees too were dusty and the leaves fell early that year. . . .[5]

The authorial audience infers Hemingway's negative attitude toward the troops, his message about their disruption of nature: the appealing vision of river, plain, and mountains, of the boulders and pebbles of the riverbed and the clear, blue water of its channels is disrupted by the entry of the troops whose marching eventually leads to the unnatural, early falling of the leaves. Because Frederic, however, is just describing and not analyzing—we supply the causal links, he piles up the "ands"—it is questionable whether he shares in this communication between Hemingway and the authorial audience. This question persists as Hemingway uses Frederic's narration to show us a connection between the rain and the destruction of life, a connection that also is established in part through descriptions of the trees: "in the fall when the rains came the leaves all fell from the chestnut trees and the branches were bare and the trunks black with rain. The vineyards were thin and bare-branched too and all the country wet and brown and dead with autumn" (p. 4). The final sentences of the chapter answer the question. "At the start of the winter came the permanent rain and with the rain came the cholera. But it was checked and in the end only seven thousand died of it in the army" (p. 4).

The authorial audience blanches at that "only" and at the restricted concern with the "army." Even acknowledging that a cholera epidemic could easily wipe out more than seven thousand, we cannot overlook the callous attitude toward those troops (and an untold number of civilians) that is expressed in the sentence. Frederic seems to be mouthing here the party line, the official account of what happened, just as in his later debate with Passini he will mouth the official line that defeat is worse than war. In sum, by the end of the first chapter the authorial audience knows that it is being addressed by a narrator whose knowledge of his own situation is more limited than its own and whose values are rather distant from those of his author.

The progression is then further complicated by the introduction of the major instabilities: Frederic's situation as an American in the Italian army and his relation with Catherine. Here too we recognize a distance between him and Hemingway: he has simply drifted into the war, and he feels distant from it. "Well, I knew I would not be killed. Not in this war. It did not have anything to do with me. It seemed no more dangerous to me myself than war in the movies" (p. 37). He becomes interested in Catherine because pursuing her "was better than going every evening to the house for officers where the girls climbed all over you and put your cap on backward as a sign of affection between their trips upstairs with brother officers" (p. 30). He does not recognize her own insight into the games they are playing, does not realize all the ways in which she is in control of what happens between them.

In short, at the outset of the narrative, Hemingway asks us to regard Frederic as a callow, unreflective, self-centered youth, who is in over his head both in the war and in his relationship with Catherine. The complications of the main instabilities follow a path that gradually also leads to a resolution of the initial tension. The progression traces Frederic's slow evolution into a mature man who both learns and faces up to what the narrative presents as the overwhelming truth of his existence. He is in danger not just from the war but from the world itself, which is inevitably and wantonly destructive. In his initial stumbling through this world, he is introduced by Catherine to the possibility of an alternate world. He slowly realizes what that world is all about, slowly realizes its difference from and superiority to the world of the war that he has been living in, and he eventually commits himself to a life with Catherine in which they try to live in that alternate world.

When Frederic first sees Catherine walk into his hospital room in Milan, he claims that "I was in love with her" (p. 89). But Hemingway does not give his authorial endorsement to Frederic's claim. Instead Hemingway shows that although Frederic has moved beyond preferring Catherine to the whores at the front, his love is stll seriously deficient. Frederic is in love with Catherine's physical beauty, but he still does not commit himself fully to her, as Hemingway indicates through Frederic's selfish reaction to the news of her pregnancy and through his characteristically unthinking decision to leave her and head back to the front. Both actions also maintain the tension, because they show that he still does not know what we—and Catherine—know about the world. After the disastrous retreat from Caporetto that leads Henry to make his separate peace, one of the major instabilities is all but resolved. Frederic and Catherine need to get fully clear of the army and the war, as they eventually do in the flight to Switzerland, but Frederic's symbolic baptism in the Tagliamento signals the end of his own involvement in the war.

By this point, however, the authorial audience has seen so much evidence of Hemingway's view of the world that a new kind of instability replaces that one—and in fact carries the narrative through to the end. Once we know that the world is destructive, then we know—in general terms at least—the outcome of the narrative. We read on both to see how that outcome will emerge and to see whether Frederic will come to know what Hemingway, the authorial audience, and Catherine already know. This instability becomes even more prominent because once Frederic returns to Catherine the instability about his commitment to her is resolved. "Often a man wishes to be alone and a girl wishes to be alone too and if they love each other they are jealous of that in each other, but I can truly say we never felt that. We could feel alone when we were together, alone against the others. It has happened to me like that once. I have been alone while I was with many girls and that is the way you can be most lonely. But we were never lonely and never afraid when we were together" (pp. 238–39). As this passage indicates, the final section of the narrative shows Frederic's growing knowledge of the world, a knowledge ultimately attained through his witnessing of the death of his child and especially the death of Catherine. The separate world he and Catherine have sought to create has not been expanded but destroyed, and Frederic is left to live out his life with the knowledge of what he has lost and the certainty that there is no escape from the destruction he has just experienced.

The emotional quality of this progression is similar to that we associate with tragedy, but its trajectory is different from the classical pattern. Given Hemingway's view of the world, Frederic's doom is a condition of existence, not something that he is even partly responsible for: there is no moment of tragic choice here. And unlike Oedipus, Hamlet, Macbeth, Othello, and King Lear who become increasingly ravaged as their tragedies unfold, Frederic actually grows in wisdom and grace. As he slowly changes, he becomes more and more aligned with Hemingway's norms—and thus more estimable in the eyes of the authorial audience. The last step in that growth is not made until the last sentences of the narrative, which provide both completeness and closure as they depict Frederic's response to his loss.

His initial impulse is to have one final romantic scene with Catherine, and he chases the nurses out of the hospital room to be alone with her. "But after I got them out and turned off the light it wasn't any good. It was like saying good-bye to a statue" (p. 314). As Eugene B. Cantelupe has noted, Frederic's earlier reflections on the marble busts in the hospital at the front have loaded the simile with great force: "They had the complete marble quality of looking alike. Sculpture had seemed a dull business . . . marble busts all looked like a cemetery" (p. 28).[6] Frederic now must face the reality of Catherine's death and respond to that. The very last sentence of the narrative, "After a while I went out and left the hospital and walked back to the hotel in the rain" (p. 314), conveys the knowledge (after a while) and the grief (it was what makes him move so slowly) and the control (he moves nevertheless, even as he is being hit in the face with the destructive rain) behind his very deliberate action. The instabilites and tensions are all resolved here. There is nothing left for him to do for Catherine. There is no longer any gap in either his knowledge about or his experience of the world's destructiveness. His doom is complete. And yet in spite of his knowledge and in spite of his experience, he is not crushed but takes a step that indicates he may become one of those who are strong at the broken places.

If even this partial analysis of the progression has merit, then, as noted above, it casts strong doubt on much of Fetterley's indictment. If Frederic's treatment of Catherine throughout much of the book is not endorsed by Hemingway, then it cannot be used as evidence of Hemingway's view of women. At the same time, this analysis leaves parts of the indictment untouched. Fetterley's point about the covert message of Frederic's treatment of women in authority or without appropriate competence does correspond to a pattern in the overt story that the progression neither requires nor transforms. But of course the crucial issue for assessing Fetterley's resistance is the narrative's treatment of Catherine, the subject to which I now turn.

IV

Though incomplete, the above analysis of the progression indicates that for the novel to be effective Hemingway needs to accomplish at least three synthetic tasks: (1) provide some means to bring about Frederic's change; (2) incorporate evidence that the world is in fact destructive; and (3) create the sense that Catherine's death is not the fault of anything or anyone except the impersonal "they" who kill everyone eventually, hurrying after only the very good and the very gentle and the very brave. Significantly, Hemingway gives Catherine synthetic functions that contribute to his accomplishing all three of these tasks.

More than anything or anyone else Catherine is responsible for the change in Frederic, for his growth in knowledge about the world and for his corresponding growth in unselfish love. To be sure, Henry's experiences in the war contribute to his knowledge about the world but it is his life with Catherine that enables him to understand the significance of those experiences. Hemingway shows us, for example, that even after watching Passini die a very painful death and having his own knee blown up, Frederic is blind to the nature of the war. Immediately before those events Frederic and Passini argue about the war: the Italian driver claims that nothing is worse, while Frederic rather weakly maintains that defeat is worse.

> "It could not be worse," Passini said respectfully. "There is nothing worse than war."
> "Defeat is worse."
> "I do not believe it," Passini said still respectfully. "What is defeat? You go home." . . .
> "Tenente," Passini said. "We understand you let us talk. Listen. There is nothing as bad as war. We in the auto-ambulance cannot even realize at all how bad it is. When people realize how bad it is they cannot do anything to stop it because they go crazy. There are some people who never realize. There are people who are afraid of their officers. It is with them the war is made."
> "I know it is bad but we must finish it."
> "It doesn't finish. There is no finish to a war."
> "Yes there is."
> Passini shook his head.
> "War is not won by victory. What if we take San Gabriele? What if we take the Carso and Monfalcone and Trieste? Where are we then? Did you see all the far mountains to-day? Do you think we could take them all too? Only if the Austrians stop fighting. One side must stop fighting. Why don't we stop fighting? If they come down into Italy they will get tired and go away. They have their own country. But no, there is a war." (Pp. 49–50)

At this point, Frederic essentially gives up the argument by commenting on Passini's delivery rather than replying to the substance of his remark: "You're an orator" (p. 50).

With this argument as backdrop, Frederic's description of the shelling that kills Passini and injures himself takes on more significance:

> Through the other noise I heard a cough, then came the chuh-chuh-chuh-chuh—then there was a flash, as when a blast-furnace door is swung open, and a roar that started white and went red and on and on in a rushing wind. I tried to breathe but my breath would not come and I felt myself rush bodily out of myself and out and out and out and all the time bodily in the wind. I went out swiftly, all of myself, and I knew I was dead and that it had all been a mistake to think you just died. Then I floated, and instead of going on I felt myself slide back. . . . In the jolt of my head I heard somebody crying. I thought somebody was screaming. I tried to

move but I could not move. I heard the machine-guns and rifles firing across the river and all along the river. There was a great splashing and I saw the star-shells go up and burst and float whitely and rockets going up and heard the bombs, all this in a moment, and then I heard close to me some one saying "Mama Mia! oh, Mama Mia!" I pulled and twisted and got my legs loose finally and turned around and touched him. It was Passini and when I touched him he screamed. His legs were toward me and I saw in the dark and the light that they were both smashed above the knee. One leg was gone and the other was held by tendons and part of the trouser and the stump twitched and jerked as though it were not connected. He bit his arm and moaned, "Oh mama mia, mama Mia," then, "Dio te salve, Maria. Dio te salve, Maria. Oh Jesus shoot me Christ shoot me mama mia mama Mia oh purest lovely Mary shoot me. Stop it. Stop it. Stop it. Oh Jesus lovely Mary stop it. Oh oh oh oh," then choking "Mama mama mia." Then he was quiet, biting his arm, the stump of his leg twitching. (P. 54)

When the priest then visits Frederic in the hospital, he tells Frederic, "You do not mind the war. You do not see it. You must forgive me. I know you are wounded." Henry replies, "That is an accident." The priest: "Still even wounded you do not see it" (p. 68). Yet when Frederic and the priest next discuss the war—upon Frederic's return to the front after his summer of convalescence in Milan—Frederic adopts Passini's position. He tells the priest that victory may be worse than defeat because it prolongs the war and that "the peasant has wisdom because he is defeated from the start." Reflecting on these statements, Frederic says, "I do not think and yet when I begin to talk I say things that I have found out in my mind without thinking" (p. 172).

For the authorial audience, however, the experience of reading the preceding chapters describing Frederic's life with Catherine in Milan leads to a more concrete source of Frederic's mental turnabout— Catherine herself. As Spanier points out, Catherine knows what the war—and the world—are like before she meets Henry. During their first conversation, she says, "People can't realize what France is like. If they did, it couldn't all go on. He didn't have a sabre cut. They blew him all to bits" (p. 20).[7] Much of her behavior in the novel, especially her willingness to give herself to Frederic and to construct their alternate world, is a response to this knowledge. Given the belief that the world is inevitably destructive, she doesn't care any more about her own soon-to-be-destroyed identity; she cares instead about living for as long as she can in a world built on the values of gentleness, service, and communion. Catherine occasionally articulates pieces of this knowledge, but it is her behavior that affects Frederic. To move as Frederic does from life with Catherine to life on the front is to move from a world of tenderness and gentleness to a world of impersonal violence and destruction. It is no wonder that upon returning to the front Henry is suddenly able to articulate his newfound appreciation for defeat and the gentleness that accompanies it.

Similarly it is also not surprising that he articulates his knowledge of the world directly after the account of his reunion with Catherine in Stresa. Although the shift in tense indicates that he has attained this knowledge only after the events of the narrative, his placement suggests how strongly he associates that knowledge with Catherine. Thus, the apparently abrupt transition from his thoughts about Catherine to his thoughts about the world is striking but logical—it is she who has taught him:

> I know that the night is not the same as the day: that all things are different, that the things of the night cannot be explained in the day, because they do not then exist, and the night can be a dreadful time for lonely people once their loneliness has started. But with Catherine there was almost no difference in the night except that it was an even better time. If people bring so much courage to this world the world has to kill them to break them, so of course it kills them. The world breaks everyone and afterward many are strong at the broken places. But those that will not break it kills. It kills the very good and the very gentle and the very brave impartially. If you are none of these you can be sure it will kill you too but there will be no special hurry. (Pp. 238–39)

As Catherine teaches Henry, she also teaches the authorial audience—though she is not the only element of the novel providing evidence for Hemingway's case that the world is malevolent. Frederic's unreflective descriptions of the war, the rain, the cholera, and the various injuries and deaths he witnesses are what give us this instruction most strongly. But once these descriptions illustrate Hemingway's view, he can then use Catherine to speak about the world for him in order to reinforce or extend this view. "I'm afraid of the rain because sometimes I see me dead in it" (p. 121). "There's only us two and in the world there's all the rest of them. If anything comes between us we're gone and then they have us" (p. 134). "I'm not brave anymore, darling. I'm all broken. . . . They just keep it up till they break you" (p. 306). As the narrative progresses and Hemingway uses Frederic's descriptions and Catherine's comments to make his world view clearer and clearer, our knowledge that Henry and Catherine are doomed becomes firmer and firmer—and part of our knowledge is that this doom is a condition of existence, not the responsibility of any human agent.

Fetterley's neglect of these synthetic functions in the overt story is a serious omission in her analysis. As Hemingway has Catherine perform these functions, he in effect stands with her as they both look down upon Frederic. To argue that there is an underlying hostility in this major aspect of Hemingway's characterization is to argue that Hemingway is using Catherine to express hostility toward himself. That line of argument may have a certain appeal, but it would lead to a very different covert story from the one Fetterley recounts. Nevertheless, what we have seen so far is not the whole story of Catherine's role in the narrative.

In addition to the synthetic functions traced above, Catherine performs one more in her death, for that event is not only the final sign of the world's malevolence but also the final test of Frederic's growth. As noted above, to know the nature of the world abstractly is one thing, to experience its destruction in the most painfully personal way is another, and to respond to that pain without being destroyed even further yet another. Frederic is able to survive this test, and for that Hemingway asks us to admire him. The point I want to stress now is that in this synthetic function, as in the others, Catherine is subordinated to Frederic; her death provides the occasion for the last stage of his growth. Whether there is an offensive covert implication here is a question that we can better answer after considering Catherine's mimetic and thematic functions and their relations to these synthetic ones. Since Catherine's mimetic function has been especially problematic, I shall begin with it.

Setting aside for the moment the extent to which she is the product of a male fantasy, we can recognize that she possesses the following traits: she is tall, blond, attractive, and slim-hipped; she is self-effacing, gentle, and compliant; sexually inexperienced but knowledgeable about the world; despite her gentleness, tough in the face of danger or pain. As Fetterley notes, critics have often found this group of traits to result in an incoherent character—sometimes tough, sometimes gentle, sometimes a partner who acts as Hemingway's version of the good man, sometimes a companion who is the essence of the feminine. Yet if we can grant Hemingway his premise that the shock of her first boyfriend's death has jolted Catherine into knowledge of the world, then I think that she can be more accurately seen as having a coherent mimetic function. The basis of her character is her toughness, but the basis of her behavior is her knowledge of the world. Starting with the belief that doom is a condition of existence, that the world will visit its impersonal violence on her, Catherine acts to establish a life based on opposing principles, on the values of gentleness, tenderness, and union with another human being. To the extent that the other also appreciates those values, she will succeed in creating that alternate though temporary life. It takes a long time, but I think that Hemingway wants us to see Frederic in Switzerland becoming such another.[8] At the same time, because Catherine is fundamentally tough, she is able to stand up to the problems along the way: the pregnancy, Frederic's going back to the front, the flight into Switzerland, the pain of her childbirth.

Of these many attributes, only some become the basis for thematic functions. Consider, for example, the different ways the progression leads us to regard two of Catherine's physical traits, her long hair and her narrow hips. As previous critics have noted, Catherine's long hair is a sign of her feminine sexuality, but over and above that it becomes a sign of the temporary but important barrier Catherine and Frederic attempt to erect between themselves and the world's destruction.

> I loved to take her hair down and she sat on the bed and kept very still, except suddenly she would dip down to kiss me while I was doing it, and I would take out the pins and lay them on the sheet and it would be loose and I would watch her while she kept very still and then take out the last two pins and it would all come down and she would drop her head and we would both be inside of it, and it was the feeling of inside a tent or behind a falls. (Pp. 109–10)

With Hemingway's implicit endorsement of the feelings expressed here, the long hair, while perhaps not being converted into a separate thematic function, certainly participates in and contributes to the thematic function carried by her traits of toughness and gentleness, namely, indicating the best responses to the world's malevolence.

I will say more about that function shortly, but first note that if I am right about the progression's emphasis on destruction as a condition of existence, then Catherine's narrow hips have no analogous function—not even in the covert story. They do provide a mimetic—and medical—explanation of why Catherine dies in childbirth, but the progression works against the inference that the width of Catherine's hips is the real cause of her death. It implies instead that the cause is the nature of the world; if it had not been her hips, it would have been something else; if it had not been in childbirth, it would have been some other time. Fetterley's complaint about Hemingway's deflecting responsibility from the doctor seems to miss this whole element of the overt story: to make the doctor responsible would be to undermine the thematic point of the whole event, since it would imply that if they had chosen a different doctor, things could have turned out differently. Even as the progression suggests that if the doom had not come this way it would have come another, it supplies an implicit logic for this mechanism. By making the efficient cause related to Frederic and Catherine's lovemaking, which is itself so connected to their attempts to construct an alternate world, the progression reinforces the point about the world's malevolence. Second, by making Catherine the one who dies, the progression recalls Frederic's earlier conclusion that the world goes after the very good and the very brave and the very gentle first. To argue that the covert message here is that Catherine dies because of her female biology is, I think, not to resist the overt story but to ignore it.

Now consider Catherine's gentleness and her toughness. Together these traits form the basis of her identification as one of those who is strong at the broken places and as one of the very good and brave and gentle. In short, Catherine's response to her knowledge of the world—her attempt to establish an alternate way of life—and her tough response to pain and danger, especially to her own impending death during childbirth, serve the thematic function of demonstrating how one should act in the face of such knowledge. In performing this thematic function, Catherine again stands with Hemingway, or as Spanier puts it, she fulfills the role of a code hero-ine.[9] Furthermore, the strong connection between Catherine's synthetic functions and this thematic function gives it a prominent place in the progression of the whole narrative.

But this is still not the whole story. Even as the progression points to this dominant thematic function, it also creates another, more problematic one connected with Fetterley's complaint about Catherine's constant desire to serve Frederic and his contentment in having her serve. Throughout their time together, both in Milan and in Switzerland, Catherine's first concern is to serve Frederic, and as she does so, he repeatedly tells us, apparently with Hemingway's approval, "we had a fine life." To enter the authorial audience, we are asked to agree, and thereby to assent to a definition of the fine life in which the female is endlessly self-effacing, tirelessly available, and continually sacrificing. In other words, Frederic's descriptions and commentary, even of their life in Switzerland, convert these traits of Catherine into a thematic function that can only be described as hopelessly sexist. In this respect, Catherine does appear to be the projection of a male fantasy.

Let us examine more closely the relation between Catherine's positive and negative thematic functions. The conclusion that the positive function has a prominent role in the progression suggests that the negative function might in fact be what Ralph Rader has called an unintended negative consequence of a positive intention: in order for Catherine to fulfill her synthetic role as the agent of Frederic's change and her other thematic role as the exemplary respondent to the world, she unavoidably appears as the image of a sexist male's view of an ideal woman.[10] Although this explanation has the appeal of coherently relating the functions, it is, I think, finally unsatisfactory because the allegedly unintended consequences are actually avoidable, or in other words, they appear as intended as the positive intention. The hypothesis that lets Hemingway off the hook does not pay sufficient attention to the way that the progression itself calls attention to the "fine life" with Catherine as the image of the "fine" woman, to the way that the emphasis on both this life and Catherine's subservience are prominent parts of the narrative. As Fetterley notes, Catherine does define herself in terms of men and that mode of definition appears to be taken for granted as a natural occurrence by Hemingway.

Furthermore, the explanation is not sufficiently reflective about Hemingway's alleged positive intention; instead, it is willing to start where he starts, willing in other words to take the givens of the narrative situation for granted, willing to silence by critical fiat the voices who want to argue. Fetterley certainly wants to reflect on those givens, and everyone who reads her is likely to do the same. *A Farewell to Arms* is after all a man's story and a story in which we are asked to focus on and admire the man's growth. So far so good—or at least no problem. But notice what happens: in a parallel to the way Catherine serves Frederic on the mimetic level, she also serves him—and Hemingway—on the synthetic level. The woman's initially more mature vision becomes important largely for its use in our measurement of the man. And as we have seen, the logic of the narrative dictates that the woman be sacrificed as the final test for the man's growth. Furthermore, Frederic's resentment of women in authority and his contempt for those who are not fully competent also contribute to the narrative's overall subordination of women. Finally, why should Catherine and Henry's stillborn child be male rather than female? The implicit assumption there seems to be that the death of a son will be a greater blow to Frederic than the death of a daughter. It is in short another sign of how the narrative takes for granted the subordination of women to men. To accept uncritically the invitation offered by the work, to join the authorial audience without reservation, is also to take that subordination for granted. In this context, the adjective in the phrase, "Hemingway's positive intention," becomes extremely problematic.

Once one registers these problems and registers further the facts that the work shares its premises with many, many others and that it has a firm place in the canon of American literature, many flesh and blood readers will be impelled to argue with Hemingway's characterization of Catherine. Yet at the same time, to focus only on those problems is to miss some of the genuine power of the book, including that offered by the more successful aspects of Catherine's characterization, especially Hemingway's ability to make many of Catherine's mimetic, thematic, and synthetic functions reinforce each other and contribute to the emotional power of the progression. For readers who are concerned both with entering the authorial audience and holding on to a belief in the equality of the sexes, Hemingway's treatment of Catherine makes the experience of reading *A Farewell to Arms* almost dizzying in its complexity and contradictions: the combination of admiration and objection, of positive and negative evaluation that the narrative invites and that I have expressed and reasoned to in my allegedly neat and linear argument sometimes exists as a single, simultaneous response to the narrative. There can, consequently, be no neat and simple outcome to the reader's response to the invitation Hemingway offers in *Farewell*. Hemingway's characterization of Catherine is indeed sexist, but that sexism does not entirely destroy the power of the narrative or even of her own role in it, because that sexism does not exist in isolation from the more positive features of the characterization and the narrative as a whole.

V

But even this is not yet the whole story. For those readers who want to question thoroughly the relation between our values and those we are asked to adopt as we enter the authorial audience, there is at least one more expository event to endure. In making the case for Catherine's positive synthetic and thematic functions, I have argued that she stands with Hemingway in her knowledge of the world and in exemplifying how to respond to that knowledge. Once we step outside the authorial audience, we recognize that this "knowledge" is actually a belief, and clearly a belief that will not be shared by all members of Hemingway's flesh-and-blood audience. As we have seen, Fetterley does not take the belief at all seriously but views it as Frederic's false justification of his sense of betrayal. Other critics such as Gerry Brenner view the passages in which Frederic expresses those beliefs as "self-pitying essayettes."[11] Even if such critics were, for the sake of argument, to accept my point that Hemingway stands behind Frederic in the "If people bring so much courage to this world" speech, then they would argue that Hemingway is standing behind a flawed philosophy, a false truth, an erroneous belief. One consequence of that argument would of course be to undermine the grounds of my partial defense of Hemingway's treatment of Catherine. But how would those critics make such a case? Alternatively, how would defenders of Hemingway make a persuasive case for the validity of his beliefs?

One way of arguing either side of the case is simply to invoke one's own beliefs about—and one's own experience in—the world: "that's simply not true;" "Hemingway needs to find Jesus;" "Hemingway captures my experience of living in this awful world." Flesh-and-blood readers always make such evaluations, and those evaluations are always a significant part of their responses to a narrative. Because the values, beliefs, and experiences of those readers are almost infinitely various, I cannot consider them all, and I have no ambitions to determine what everyone should believe. Yet notice that neither Fetterley nor I have hesitated about saying that a sexist presentation of Catherine ought to be judged negatively by all readers. Our willingness to speak against the values implicit in sexism is in part a reflection of a cultural norm held by the members of our social class: the feminist movement has arguably had its most consistent (if not its most significant) success among the upwardly mobile, politically liberal members of the American academy. Indeed, to speak in defense of Catherine may be to put in question one's credentials as a politically correct literary critic.

Be that as it may, the social pressure in the academy that reinforces the norm against sexism only partially warrants the complaints about sexism. Underneath that pressure is a clear ethical position that can legitimately claim to transcend the differences among the various specific belief systems of Western culture: To assume that women are inherently inferior to men is to deny full humanity to women.[12] The norms, however, that may be invoked either for or against Hemingway's world view—those, say, of existentialism on the one side and Catholicism on the other—do not transcend the differences among specific belief systems and, thus, do not imply any ethical norm as widely shared as the one against sexism. Yet if we look closely at the method controlling the assessment of Hemingway's uses of Catherine to this point, we can still find some guidance for evaluating Hemingway's beliefs about the world—and by extension Catherine's roles that are connected with it.

My method so far has been to explore two questions: (1) How well has Hemingway incorporated Catherine's mimetic, synthetic, and thematic functions into the larger progression of the distinct narrative tragedy that he is writing? (2) What are the ethics of reading Catherine as the authorial audience is asked to do? Or, what ethical position must one adopt to enter fully into the authorial audience's expected responses to Catherine's functions? The negative element of my evaluation stems from the conclusion that to enter into the authorial audience is occasionally to participate in and give consent to the deficient ethics of sexism. The analogous questions about Hemingway's world view, then, are: (1) How well is it incorporated into the narrative so that a flesh-and-blood reader may be induced to enter the authorial audience and adopt that view at least for the time that she is reading the narrative? And (2) what are the ethical consequences of adopting this world view?

Hemingway, I think, takes great pains to incorporate convincingly his world view into the narrative as a whole. The key problem he faced was one of appropriate generalization: most readers would be willing to agree that war is inevitably destructive, but how could he extend their belief about war to a belief about the world? His first device, one which I think is overdone, though not fatally so, is to establish the link between rain and destruction, a link that allows him to introduce in the very first chapter destruction from a source other than the war—the cholera epidemic. His second technique is to represent virtually all the destruction of the war itself as impersonal. The death of Catherine's first boyfriend is presented as just something that happens in war. The shelling that kills Passini and injures Frederic is associated not with any malicious Austrian general but with the nature of things: go near the front and you may be blown up while eating cheese. Similarly, the bullet that kills Aymo during the retreat comes suddenly from some unspecified gun. The executions at the Tagliamento are as much a sign of the breakdown of the Italian army as they are a sign of the problems with the individuals carrying them out. Hemingway's third technique is to use from time to time Catherine's own articulations of her knowledge. The result is that by the time Frederic articulates the world view in Chapter 34, we have been accumulating evidence for it for some time. Since the evidence is generally easy to accept piece by piece, we are well prepared to accept the grand conclusion.

At the same time, the "If people bring so much courage to this world" passage itself is somewhat problematic. First, Frederic's departure from his normally flat "just-giving-the-facts" narration clearly marks the passage as a set piece of Hemingway's and runs the risk of appearing overwritten. In that respect, it is different from Frederic's articulation of similar beliefs during the agony of Catherine's childbirth. His "That was what you did. You died" commentary more clearly grows out of the immediate action. Second, the passage's claim—absent from the later passages—that the world is not just destructive but selective in its decisions about whom to destroy first strains one's credulity beyond the evidence of the narrative. Yes, Aymo appears to be one of the very good. And so does Catherine. And Passini too. But what about all the victims of the cholera? Or the soldier who bleeds to death above Frederic on the way to the field hospital? Or the men being executed at the Tagliamento? On the other hand, if we recall that Frederic expresses these thoughts immediately after he is writing about his happiness with Catherine, we can attribute this part of the generalization to his thoughts of her as very good, brave, and gentle. But the sense of the passage as a Hemingway set piece blocks that solution to the problem of overgeneralization. We are asked to see Frederic speaking for—indeed, with—Hemingway here. In summary, Hemingway's artistry in leading up to this passage and those that come later works well to win his reader's assent to the world view, though the passage itself is not fully successful in clinching the case. On balance, the artistic inducements for the flesh-and-blood audience to adopt Hemingway's beliefs about the world, while not perfect, are sufficient for me to maintain my claim that Catherine's functions connected with the communication of those beliefs are positive ones.

The best way to assess the ethics of Hemingway's world view, I think, is to consider the apparent consequences it has for those characters who share it. And in examining its consequences for Catherine, we need to face the question of whether the belief in the world's malevolence is connected with the sexist elements of the narrative. Is Catherine's willingness to be subservient to Frederic because of her knowledge of the world just another sign of Hemingway's automatic assumption of the subservience of women? We can better answer this question after a look at Count Greffi and the Frederic of Book V.

Hemingway uses his creation of Count Greffi to perform the synthetic function of showing his audience a character who lives with grace and dignity in the face of his own impending death. He would probably never make a speech such as Frederic's "If people bring so much courage to this world," but Hemingway lets him say enough so that the authorial audience can infer that his beliefs are similar to the later Frederic's. Greffi says that he values most "someone I love," that the war is "stupid," that he values life because "it is all I have," that he has expected to become religious as he has grown older "but somehow it does not come" (pp. 250–51). The ethical consequences of Greffi's beliefs all appear to be positive: he is gentle, kind, and solicitous with Frederic; he doesn't take himself too seriously yet he is content with who he is. In the face of his coming death, he goes on much as he always has, giving his birthday parties, playing billiards, drinking champagne, wondering if he will become religious. If Hemingway's beliefs about the world lead to this kind of behavior, then we ought to have no qualms about adopting them.'

As the example of Greffi indicates, in considering the ethical dimension of Hemingway's beliefs about the world's malevolence, we are concerned both with the beliefs themselves and and his view of the proper responses to that malevolence. Like Catherine, Greffi performs the thematic function of indicating how to live with the knowledge of the world. He is an image of what Frederic might become in his old age. The Frederic we see in Book V is moving in this direction. He is content with the small things of his life, his equivalent of Greffi's billiards and champagne: he gets excited watching the hairdresser wave Catherine's hair; he loves to go riding along the country roads with her. More important, he treats Catherine more gently and solicitously than he ever has before. Again, while we could all easily imagine higher standards of ethical conduct than Frederic exhibits, the ethical consequences of Hemingway's beliefs all seem positive.

If, as these examples suggest, adopting the world view itself leads the male characters to be gentle and solicitous, to become like Catherine, then we can, at least to some extent, separate the beliefs about the world from the sexism. Neither is necessarily implicated in the other. In fact, the ethical consequences of Hemingway's beliefs about the world appear to lead one away from rather than toward sexism. Nevertheless, Hemingway's deeply ingrained assumption that women are subordinate to men does intersect with those beliefs, most visibly in the implicit messages about how men and women respond to them. Both Greffi and the later Frederic have a kind of independence that is never even presented as an option for the male-identified Catherine. The men can live in the destructive world without women, whereas the woman "naturally" turns to another man. Thus, Catherine's subservience is a point where two of Hemingway's otherwise independent views intersect: his portrayal of her subservience grows out of both his views of the relation of men to women and of how best to respond to the knowledge of the world's destructiveness. In that respect, this subservience is another instance of what I referred to earlier as the way in which reading Catherine's character can be dizzying in its complexity and contradictions. But this intersection of the beliefs and its consequences for the characterization of Catherine do not point to any negative ethical consequences of Hemingway's beliefs about the world; instead they once again show the negative consequences of the sexism and the way in which Hemingway's second-nature assumption about the subordination of women to men infects the whole narrative.

Thus, as we move to the end of my story of Catherine's functions, we have good cause to evaluate positively her synthetic and thematic functions related to Hemingway's communication of his beliefs about the world, just as we have good cause to evaluate negatively the thematic functions related to his sexism. As a coda to the story, I would like to point out an interesting by-product of this final event, one connected not with the conflict between author and audience caused by the sexism but rather with potential conflicts caused by different beliefs about the nature of the world.

If my analysis in this last section holds up, then we can understand why flesh-and-blood readers whose beliefs about the world are considerably more optimistic than Hemingway's can still adopt his and be moved by the narrative. Such readers do not simply give in to the narrative illusion—and they do not end up hating themselves in the morning—because they are very likely not only to accept but to admire (and perhaps even aspire to) the ethical consequences Hemingway draws from that world view. In other words, both existentialists and fundamentalists can enter Hemingway's authorial audience without compromising their ethical standards. At the same time of course, fundamentalists will find themselves resisting the bald statement of the world view, but the very experience of being moved by the narrative can establish a very productive relationship with it, one arguably more productive than that of the existentialists who will merely have many of their beliefs reinforced. The combination of intellectual resistance and emotional suasion has the potential of making one rethink—and rejustify or reject—one's own world view.

For another variation on the same phenomenon, consider the feminists who are opposed to marriage and in love with Jane Austen's novels. The potential for conflict between author and readers there is of course initially reduced by Austen's concern not with marrying per se but with marrying for the best. Thus, the ethical dimension of reading *Pride and Prejudice* or *Emma* involves measuring the characters (and to some extent oneself) against the ethical norms of the narrator, norms which are at once appealing and challenging. For readers opposed to marriage as an institution, the marriages themselves may become incidental to the core experience of following the carefully nuanced, yet clear, ethical paths that the heroines eventually walk. For others, of course, the conflict between the ethical dimension of reading and the value Austen places on marriage may be too great to overcome. But again, for some subset of those readers that conflict can be very productive.

Not surprisingly, then, the rhetorical consequences of resisting reading will be likely to vary from narrative to narrative. The act of repudiating a narrative more fully than I have done here may be relatively empty if the repudiation is easy and dependent on an inadequate reconstruction of the narrative's design. The resistance is empty because there is little genuine encounter between the text and the reader. Even if the reconstruction is careful, the repudiation may be relatively unsatisfying if the ethical basis of the work is easily rejected. In such cases the degree of satisfaction will be at least partially dependent on the cultural status of the repudiated text: repudiating Faulkner is likely to be more satisfying than repudiating Ferber. Resistance is more likely to be satisfying and productive when it is partial, when we find ourselves in genuine disagreement with some parts of a work without entirely losing our respect for it. In these cases, we talk with the text and its author more as equals, acknowledging their power, but for that very reason, required to think hard about the nature and meaning of their limits. The dialogue established in these encounters can go on for a long time and can lead us to rethink some of our most fundamental commitments and beliefs.

Conclusion
Extensions and Reconsiderations

I

The resources of narrative and the inventive capacities of human story-
tellers are, I think, too vast and various for the multitudinous interactions of character and progression to be analyzed in a single study.
Every reader can no doubt think of numerous narratives where the
interaction of character and progression is different from the patterns
examined here. Given this situation, this inquiry does not attempt
to be exhaustive. It does, however, retain the vaulting ambition of
comprehensiveness, the goal of establishing—and demonstrating in
operation—theoretical categories and principles rich enough to have
substantial predictive value and flexible enough to apply to new
cases. Consequently, it has sought that richness and that flexibility by
working with examples that would satisfy the twin criteria of representativeness and range. More specifically, through its choice of narratives and critical positions, this study has been attempting (1) to
describe and analyze both typical and unusual relations among the
components of character; (2) to investigate a wide spectrum of principles of progression; and (3) to undertake a broad sweep of the interpretive issues connected with viewing character and progression
from a rhetorical perspective.

In this final chapter, I want first to make another step toward comprehensiveness by demonstrating the flexibility of the categories and
principles already established, and then second, to move beyond the
quest for comprehensiveness by reflecting on the predictive power of
the theory, including the limits on that power. Rather than undertaking full-scale analyses of new narratives as I approach argument's
end, I will seek to demonstrate flexibility by addressing some specific
issues raised by three very different works: Norman Mailer's *The Armies of the Night*, George Eliot's *Middlemarch*, and Virginia Woolf's
Mrs. Dalloway. *The Armies of the Night* is the flip side of *If on a winter's*

189

night a traveler: a narrative where the protagonist is not a fictional construct but a historical person. What happens to the mimetic-synthetic relationship there? To what extent can Mailer the author's presentation of Mailer the character be considered synthetic? How does such a nonfictional protagonist perform thematic functions? *Mrs. Dalloway* poses the question of how the interaction between character and progression works in a narrative where so much of the progression is itself a gradual unfolding of character. The question is complicated further because Clarissa, though obviously central, is one among several characters whose inner lives Woolf opens to her audience. In answering the question, I will find it useful to examine Eliot's handling of the Fred Vincy-Mary Garth subplot in *Middlemarch*. What Eliot does there in elaborating the subordinate action while making it serve the main plot lines both looks back to what Austen does with Charlotte Lucas and Dickens with Wemmick and ahead to what Woolf does with Septimus Smith. In explaining how the subordinate characters function in those different progressions, the study will complete one strand of its own progression.

II

In the last paragraph of Book One of his account of the October 1967 march on the Pentagon to protest American involvement in the Vietnam War, Mailer the narrator describes the process by which Mailer the character became Mailer the author.

> Then he began his history of the Pentagon. It insisted on becoming a history of himself over four days, and therefore was history in the costume of a novel. He labored in the aesthetic of the problem for weeks, discovering that his dimensions as a character were simple: blessed had been the novelist, for his protagonist had been a simple of a hero and a marvel of a fool, with more than average gifts of objectivity—might his critics have as much!—this verdict disclosed by the unprotective haste with which he was obliged to write, for he wrote of necessity at a rate faster than he had ever written before, as if the accelerating history of the country forbade deliberation. Yet in writing his personal history of these four days, he was delivered a discovery of what the March on the Pentagon had finally meant, and what had been won, and what had been lost, and so found himself ready at last to write a most concise Short History, a veritable precis of a collective novel, which here now, in the remaining pages, will seek as History, no, rather as some Novel of History, to elucidate the mysterious character of that quintessentially American event.[1]

From our perspective, there are two especially noteworthy elements of this passage. First, although it claims that the writing of Book One made possible the writing of Book Two, the passage reveals almost nothing about the precise relation between them, about, for example, how the two parts constitute a single narrative or what the nature of that narrative might be. Second, the passage points to the irreducibly synthetic component of character even in nonfiction narrative: "[H]is dimensions as a character were simple: blessed had been the novelist, for his protagonist had been a simple of a hero and a marvel of a fool, with more than average gifts of objectivity." Like Huck Finn in civilization, we've been here before, and like Huck, we've learned not to take everything at face value. As we have seen in *The French Lieutenant's Woman*, when the narrator of a fictional narrative claims that the narrative is taking its direction from a character's mimetic function, that claim actually foregrounds the synthetic component of the character. The same logic applies here. If Mailer the character is a "simple of a hero" and a "marvel of a fool," it is because Mailer the author has emerged from his labor "in the aesthetic of the problem" with a decision to represent himself that way. Understanding the rationale for that decision will enable us to understand the connection between Books One and Two.[2]

Mailer begins his narrative by quoting *Time* magazine's account of his performance during the weekend of the March:

A Shaky Start

Washington's scruffy Ambassador Theater, normally a pad for psychedelic frolics, was the scene of an unscheduled scatological solo last week in support of the peace demonstrations. Its antistar was author Norman Mailer, who proved even less prepared to explain Why Are We in Vietnam? than his current novel of that title.

Slurping liquor from a coffee mug, Mailer faced an audience of 600, most of them students, who had kicked in $1,900 for a bail fund against Saturday's capers. "I don't want to grandstand unduly," he said, grandly but barely standing.

It was one of his few coherent sentences. Mumbling and spewing obscenities as he staggered about the stage—which he had commandeered by threatening to beat up the previous M.C.—Mailer described in detail his search for a usable privy on the premises. Excretion, in fact, was his preoccupation of the night. "I'm here because I'm like LBJ," was one of Mailer's milder observations. "He's as full of crap as I am." When hecklers mustered the temerity to shout "Publicity hound!" at him, Mailer managed to pronounce flawlessly his all-purpose noun, verb and expletive: "**** you."

Dwight Macdonald, the bearded literary critic, was aghast at the barroom bathos, but failed to argue Mailer off the platform. Macdonald eventually squeezed in the valorous observation that Ho Chi Minh was really no better than Dean Rusk. After more obscenities, Mailer introduced poet Robert Lowell, who got annoyed at requests to speak louder. "I'll bellow but it won't do any good," he said and proceeded to read from *Lord Weary's Castle*.

By the time the action shifted to the Pentagon, Mailer was perky enough to get himself arrested by two Marshals. "I transgressed a police line," he explained with some pride on the way to the lockup where the toilet facilities are scarce indeed and the coffee mugs low-octane. (Pp. 13–14)

Mailer's comment on the account, "Now we may leave *Time* in order to find out what happened," conveys a withering judgment on its accuracy, but his own subsequent description of his initial involvement in the march and of his behavior at the Ambassador seems to confirm the *Time* reporter's assessment of him.

The mimetic portrait Mailer draws of himself in the early scenes is that of a man who is not only a marvel of a fool but also a giant of an ego. Reluctantly drawn in to participating in the March, he anticipates it with all the eagerness of a blueblood MBA about to spend a weekend with a UAW local: "It was going to prove a wasteful weekend he decided with some gloom—he could have spent it more profitably cutting his new movie. . . . Mailer wished as the Washington weekend approached that the Washington weekend were done" (pp. 20–21). In his verbal jousting with Robert Lowell at the party before the Thursday night rally at the Ambassador, he replies to Lowell's compliment that Mailer is the finest journalist in America by saying, "Well, Cal, there are days when I think of myself as being the best writer in America" (p 33). When asked by Ed de Grazia, the organizer of the rally, if he would like to speak first—before Lowell, Dwight Macdonald, and Paul Goodman—Mailer replies, "There'll be nothing interesting to follow me" (p. 39). He jumps at the chance de Grazia offers him to be M.C., and takes pleasure in "thoughts of the subtle annoyance his role as Master of Ceremonies would cause the other speakers" (p. 39).

The gigantic proportions of the Mailer ego are nowhere more evident than they are in the events at the Ambassador, where Mailer, now drunk, acts the part of the self-indulgent M.C., and assesses the whole evening according to how well he is doing with the audience. He presents his own speech as an attempt to win greater applause from the audience than Lowell: "They gave Lowell a good standing ovation, much heartiness in it, much obvious pleasure that they were there in Washington on a night when Lowell had read from his work. . . . to Mailer it was now *mano a mano"* (p. 61). Mailer's own speech—and the asides he makes about it in the narration—are comic enough to prevent it from being an utter disaster ("'they [reporters] alone have done more to destroy this nation than any force in it.' They will certainly destroy me in the morning . . ."), but the speech is another egregiously self-indulgent and egotistical performance. Mailer claims to be the dwarf alter ego of Lyndon Johnson and delights in spewing obscenities with his adopted Texas accent. His report of his behavior fleshes out the account given in *Time*, but it leads the reader to conclude that Mailer got off easy at the hands of the Luce-ites. If John Marcher's main trait is his obsession, Mailer's—at this point in the narrative—is his egotism.

Slowly, however, Mailer's attitude toward participating in the events of the weekend changes and so too does the resulting character portrait. At the demonstration at the Justice Department on Friday afternoon, Mailer begins to feel a "deep modesty on its way to him" (p. 93). As faculty members walk up and deposit their draft cards in a bag to be turned over to the Justice Department,

> he stood in the cold watching [them], yes always one by one, and felt his hangover which had come in part out of his imperfectly swallowed contempt for them the night before, and in part out of his fear, yes now he saw it, fear of the consequences of this weekend in Washington, for he had known from the beginning it could disrupt his life for a season or more and in some way the danger was there it could change him forever. (P. 93)

That night Mailer, Lowell, and Macdonald agree that they will seek to get arrested on the March. But Mailer wants to get arrested early so he can go back to New York for a party on Saturday night.

By the time that Mailer emerges from jail on Sunday morning, however, his change is complete. The experience of the march, his arrest for "transgressing a police line," his night in Occoquan jail amid the company of numerous other demonstrators, his witnessing of his lawyer's argument with the U.S. Commissioner that eventually won him a suspended sentence: all these events have immersed Mailer in the weekend he wanted to avoid, and that immersion has humbled him, got him out of himself, and focused him on the significance of the march. Just as the narrative begins with a report of a speech he made, so it ends with such a report, this time from the *Washington Post*:

> Novelist Norman Mailer, using a makeshift courtroom to deliver a Sunday sermon on the evils of the Vietnam War, received the only

prison sentence yesterday as justice was meted out in wholesale lots for hundreds of anit-war demonstrators.

In his courtroom speech Mailer said, "They are burning the body and blood of Christ in Vietnam."

"Today is Sunday," he said "and while I am not a Christian I happen to be married to one. And there are times when I happen to think that the loveliest thing about my dear wife is her unspoken love for Jesus Christ. . . ."

Mailer said he believed that the war in Vietnam "will destroy the foundation of this republic, which is its love and trust in Christ." Mailer is a Jew. (P. 240)

In this case, however, the gap between what the press reports and what Mailer's audience sees is very large. Mailer's speech is not prompted by a desire to parade his ego before what he hopes will be an appreciative audience but to express a feeling that the cumulative experience of the weekend has given him:

standing on the grass, he felt one suspicion of a whole man closer to that freedom from dread which occupied the inner drama of his years, yes, one image closer than when he had come to Washington four days ago. The sum of what he had done that he considered good outweighed the dull sum of his omissions these same four days. So he was happy, and it occurred to him that his clean sense of himself, with a skin of compassion at such rare moment for all . . . this nice anticipation of the very next moves of life itself . . . must mean, indeed could mean nothing else to Christians, but what they must signify when they spoke of Christ within them. . . . (P. 238)

Mailer's turn to the idea of Christianity here recalls his earlier explanation in the chapter "Why Are We in Vietnam?" (the explanation delivered by the author as the character sleeps in Occoquan) that the war represents a suppressed schizophrenia in the American character: Americans worshiped the Mystery of Christ and the no Mystery of the Corporation and found an outlet for the conflict in the war, which at least opened up one's emotions for the soldiers and the orphans.

Now that he sees his own connection to the mystery of Christianity, he gives his speech, the second paragraph of which was not reported in full by the *Post*:

"Some of us," said Mailer to the reporters and the photographer and the microphone, "were at the Pentagon yesterday, and we were arrested in order to make our symbolic protest of the war in Vietnam, and most of us served these very short sentences, but they are a harbinger of what will come next, for if the war doesn't end next year," then said he, feeling as modest as he had felt on the steps of the Department of Justice, "why then a few of us will probably have to take longer sentences. Because we must. You see, dear fellow Americans, it is Sunday, and we are burning the body and blood of Christ in Vietnam. Yes, we are burning him there, and as we do, we destroy the foundation of this Republic, which is its love and trust in Christ." (P. 239)

Viewed in this broader context, the speech seems sane rather than farfetched; although it is not an immortal speech, it does present Mailer making the kind of gesture for the whole antiwar movement he would have been incapable of four days before. This point is underlined by the final part of the coda to his own story. "As the days went by, he contracted to write an account of the March on the Pentagon, and wrestled with the difficulties of how to do it, and appeared on a television show and amazed himself. For if he had been half as conservative as Russell Kirk in prison, he was half as militant on television as H. Rap Brown" (p. 241).

In short, the narrative of Book One is the narrative of Mailer the character's alteration from the egotist who is greater than the event to the more modest man who is transformed by the event. Even as the narrative claims to be truthful, it also gives the protagonist a clear synthetic function: Mailer the character functions in the narrative in much the same way as a protagonist does in a Bildungsroman: he makes the passage from ignorance to knowledge. The thematic component of Mailer's character is more like that of Fowles's Charles Smithson than that of any other character we have seen. In one respect of course, Mailer and Smithson are very different: where Fowles emphasizes the extent to which Charles is typical of his class and his age, Mailer the author makes no such claims for representativeness. Nevertheless, the thematic function of the character is carried by the whole narrative rather than by particular traits being thematized. Charles functions as part of Fowles's narrative explanation of the shift from the Victorian Age to the modern, and Mailer functions to show the power of the march upon those who participated in it: it transformed even so great an egotist as himself.

Mailer's decision to treat himself this way has some further consequences for our understanding of the progression of Book One and for the relation between it and Book Two. By incorporating the reports of *Time* and the *Washington Post* and other newspapers into this narrative which focuses on his own participation in the march, Mailer is implicitly contrasting their methods for getting at the significance of the events with his own. Their methods of course lead to reporting which flattens out the events, diminishes them, grinds them up in the great mix of personality and one-upmanship they seem so intent on pursuing. Mailer's methods are unusual, but they communicate a substance to the events that is conspicuously lacking in the mass media reports.

One of the most notable features of Mailer's method in Book One is that his account of all the events is largely restricted to the vision of Mailer the character. The narrative of the events at the Ambassador Theater is not interrupted by the more mature vision of the post-march Mailer the way that, say, the narration of *Great Expectations* is interrupted by the vision and voice of the mature Pip. One consequence of this technique is that the authorial audience may be repulsed not just by Mailer the character but also by Mailer the author. Because the authorial audience knows that Mailer the author and Mailer the character are, in some sense, the same person, our impulse is to view the author and the character as closely aligned: we may then conclude that the jerk up on the stage is also the jerk who wrote this book. Mailer employs various means—especially displaying a sharp wit and a style commanding in its flexibility and range—to prevent the authorial audience from simply giving up on him, but we may wonder why he would run the risk. The reason, I think, is not far to seek. By presenting the unmitigated view of Mailer the egotist at the outset, Mailer makes the effect of the transformation, gradual as it is, that much more powerful.

In Book Two, the Novelist, as Mailer says, "passes the baton to the Historian" who broadens his focus considerably and offers an account of the whole event from its planning to its execution to its last minutes and some of its aftermath. The history has a clear thesis: despite the failure of the American press to recognize what was going on, the March on Washington was a significant event in the history of the United States, one that planted the seeds for a new positive growth in the character of the whole country. This thesis comes through frequently, but it is perhaps most notable in three places, the first of which is Mailer's description of the rite of passage undergone by those who remained at the Pentagon after the battle of the wedge Saturday night and on into Sunday morning:

> each generation of Americans had forged their own rite, in the forest of the Alleghenies and the Adirondacks, at Valley Forge, at New Orleans in 1812, with Rogers and Clark or at Sutter's Mill, at Gettysburg, the Alamo, the Klondike, the Argonne, Normandy, Pusan—the engagement at the Pentagon was a pale rite of passage next to these, and yet it was probably a true one, for it came to the

spoiled children of a dead de-animalized middle class who had chosen most freely out of the incomprehensible mysteries of moral choice, to make an attack and then hold a testament before the most authoritative embodiment of the principle that America was right, America was might, America was the true religious war of Christ against Communist. (P. 311)

The thesis about the significance of the march again emerges clearly in Mailer's penultimate chapter. He says that the real end of the march was probably in Occoquan and the jail in Washington, D.C., especially among a group from a Quaker farm in Connecticut who continued the protest by practicing noncooperation: "some of them refused to eat or drink and were fed intravenously. Several men at the D.C. jail would not wear prison clothing. Stripped of their own, naked, they were thrown in the Hole. There they lived in cells so small that not all could lie down at once to sleep. For a day they lay naked on the floor, for many days naked with blankets and mattress on the floor. For many days they did not eat nor drink water. Dehydration brought them near to madness" (p. 318).

Mailer speculates about the significance of their actions:

Did they pray, these Quakers, for forgiveness of the nation? . . . The prayers are as Catholic as they are Quaker, and no one will know if they were ever made. . . . But if the end of the March took place in the isolation in which these last pacifists suffered naked in freezing cells, and gave up prayers for penance, then who was to say they were not saints? And who to say that the sins of America were not by their witness a tithe remitted? (Pp. 318–19)

From here Mailer moves to the difficult—and poorly managed—metaphors of the final page, where he sets forth his vision of America about to give birth to either "the most fearsome totalitarianism the world has ever known" or "a babe of a new world brave and tender, artful and wild" (p. 320).[3]

The power and persuasiveness of Mailer's thesis about the march depend of course on the kind of analysis of its events he offers in Book Two, but it depends more crucially on the representation of himself in Book One. First, Mailer's analysis is frequently imaginative and speculative: his audience's willingness to follow him through his swoops depends upon the extent to which Book One allows us to feel he has earned the right to make them. Second, Book One implicitly but powerfully bears witness to the thesis about the significance of the march: the change in Mailer the character exists as a sign of the event's power to change the country. Then, finally, the two books together serve as a final testament to the power of the march and the change in the character. Where he once looked upon the event as something to be gotten through, he has ended up being moved to write this extraordinary narrative about it. *The Armies of the Night*, in short, is an example of a narrative that uses the mimetic function of the protagonist in service of a thematic point about the whole event in which that protagonist played a small part.

III

In the discussion of *Pride and Prejudice* in Chapter 2, we have seen that Austen uses Charlotte Lucas's decision to marry Collins as a way to enhance the mimetic power and thematic force of Elizabeth's decision to refuse Darcy's marriage proposal. Because Charlotte takes on the thematic function of illustrating the power of the marriage market, Elizabeth's refusal develops her own thematically significant independence from the market's norms even as it further develops the authorial audience's undersanding of her as a possible person. Dickens's use of Wemmick in *Great Expectations* is, in a sense, an elaboration of the same principle of narrative construction: the actions of the minor character, though not significantly advancing or retarding the actual forward movement of the narrative, take on a thematic function that plays a significant part in the progression by affecting the response of the authorial audience to the mimetic and thematic functions of the protagonist. Our sense of both the nature and significance of Pip's difficulty in relating his connection to the lower class with his existence in the upper is enhanced by Dickens's inventive use of Wemmick. Eliot in effect takes this same Principle of Indirect Affective Relevance about as far as possible by elaborating the role of the minor characters to such an extent that they have their own recognizable subplot.

The nature and purpose of Eliot's development of the sometimes complained about Fred Vincy-Mary Garth subplot can perhaps best be explained if we begin by noticing a curious feature of the novel's famous final paragraph:

> Her finely-touched spirit had still its fine issues, though they were not widely visible. Her full nature, like that river of which Cyrus broke the strength, spent itself in channels which had no great name on the earth. But the effect of her being on those around her was incalculably diffusive: for the growing good of the world is partly dependent on unhistoric acts; and that things are not so ill with you and me as they might have been, is half owing to the number who lived faithfully a hidden life, and rest in unvisited tombs.[4]

What is curious here is that the authorial audience is very willing to accept the narrator's claims about Dorothea's contributions to the growing good of the world, but the narrative itself has repeatedly shown us Dorothea's difficulties in making such contributions. Indeed, for most of the narrative Dorothea's mimetic portrait emphasizes both her good intentions and her relative ineffectuality. Even her unselfish intercession in Lydgate and Rosamond's marital difficulties has only a temporary positive effect: it neither prevents Rosamond from bending Lydgate to her will nor gives Lydgate enough solace and resolution to keep him from calling Rosamond his basil plant.

Why then does the authorial audience give credence to the narrator's claim here? Or, to begin with the prior question, why doesn't Eliot do more to show us Dorothea contributing to the growing good of the world? Another way of getting at the same point is to ask why the paragraph's assertions about both Dorothea and the growing good of the world are so carefully qualified—the growing good of the world is only "partly dependent" on such unhistoric acts as Dorothea's; our own situation is referred to as "not so ill," and for that we are only "half" in debt to those living a hidden life. The penultimate paragraph not only provides the basis for an answer but indicates that the final paragraph is less a summary of Dorothea's narrative than the final step in the completion of her story line. That penultimate paragraph provides a more accurate summary, and thereby underlines the major thematic point of Dorothea's story, one to which our attention has been directed from the very first page of the Prelude:

> there is no creature whose inward being is so strong that it is not greatly determined by what lies outside it. A new Theresa will hardly have the opportunity of reforming a conventual life, any more than a new Antigone will spend her heroic piety in daring all for the sake of a brother's burial: the medium in which their ardent deeds took shape is forever gone. But we insignificant people with our daily words and acts are preparing the lives of many Dorotheas, some of which may present a far sadder sacrifice than that of the Dorothea whose story we know. (Pp. 577–78)

In other words, Eliot did not show us Dorothea doing more to contribute to the growing good of the world, and she does not leave her assertions about the world's progress unqualified because of the weight Dorothea's narrative has given to this major thematic point. Both Dorothea's good intentions and her ineffectuality have been thematized. To show Dorothea doing more to contribute to the world would be to run the risk of undermining the thematizing of her ineffectuality. At the same time to give Dorothea's story its final development in the concluding paragraph, Eliot needed to find some mechanism to incorporate into the novel this secondary thematic point that, despite the impossibility of heroic action, the world can nevertheless improve. As Ralph Rader has suggested, her setting the action at the time of the Great Reform Bill is part of that mechanism.[5] Over and above her choice of setting, Eliot establishes the mechanism both within and without Dorothea's story line—that is, in what she does in the progression of Dorothea's own story and in the creation and elaboration of Fred and Mary's.

As noted above, Eliot uses Dorothea's own story line primarily to demonstrate the narrative's major thematic interest. Yet the crucial events in the climax of the story line suggest the potential for a different emphasis. When Dorothea undergoes her dark night of the soul, we see her both openly acknowledging her own emotional needs in a way that she never has before—there is a new development in the mimetic component of her character—and going beyond them to think about the good of others. "What should I do—how should I act now, this very day, if I could clutch my own pain, and compel it to silence, and think of those three?" (p. 544). Through the events of this night and Dorothea's long talk with Rosamond the next day, Eliot establishes with great authority and emotional power that Dorothea has the *capacity* to contribute to the growing good of the world. Indeed, in bringing Rosamond and Lydgate more closely together, at least for a time, Eliot does allow us to see that Dorothea can be a positive force for good: she is not totally ineffectual. Yet in a larger sense her contribution to Lydgate comes too late; the good it does is very severely qualified, not only in the Finale but even in the narrator's summary comments after Dorothea's visit to Rosamond:

> Poor Rosamond's vagrant fancy had come back terribly scourged—meek enough to nestle under the old despised shelter. And the shelter was still there: Lydgate had accepted his narrowed lot with sad resignation. He had chosen this fragile creature, and had taken the burthen of her life upon his arms. He must walk as he could, carrying that burthen pitifully. (P. 552)

The reason that Eliot does not do more with the positive effects of Dorothea's intervention is of course tied up with what she has already done with Lydgate's story line. She has developed there a mirror reflection of Dorothea's own plot: a character with ardent desires to make the world better, through a series of his own mistaken choices in combination with the forces of Middlemarch society, is unable to translate those desires into effective action. In that respect, Eliot has also developed the Lydgate plot to elaborate the primary thematic interest. But there are two major differences between the two story lines: (1) Lydgate does not face the obstacle to effective action that Dorothea's womanhood represents for her; and (2) he more clearly represents the way in which the idealistic individual's own egoism may contribute to society's frustration of his ideals; in that sense, he has a thematic function that Dorothea lacks. Because of his egoism, Lydgate is defeated more thoroughly than Dorothea, and because of his greater initial advantages the fall has a far greater impact than it would otherwise. In this respect, we can see that the Lydgate story is itself being summarized in the novel's penultimate paragraph, and we can apply the narrator's comments about Dorothea to him as well: indeed, he can be seen as having experienced a far sadder sacrifice than the sacrifice of the "Dorothea whose story we know." If Eliot were to show Dorothea's intervention as having more positive effects, she would undermine the way in which the progression has been thematizing the Lydgate story line.

Thus, Eliot needs another means to make possible the final development of Dorothea's story—and to develop the secondary thematic point. And the means she chose, I believe, is the Fred and Mary story line. Critics have sometimes complained that this strand of the narrative pales by comparison to the two major story lines, but I think that its differences from them are both purposeful and necessary. Even without a detailed look at their mimetic traits, we can see that Fred and Mary provide a counterpoint to Dorothea and Lydgate because they are less worried about reforming the world than about finding a place in it; they are in effect the representatives of the world that Lydgate and Dorothea would so much like to help. At the same time, they are individualized in such a way—Fred combines good nature and indolence, Mary common sense, industry, and loyalty—that the traits themselves provide both a good part of the basis for the instabilities in their story line and the grounds for the authorial audience to desire their union. Because their story line consists of the working out of that happy union through the unhistoric acts of many characters, it provides a very strong warrant for our belief in the narrator's assertion about the growing good of the world. Through Mary's constancy and Caleb's generosity, Fred is able to find a purpose for his life.

Even more dramatically, Fred is able to marry Mary through the unhistoric acts of Farebrother. Like Dorothea, Farebrother is able to put self to one side and not only intercede with Mary for Fred, but then later to sway Fred from his gambling. Furthermore, in Fred and Mary's eventual succession to Stone Court (itself made possible by

Bulstrode's desire to make amends to Harriet by doing something for her family) the narrative presents the reclamation of one notable Middlemarch property. The transformation of Stone Court from the home of old Peter Featherstone to the place where Bulstrode is involved in the "murder" of Raffles to the scene of Fred and Mary's domestic happiness is the narrative's most visible sign of the growing good of the world.

From this vantage point, we can see that the effects created by this plot are, like those created by Charlotte Lucas and Wemmick, powerful because they complement the narrator's functions. Eliot's narrator can talk about the growing good of the world in the last paragraph because she has presented the narrative evidence to support her position. Without Eliot's elaboration of the Fred and Mary subplot the last step in the completion of Dorothea's story—indeed, in the completion of the whole narrative—would seem unearned; with them it works very powerfully. In sum, the Fred and Mary subplot is as crucial to the effectiveness of the final development of the Dorothea story line as Dorothea's own reactions in her dark night of the soul.

Although there is of course a lot more one could say about the complex interaction of the characters and subplots of Eliot's narrative,[6] this account of the Indirect Affective Relevance of the Fred and Mary story line is sufficient to help explain some salient features of the relation between character and progression in *Mrs. Dalloway*. Woolf's novel offers a different kind of progression from anything we have analyzed to this point. After we are plunged *in medias res* by the opening sentence, "Mrs. Dalloway said she would buy the flowers herself,"[7] we are plunged inside Clarissa's consciousness (what a lark!), and the forward movement of the narrative is governed by Woolf's progressive revelation of her character; this technique emphasizes the mimetic component of her character. In effect, the opening plunge produces a tension of unequal knowledge about Clarissa between author and authorial audience. Clarissa emerges from the initial pages as a highly particularized, if unextraordinary, woman of the British upper class. She has a love of life and an awareness of its chaos; she dislikes discord and seeks to please others; she has the gift of knowing others by instinct; she wonders about the course of her life, whether she should have married Peter Walsh instead of Richard Dalloway.

Some of this revelation of the character contains a potential for further development in the progression: Clarissa's love of life and her fear of its imminent chaos exist as a potential instability. The narrative does not build upon it directly, but it remains an opening to be exploited, and an issue to be explored in later sections of the narrative. Woolf soon does complicate the progression by tension in several ways. First, she introduces Peter Walsh, who among other things, raises questions about the significance of what it means to be Clarissa Dalloway in these circumstances; his most famous question of course is "What is the sense of your parties?" In a sense, Peter is asking the question analogous to one asked by the authorial audience: so, what's the point, or more politely, is the point the same as that of a dramatic monologue—fleshing out the mimetic portrait of the character—or is there also a thematic function associated with the character? Second, Woolf's technique of offering shifting and limited access to the consciousnesses of many characters and the repetitions of imagery within those different consciousnesses work together to suggest an underlying connection between them all. The third complication depends in part on this second method: Woolf develops the consciousness of Septimus Smith as, in effect, one side of Clarissa's own consciousness. Septimus is an example of a mind that has been overpowered by the chaos that Clarissa fears.

The previous analysis of *Middlemarch* helps explain what is distinctive about Woolf's use of Septimus here. The attention given to the revelation of his consciousness is again largely a part of a progression by tension rather than one by instability. To be sure, there is a progression towards his suicide that arises out of the developing instability between his mental state and the treatments suggested by Holmes and Bradshaw, but the narrative pays more attention to revealing his state than to generating expectations about his eventual fate. But just as the Fred and Mary plot serves to demonstrate that the world can become progressively better, so too this revelation serves to reinforce the power of Clarissa's anxiety about the danger of living. Just as Fred and Mary's story has its own independent development, so too does Septimus's. But that development does not follow the progression of an action; it is in effect a subplot of character. Woolf brings the two strands of the narrative more directly together than Eliot does: at the party, Woolf brings the internal instability within Clarissa to its climax as she comes face to face with the chaos brought into her party by the news of Septimus's death. At this point all the previous complications of the progression come together. The potential for the internal instability between Clarissa's attitudes toward life is now actualized: will her fear overcome her love? In coming to the fore, this instability also functions as a test of the significance of Clarissa's life. She has defended herself against Peter's questions by saying that her parties were "an offering" (p. 184) to life, a way of bringing together people who would not otherwise be

brought together. At this juncture, her ability to make such an offering and her faith in it is severely tested: "Oh! thought Clarissa, in the
middle of my party, here's death, she thought" (p. 279). And at the
same time, her ability to work through the instability depends upon
her capacity to integrate Septimus's death into the life that continues
around her. Withdrawing from the main room, she thinks,

> Somehow it was her disaster, her disgrace. It was her punishment
> to see sink and disappear here a man, there a woman in this pro-
> found darkness, and she forced to stand here in her evening dress.
> She had schemed; she had pilfered. She was never wholly admi-
> rable. She had wanted success. Lady Bexborough and the rest
> of it. . . .

Yet in the course of looking out the window, Clarissa is able to turn
the disgrace into gladness.

> She parted the curtains; she looked. Oh, but how surprising!—in
> the room opposite the old lady stared straight at her! She was
> going to bed. . . . She was going to bed, in the room opposite. It
> was fascinating to watch her, moving about, that old lady, crossing
> the room, coming to the window. Could she see her? It was fasci-
> nating, with people still laughing and shouting in the drawing-
> room, to watch that old woman, quite quietly, going to bed. The
> young man had killed himself; but she did not pity him; with the
> clock striking the hour, one, two, three, she did not pity him, with
> all this going on. There! the old lady had put out her light! The
> whole house was dark now with this going on, she repeated, and
> the words came to her, Fear no more the heat of the sun. She must
> go back to them. But what an extraordinary night! She felt some-
> how very much like him—the young man who had killed himself.
> She felt glad that he had done it; thrown it away. The clock was
> striking. The leaden circles dissolved in the air. He made her feel the
> beauty; made her feel the fun. But she must go back. (Pp. 283–84)

Sparked by her connection with the old lady who goes on with this
thing called life in a way very different from that of Clarissa, Mrs.
Dalloway is able to enter imaginatively into both the old lady's life
and Septimus's. She recognizes his suicide as a positive step, yet
something very different from her own offering. In effect, Clarissa is
able to accept her fear of life's chaos and subsume it under her love
for life in all its variation. Woolf then ends the narrative by affirming
the importance of Clarissa. Filled with new vitality by her integration,
Clarissa does return to the others, and, as the final sentences indicate,
produces an extraordinary effect upon her biggest doubter.

"I will come," said Peter, but he sat on for a moment. What is this terror? what is this ecstasy? he thought to himself. What is it that fills me with this extraordinary excitement?
It is Clarissa, he said.
For there she was. (P. 296)

The mimetic portrait of the character is complete, her thematic functions of illustrating the connectedness of disparate individuals and of demonstrating the possibility of affirming life in the face of its own terror are complete, and the author's implicit case for the value of such a character is complete. But no substantial change in Clarissa's fate or fortune has occurred. Her moment of integration may or may not signal a new permanent attitude toward life and her role in it. The narrative leads us to see it as an important victory for her, but it does not provide assurances that her fear of life's chaos has been overcome completely. Similarly Peter's acknowledgment of her importance to him is not presented as something that will significantly alter their relationship. The ending, in short, is in keeping with the rest of the narrative, which gives us a progressive revelation of character rather than the progression of an action.

Woolf's use of Peter Walsh represents a kind of thematizing that we have not encountered before—and helps us more fully understand the mimetic-thematic relationship of Clarissa's character. Peter's progression from questioning her value to affirming it does not direct the authorial audience to any specific thematic conclusion (the moment of integration does that) but points to the significance of this apparently unextraordinary woman. The thematic force here is subordinated to the mimetic portrait; it is Clarissa we are to focus on most fully, but through Peter we are told that this kind of a woman, with her flowers, her fears, and her festive parties, has a significance rivalling that of any of the great personages who linger on the fringes of the book. In one sense, Woolf uses Peter Walsh to supply an element of her portrait of a lady that Browning did not need in his portrait of a duke: Browning could let the Duke's remarkable actions and character speak for themselves; it is easy for audiences to accept the implicit significance and interest of the Duke and his actions. Woolf, on the other hand, needs a way to build the authorial audience's acceptance of Clarissa's significance into the narrative. Peter Walsh is that way—which is to say, Peter performs that synthetic function.

IV

I have suggested above that the comprehensiveness of this theory of character and progression ought to be judged by both the predictive power and the flexibilty of its theoretical principles; I now want to look more closely at their predictive power. The principles in a sense both lead one to predict and cause one to shy away from predictions—and that double movement is, I think, a source of strength. They lead one to predictions because they establish a set of categories for examining character, and the results of their application here represent a good cross-section of the possible relations among the postulated components of character. We have seen mimetic functions subordinated to thematic ones (*1984*, *The French Lieutenant's Woman*, *The Armies of the Night*) and to synthetic ones (*If on a winter's night a traveler*). We have seen thematic functions subordinated to mimetic ones ("My Last Duchess," *Mrs. Dalloway*). We have seen mimetic and thematic functions move along parallel tracks where one is not clearly subordinated to the other, though one may be more centrally related to the progression of the narrative (*Pride and Prejudice* and, on the other side of the station, *Middlemarch*). We have seen the synthetic function of characters remain firmly in the background of works ("My Last Duchess," *Pride and Prejudice*, *A Farewell to Arms*), and we have seen it move intermittently into the foreground (*1984*, *The French Lieutenant's Woman*, *Great Expectations*). We have seen the mimetic and thematic functions of characters fused ("The Beast in the Jungle") and the synthetic and thematic functions fused (*If on a winter's night a traveler*). We have seen thematic functions in harmony (most of our examples) and in ethical conflict (*A Farewell to Arms*). These kinds of relationships, for the most part, are not unique to the individual narratives in which they appear, and so the analyses here can serve as a guide to possible patterns of character in other narratives.

Yet as the above parenthetical groupings indicate, the theory must move away from prediction because not all the generally similar relationships among the components of character get established in the same way. To take perhaps the clearest example, the progressions of the three narratives that I identify as all subordinating the mimetic to the thematic—*1984*, *The French Lieutenant's Woman*, *The Armies of the Night*—are very different from each other. There are of course general patterns of progression too, and these patterns allow us to make such general predictions as (1) representations of actions will typically have mimetic and thematic functions of the main characters moving along parallel tracks while the synthetic functions remain in the background and (2) novels with a central thematic point such as *1984* will subordinate the mimetic function to the thematic function. The trouble with these generalizations, however, is precisely that they are too general. They do not tell us much more about any given narrative than its generic classification does. Once we notice a general similarity between, say, the two tragic-like patterns we have seen—"The Beast in the Jungle" and *A Farewell to Arms*—we can only become more aware of how far removed the generalizations are from the ways in which a specific progression will establish the relations among the components of character. Noticing the differences between these two narratives—and indeed, among all the other narratives we have examined—will force us back from predictions about character and progression in any given narrative to the principles for analyzing it. Our narratives have given us numerous examples of when and how instabilities and tensions can be introduced, complicated, and re-solved and those examples can function as a guide to others, but clearly not as a set of pre-formed molds into which others may be poured. In this respect, the demand for flexibility is more honored than the demand for predictive power; such a relationship is appro-priate to the extent that the relation between character and progres-sion in narrative is as diverse as I claim.[8]

The comprehensiveness of this inquiry needs to be considered in another way. What exactly are the nature of my theory's claims for comprehensiveness vis-à-vis other theories of character and progres-sion? Does it purport to sweep all other approaches out of the way? What are its limitations? First, it claims to be a comprehensive *rhetori-cal* theory of character, not *the* comprehensive theory. As the intro-duction briefly suggests in its discussion of the structuralist approach to character, this theory is designed to enable its practitioner to achieve a certain kind of knowledge about texts, knowledge about them as communicative transactions between author and reader. It defines the text as the site of that rhetorical transaction, and it views those transactions as having both a formal and an affective structure. In effect, the study says that if you want to know how character and progression participate in these transactions between an author and his hypothetical audience, then read me. If, however, you want to read literature as, say, a sign of its creator's psyche and thus analyze the ways in which it reflects or reveals that psyche, then you are in-terested in a different kind of knowledge, one that for some critical purposes is more important than the kind offered here, but not one that this study claims to offer or conflict with. Such a study would take up what we might call the expressive component of character, the way in which at some level it is a part of its creator's character or personality. Such a study might usefully complement the conclusions of this one, but there is no necessary logical connection between them, i.e., the expressive analysis can neither convincingly confirm nor deny the conclusions of the rhetorical and vice versa.

At the same time, my attempt to develop a rhetorical theory of character does not mean that my principles and conclusions will never come into conflict with other approaches to the text. To the extent that Levin, Scholes, Brooks, and Fetterley have been concerned with establishing principles relevant to the transactions between authors and readers offered by texts, their somewhat different frameworks overlapped with mine, and I have tried to keep my discussions of them within the boundaries of the overlap. My response to Levin focused on our shared goal of developing interpretive methods that would correspond to the "literal particulars" of the text in an a posteriori rather than an a priori way; my analysis of Scholes focused on our shared principle that interpretations ought to meet the test of explanatory adequacy; my discussion of Brooks focused on his similar purpose of explaining "reading for the plot" rather than on his use of psychoanalysis per se; or, again, my concern with Fetterley was not with the value of her own response to the text but rather with the validity of her claim that accepting the overt story of *A Farewell to Arms* means buying into the covert one she identifies. I have had to work through the differences, within the areas of overlap, between my principles and those of these four critics in order to establish the particular claims of comprehensiveness and validity that I wanted to make.

Even within this restricted definition of comprehensiveness, some features of the theory may seem either strange or too limited or both. Because the theory may seem to read narratives written over a two-hundred-year span (from *Tristram Shandy* to *If on a winter's night a traveler*) in essentially the same way, it may seem to be traveling under the banner "Never historicize!" Can the differences of sociohistorical situatedness between Austen and Calvino be as irrelevant to the rhetorical transaction as the theory seems to indicate? The first part of the answer is that the appearance of irrelevance is deceptive. Since authors typically assume that their audiences know many things, including social and cultural codes extant at the time of their writing, those elements of sociohistorical situatedness are very much a part of the transaction and very relevant to the analysis of these narratives, though sometimes, like the synthetic function of characters, they remain in the background. Reading *Pride and Prejudice* in the authorial audience requires one to know such things as social conventions about visiting among the upper classes, social codes about feminine delicacy, what it means to have one's estate entailed, what it means to be the daughter of a gentleman, what it means to get one's money by trade in that society, and so on. One can always read the novel to see how it is using these codes and one can always read against those uses. One might, for example, note the way that servants are used and treated in the novel and develop a critique about how Elizabeth's happiness and good fortune is juxtaposed with and dependent upon a working class that Austen herself takes for granted. Such a reading could go on to undermine any positive evaluation of both Elizabeth and the implied author. In other words, considering the sociohistorical situatedness of the narrative would in this case appear to have the effect of disrupting the congenial rhetorical transaction that I have sketched in Chapter 1—and one could imagine other such readings for the other narratives I have examined.

Notice first that the approach I have taken here does not preclude such readings but rather sketches the preliminary steps to them. To disrupt the transaction, to talk back productively to the text, one needs to know the grounds upon which it is being built, and one knows that, I claim, by analyzing the progression. In that sense, these kinds of readings are not only welcome within my approach but are variations, using both historical knowledge and ethical standards, of the kind of reading I have done of Hemingway. More generally, historical knowledge can be extremely important for the analysis of the progression, and the principles of my rhetorical approach dictate that it be used wherever relevant. For example, one must know conventions of both nineteenth- and twentieth-century Anglo-American narrative (as a minimum) in order to understand the progression of *The French Lieutenant's Woman*. Nevertheless, the necessary condition is not sufficient: knowing those conventions will not allow one to understand the functions of Fowles's playing with them. To do that, one must look at the internal logic and affective structure of the whole progression. In this respect, the rhetorical commitment of my theory will always lead me to privilege the transaction itself more than the conditions under which the transaction is produced. This commitment and this privileging do not mean that the theory wants finally to turn away from history toward the realm of the "purely literary," but rather wants to think about issues such as ethics and ideology as they are reflected in the rhetorical transaction of reading. That Hemingway was, like most men of his generation, a sexist is less important for my approach than the way the ideology of sexism is built into the rhetorical transaction of the narrative. The striking feature of that transaction, as we have seen, is how it requires the authorial audience both to watch Hemingway stand with Catherine above Frederic and to participate with him in his easy assumptions of her secondary, because womanly, importance.

As far as character itself goes, historicizing the narrative may reveal the greater significance of some attributes than others and may be required for the authorial audience's understanding of some thematic functions. But if I am right that the progression itself actualizes thematic functions and focuses our attention on specific issues of the narrative, then what one most needs to know is the narrative conventions operating at the time the narrative is written. If one knows those conventions, then using that knowledge as part of one's analysis of the progression will act as a check on one's historical knowledge: it will reveal—or sometimes fill—gaps that we can then appropriately deal with.

Again because of my focus on the rhetorical transaction, if I were to historicize my project in another way and try to write a history of character and progression in the British and American novel, it would be a very different kind of history from one that would be written by a neo-Marxist or a new historicist critic. I would be interested in such things as the power relationships among different members of society during different periods of the last three centuries, and I would be concerned about the functioning of "ideological state apparatuses," because these things would affect the conditions of narrative and an individual author's awareness of the possibilities of character and progression at a given time. These matters, however, would not be the focus of my history. Instead, I would try to construct a narrative about the development of the variety of forms of progression with particular emphasis on the uses of character within progressions. I would try to explain such things as how the novel expanded and contracted and expanded again between the eighteenth and nineteenth centuries; how changes in the conventions of mimetic representation allowed for new ways to develop thematic functions; how the principles of progression in Fielding were complicated by Thackeray and Dickens, while those of an Austen novel were complicated by a James and then transformed by Faulkner; how new principles were forged out of potentialities in eighteenth century fiction by figures such as Joyce and Woolf. To the extent that my history told a neat, linear story, I would be suspicious of it not only because of the complex relations between the development of narrative and the development of culture in general but also because narrative itself has been so various and diverse at least since the eighteenth century. A history that was somehow adequate to that diversity would, I am convinced, cause us to refashion our understanding of how narratives relate to each other—and might therefore have implications for anyone doing a sociocultural history of the novel. I would need to have far greater erudition than I can now lay claim to in order to write such a history, but the line I have drawn here from Austen to Dickens to Eliot to Woolf in discussing the Principle of Indirect Affective Relevance is a small, incomplete example of the kind of analysis this history would undertake.

In summary, then, my response to the question of the relation between my rhetorical theory and one that stresses reading through history is that the two are largely compatible, though the objects of their focus are quite different, and sometimes their findings will impinge on each other in significant ways.

Whether this theory of character and progression achieves its vaulting ambition or o'erleaps itself and falls on its face, it is with the value of the rhetorical transactions that I want to end. To participate in the progression of Winston's doomed rebellion, in Elizabeth's movement toward happiness, Marcher's struggle for tragic illumination, Charles's attempt to shed one age for another; to understand what it means to be a Wemmick or a Reader, to be tossed and turned by Hemingway's treatment of Catherine: these experiences offer no guarantee of improving our own characters but they do offer a kind of life that in its intensity and diversity would have preserved Marcher himself from the springing of the Beast. We are more fortunate than he, not simply in that we lack his obsession, but that we can live by reading Henry James—and George Orwell and Jane Austen and Charles Dickens and . . . and in doing that we live a life that by its very nature will have closure but not completeness.

Notes

Introduction

1. David Lodge, *Language of Fiction* (New York: Columbia University Press, 1966), pp. 63–64.

2. *Worlds from Words* (Chicago: University of Chicago Press, 1981), pp. 81–86.

3. I refrain from saying that the description absolutely *could not* refer to a real person because one could construct a plausible context for Lodge's sketch. But unless we had evidence to know that such an unusual context was operating, we would, by drawing on our conventional understanding of people in the real world, quickly conclude that the description was fictive discourse. For more on fictive discourse, see Barbara Herrnstein Smith, *On the Margins of Discourse* (Chicago: University of Chicago Press, 1978).

4. Joel Weinsheimer gets some useful mileage out of calling Jane Austen's protagonist "It" in "Theory of Character: *Emma*," *Poetics Today* 1, nos. 1–2 (1979): 185–211.

5. Jonathan Culler, *Structuralist Poetics: Structuralism, Linguistics, and the Study of Literature* (Ithaca, N.Y.: Cornell University Press, 1975), p. 115.

6. Although Bernard J. Paris uses the terms *mimetic, thematic,* and *aesthetic* to talk about literary character, the eventual direction and emphasis of his studies of character are very different from my own. His schema is a prelude to his discussion of the mimetic component in the terms of third force psychology. See his *A Psychological Approach to Fiction* (Bloomington: Indiana University Press, 1974) and *Character and Conflict in Jane Austen's Fiction* (Detroit: Wayne State University Press, 1978). Much of my work on character in this book also has some point of contact with numerous other works on the subject (especially those done in the past ten years), but my argument typically leaves that common point and goes on to make its own different claims. Thus, I have typically found those works to be useful supplements or contrasts to mine but have not drawn on them in an extended way. The useful works include Mary Doyle Springer, *A Rhetoric of Literary Character* (Chicago: University of Chicago Press, 1978), Martin Price, *Forms of Life* (New Haven: Yale University Press, 1983), Thomas Docherty, *Reading (Absent) Character* (New York: Oxford University Press, 1983), Baruch Hochman, *Character in Literature*

213

(Ithaca: Cornell University Press, 1985), and Robert Higbie, *Character and Structure in the English Novel* (Gainesville: University of Florida Press, 1984). See also the chapter-length discussions of character by Seymour Chatman in *Story and Discourse* (Ithaca: Cornell University Press, 1978) and by Alexander Gelley in *Narrative Crossings* (Baltimore: Johns Hopkins Press, 1987). In addition to the essay by Joel Weinsheimer cited in note 4 above, see the essay by Rawdon Wilson, "The Bright Chimera: Character as a Literary Term," *Critical Inquiry* 5 (1979): 725–49, and, for a strict structuralist account, A. J. Greimas, "Les actants, les acteurs, et les figures," in *Semiotique narrative et textuelle*, ed. C. Chabrol (Paris: Seuil, 1973). Before the proliferation of studies in the last ten years, the main book on character was Walter J. Harvey's *Character in the Novel* (Ithaca: Cornell University Press, 1965). And virtually all of these studies make reference to E.M. Forster's discussion of character in *Aspects of the Novel*, especially his famous distinction between "flat" and "round" characters.

Of these studies, Springer's shares more of my theoretical principles than any of the others, but my way of talking about character is quite different from her concern with "people like us" and my study has a much larger scope: she focuses on female characters in Henry James's novellas; I range from protagonists to minor characters in narratives from Austen to Calvino. I share Hochman's desire to defend the mimetic component, but again our studies move in different directions. Docherty provides the greatest contrast with my approach; he is far less accepting of the realist tradition in narrative and of the critical tradition of talking about the mimetic component of character. Higbie's thoughtful attempt to develop a "syncretic criticism" that can account for the psychological, structuralist, and sociohistorical elements of character has some affinities with my approach here, but there are many issues on which we part company, especially about the way in which character interacts with the other narrative elements. I have chosen not to discuss these alternative approaches to character at great length because, as will be noted later in this introduction, I felt that I could better indicate the implications and consequences of my approach by examining its consequences for issues in the interpretation of narrative that go beyond the element of character itself. I will, however, shortly compare my approach with one version of a strict structuralist approach.

7. Jonathan Culler, "Issues in Contemporary American Criticism," in Ira Konigsberg (ed.) *American Criticism in the Poststructuralist Age* (Ann Arbor: University of Michigan Press, 1981), p. 5.

8. *Structuralist Poetics*, p.235.

9. *Ibid.*, p. 236.

10. Ralph Rader, "The Dramatic Monologue and Related Lyric Forms," *Critical Inquiry* 3 (1976): 131–51.

11. Peter Rabinowitz, "Truth in Fiction: A Reexamination of Audiences," *Critical Inquiry* 4 (1977): 121–41. See also his "Assertion and Assumption: Fictional Patterns and the External World," *PMLA* 96 (1981): 408–19. Rabinowitz's book *Before Reading: Narrative Conventions and the Politics of Interpretation* (Ithaca: Cornell University Press, 1987) gives an account of the

conventions of "authorial reading" that in many ways complements the analyses I undertake in this book. Although there are some important overlaps between Rabinowitz's work and mine, for the most part we are focusing on different problems: he is concerned with conventions that govern reading in advance of our encounters with narrative; I am concerned with the dynamics of those encounters themselves; in a sense, with how texts themselves tell us which conventions apply.

12. In this connection, I find the crucial detail of the revelation to be a place where Browning can't help but let the seam between mimetic and synthetic components of the poem show. Although the Duke is someone concerned about relationships of power, his enunciating what he and the envoy both obviously know ("the Count *your master*") strikes me as motivated less by the dramatic situation and more by Browning's needs to get that information to the reader. But this rough spot makes the seamlessness of the rest of the poem even more striking.

13. Interestingly, however, many structuralists, including Culler, would want to resist any direct move from "work to world," any claim that the propositions had reference to the world beyond the text. For more on this point, see my "Thematic Reference, Literary Structure, and Fictive Character: An Examination of Interrelationships," *Semiotica* 48 3–4 (1984): 345–65, which also sets forth an early version of my account of "My Last Duchess."

14. It will be obvious by now that my conception of a rhetorical theory of character—or of literature more generally—is sharply different from the rhetorical approach to literature taken by such deconstructive critics as J. Hillis Miller in *Fiction and Repetition* (Cambridge: Harvard University Press, 1982) and Paul de Man in *Allegories of Reading* (New Haven: Yale University Press, 1979). Although these critics have their differences from each other, they share the idea that a rhetorical approach involves the analysis of rhetorical figures and tropes implied in a text's use of language. Implicitly defining the text as a linguistic structure first and foremost, they cut the language of the text off from its author and its implied audience. They then scrutinize the figures and tropes of the text and typically show how the apparent logic behind the use of these figures and tropes undermines itself. By contrast, within my rhetorical approach I define the text as a communicative transaction between author and reader carried out through the various elements of the text (including such translinguistic ones as character and action) as these are shaped and designed for a particular purpose. In one sense, because the definitions of the text within these two rhetorical approaches are so different, their rivalry is not as intense as might first appear. In effect, one approach asks, what did the author mean to communicate through this language?; and the other asks, what can the language of this text, when viewed from the logic of figuration, be construed to mean? Each might say to the other that what the approach yields is valid, given its starting point. To argue over the starting point here would require me take a detour so wide that I might never get back to the main track of my investigation. I have decided, therefore, to stay on the main track and let my findings be a partial argument for the validity of my starting point. For an argument that directly takes up Miller's

view of language and tries to indicate its deficiencies, see my *Worlds from Words*, Chap. 4.

15. For a good overview of the story-discourse model of narrative, see Seymour Chatman, *Story and Discourse* (Ithaca: Cornell University Press, 1978). My concern with the temporal movement of narrative and with the dynamics of the audience's relations with authors and narrators follows to some degree Meir Sternberg's excellent *Expositional Modes and Temporal Ordering in Fiction* (Baltimore: The Johns Hopkins Press, 1978). Since my analysis is pitched toward progression in general, it does more with action and less with exposition than his. But his book is a strong argument for the power of two critical principles that we hold in common: (1) to do justice to a narrative's effect one must pay strict attention to the interaction of all narrative elements through the temporal process of the narration; and (2) to assess an author's treatment of any individual element the critic must make reference to its interaction with others.

Other useful studies of what I am calling progression include David Richter, *Fable's End: Completeness and Closure in Rhetorical Fiction* (Chicago: University of Chicago Press, 1974), a study of the nature of endings in didactic fiction, and D. A. Miller, *Narrative and Its Discontents* (Princeton: Princeton University Press, 1981), a study that argues that ending is virtually always a problem in narrative. Marianna Torgovnick's *Closure in the Novel* (Princeton: Princeton University Press, 1981) offers a worthwhile account of many different kinds of final scenes, but does not offer a full theory of narrative closure. Peter Brooks has recently offered a psychoanalytic analysis of narrative dynamics in *Reading for the Plot* (New York: Knopf, 1984), which I shall discuss in some detail in chap. 4.

16. Ring Lardner, *The Best Short Stories of Ring Lardner* (New York: Scribner's, 1957), p. 29. Further citations will be given in page numbers in parentheses in the text.

17. To be sure, Whitey is not simply interchangeable with the other men: his nickname has a positive connotation and his general good nature sets him apart from the cruel group that accompanies Kendall in his effort to humiliate Julie Gregg.

18. Whitey's synthetic function as narrator and commentator is of course very important and I will discuss it below, but as noted earlier, Lardner, like the poet in a dramatic monologue, wants to keep the synthetic aspect of the character in the background in order to preserve the illusion that we are overhearing a real conversation.

19. Cleanth Brooks and Robert Penn Warren, *Understanding Fiction* (Englewood Cliffs, N.J.: Prentice-Hall, 1979), p. 171.

20. Judith Fetterley, *The Resisting Reader: A Feminist Approach to American Fiction* (Bloomington: Indiana University Press, 1978).

Chapter 1

1. Critical books and journals are filled with thematic interpretations of canonical works, theorists such as Gerald Graff and Robert Scholes have ex-

plicitly defended thematizing as a central act of criticism, and even someone such as Jonathan Culler, who has argued that we should move away from interpretation toward a description of literary competence or the semiotics of reading, builds into that description a "rule of significance," which in effect is a rule of thematizing. Furthermore, deconstructionists often proceed by establishing a binary opposition between two thematic issues that they then dismantle. For Graff, see "Literature as Assertions," in *American Criticism in the Poststructuralist Age*, ed. Ira Konigsberg (Ann Arbor: University of Michigan Press, 1981); for Scholes, see *Textual Power* (New Haven: Yale University Press, 1985); for Culler, see *Structuralist Poetics* (Ithaca: Cornell University Press, 1975) and *The Pursuit of Signs* (Ithaca: Cornell University Press, 1981). My formulation of the slogan of course echoes the principle that Fredric Jameson argues for in *The Political Unconscious* (Ithaca: Cornell University Press, 1981): "Always historicize!"

2. The most significant attacks on thematism are to be found in W. R. Keast, "The 'New Criticism' and *King Lear*," in R. S. Crane (ed.), *Critics and Criticism* (Chicago: University of Chicago Press, 1952), 108–37; R. S. Crane, *The Languages of Criticism and the Structure of Poetry* (Toronto: University of Toronto Press, 1953); Sheldon Sacks, *Fiction and the Shape of Belief* (Berkeley: University of California Press, 1964); and Richard Levin, *New Readings vs. Old Plays* (Chicago: University of Chicago Press, 1979). Further references to Levin will be made by page numbers in parentheses in the text. For a related attack on the kind of binary reasoning underlying much thematic criticism, see James L. Battersby, *Rational Praise and Natural Lamentation: Johnson, "Lycidas," and Principles of Criticism* (Rutherford, N.J.: Fairleigh Dickinson University Press, 1979). For discussions of the distinction between mimetic and didactic works, see Sacks's book and Elder Olson, "An Outline of Poetic Theory," in Crane, *Critics and Criticism*.

3. Much of the commentary has instead focused on the novel's ideas and politics and sometimes is less concerned with interpretation than with assessment of the ideas stipulated by the commentator. Nevertheless, Orwell has had many good critics, especially Alex Zwerdling, *Orwell and the Left* (New Haven: Yale University Press, 1974), Jennie Calder, *Chronicles of Conscience: A Study of George Orwell and Arthur Koestler* (London: Secker and Warburg, 1968), and, more recently, many of those represented in four collections: *1984 Revisited: Totalitarianism in Our Century*, ed. Irving Howe (New York: Harper and Row, 1983); *On Nineteen Eighty-Four*, ed. Peter Stansky (Stanford: Stanford Alumni Press, 1983); *The Future of Nineteen Eighty-Four*, ed. Ejner J. Jensen (Ann Arbor: University of Michigan Press, 1984); and *1984:Vision and Reality*, ed. Charles Klopp, *Papers in Comparative Studies* 4 (1985). Especially noteworthy in these collections are Mark Crispin Miller, "The Fate of *1984*," in Howe; Zwerdling, "The Psychopolitics of *1984*," in Jensen; and Calder, "Does the Past Matter? Orwell's Glass Paperweight," in Klopp. Sperber's essay, "'Gazing into the Glass Paperweight': The Structure and Psychology of Orwell's *1984*," *Modern Fiction Studies* (1980): 213–26, differs from my analysis of the progression not only in particulars of interpretation but also in overall focus: Sperber wants to connect the book to Orwell's

psychology and so is concerned, for example, with separating author and character at the end of the novel.

Orwell's novel has also come in for its share of negative evaluation. Among the most vigorous attacks are Louis Kampf, "*Nineteen Eighty-Four*: Why Read It?" in Klopp, and Patrick Reilly, "*Nineteen Eighty-Four*: The Failure of Humanism," *Critical Quarterly* 24, no. 3 (1981): 19–30.

4. George Orwell, *1984*, ed. Irving Howe (New York: Harcourt Brace Jovanovich, 1982), p. 3. Hereafter citations will be given by page numbers in parentheses in the text.

5. See Mark Crispin Miller, "The Fate of *1984*" in Howe, *1984 Revisited*.

6. In a letter to F. J. Warburg, 22 October 1948, Orwell says, "I haven't definitely fixed on the title but I am hesitating between 'Nineteen Eighty-Four' and 'The Last Man in Europe.'" Howe, *1984 Revisited*, p. 284.

7. Letter to F. J. Warburg, May 31, 1947. Quoted from Howe, *1984 Revisited*, p. 283.

8. I follow Gérard Genette here in my use of the terms "vision" and "voice"; the first identifies "who sees," the second "who speaks." See Genette, *Narrative Discourse: An Essay in Method*, trans. Jane Lewin (Ithaca: Cornell University Press, 1981).

9. Indeed, I think that this emphasis in the narrative helps explain why the space given over to Goldstein's book, despite its clear thematic significance in setting forth much of the totalitarian philosophy behind the Party's operations, seems excessive. In that space we lose—or at least suspend—the mimetic involvement that Orwell has been developing, and we do not learn enough new information to make up for that loss.

10. For a fuller discussion of Winston's concern with the past, see Jenni Calder, "Does the Past Matter? Orwell's Glass Paperweight" in Klopp, *1984: Vision and Reality*.

11. For a different reading of the significance of these scenes, see Patrocinio Schweikart, "Why Big Brother: The Maternal Subtext of *Nineteen Eighty-Four*," *Papers in Comparative Studies* 4 (1985): 69–80.

12. Zwerdling's discussion of the "Psychopolitics of *1984*" in the Jensen anthology cited in note 3 perceptively traces the transfer of Winston's feelings for his mother to Big Brother, a transfer now about to be completed.

13. Alistair Duckworth, *The Improvement of the Estate* (Baltimore: The Johns Hopkins University Press), 1971, p. 118. Hereafter references will be made by page numbers in parentheses in the text.

14. Susan Morgan, *In the Meantime: Character and Perception in the Novels of Jane Austen* (Chicago: University of Chicago Press, 1980), p. 80. Hereafter references will be made by page numbers in parentheses in the text.

15. Levin has recently published a new version of the attack, focusing this time on "Feminist Thematics and Shakespearean Tragedy," *PMLA* 103 (1988): 125–38. The principles he relies on in this essay are essentially the same as the ones I outline here, so my reply would be essentially the same as the one I make here.

16. See the works cited in the second note to this chapter.

17. Jane Austen, *Pride and Prejudice*, ed. Donald J. Gray (New York: Nor-

ton, 1966), p.1. Hereafter page numbers will be given in parentheses in the text.

18. By using Mr. Bennet this way here, Austen faces an interesting problem later when she wants to distance herself and her narrator from Mr. Bennet's values. As usual, she is equal to the task: she solves the problem by focusing on Elizabeth's own dawning sense of her father's limitations. As it dawns on her, it dawns also on us, and we can come to appreciate both the superiority and the limitations of his values, without feeling that Austen has initially misled us about his character by making him a narrator-surrogate.

19. This discussion of voices follows to some extent principles of analysis outlined by Mikhail Bakhtin, especially in his essay on "Discourse in the Novel" in *The Dialogic Imagination* (Austin: University of Texas Press, 1981). Like many others, I regard Bakhtin as one of the most important narrative theorists of this century. I have not made more extensive use of his work in this book, however, because of the differences in our focus. He wants to analyze novelistic discourse, I want to analyze character and progression. Moreover, his discussion of character presents me with a choice. For him characters become sites of languages revealing sociocultural values that interact with each other and with the languages of the narrator to produce the heteroglossia of the novel. I believe that this approach is very fruitful, but it finally does not account for—is not interested in accounting for—the mimetic component of narrative. (It would, however, account for the thematic, though in a rather different way from the one I have undertaken here.) Since I believe that the mimetic component is typically a crucial aspect of our reading of narrative, I have not followed him in folding character under language.

20. See Sacks, *Fiction and the Shape of Belief*, chap. 1. For a neo-Aristotelean analysis of the novel, see Walter Anderson, "Plot, Character, Speech, and Place in *Pride and Prejudice*," *Nineteenth-Century Fiction* 30 (1975): 367–82.

21. In one respect my argument here is in keeping with the general direction of Ralph Rader's work over the last decade or so. Dissatisfied with the fit between Sacks's theoretical descriptions of forms and many individual novels, Rader has suggested (among other modifications) that we recognize the moral purpose typically attached even to the action. See his "From Richardson to Austen: 'Johnson's Rule' and the Development of the Eighteenth-Century Novel of Moral Action," in James Engell, ed., *Johnson and His Age* (Cambridge: Harvard University Press, 1984): 461–83.

In quite another respect my argument has affinities with Gerald Graff's case in *Poetic Statement and Critical Dogma* (Chicago: University of Chicago Press, 1980; first published 1970) that both the New Critics and their Neo-Aristotelean opponents shied away from acknowledging that most literary works do make statements.

22. One possible exception here is the proposal scene itself, where one might argue that the deep feeling behind Elizabeth's accusations is necessary to make Darcy see the error of his ways. I think, however, that this interpretation underestimates Darcy's virtues. In any case, neither Elizabeth nor Darcy is grateful for the *manner* of her behavior in the proposal scene in the way that they are grateful for her behavior to Lady Catherine. Darcy is willing

to give Elizabeth the credit for the amelioration of his character, but he focuses more on the facts of her rejections and reproofs than on the feeling behind them.

23. Another variation on this pattern of thematic dimensions not being converted into thematic functions can be found in Orwell's use of Winston's optimism. The progression of Orwell's novel requires the attribute—or something like it—but the progression does not thematize the trait itself.

Chapter 2

1. Robert Scholes, *Textual Power* (New Haven: Yale University Press, 1985), p. 29. Hereafter page numbers will be given in parentheses in the text.

2. I too will undertake a quest for that grail, or more accurately, will reflect on some problems in such quests as part of my interests in the relations among the components of Catherine Barkley's character in *A Farewell to Arms* (Chapter 6).

3. My account of the progression will, I think, highlight certain features of the novella and James's method that have not been noticed before, but it seeks to deepen rather than challenge the general reading of the tale that has been offered by or implicit in most of the criticism: "The Beast" is the tragic story of a man, who, believing that life has singled him out for some grand fate, wastes his life waiting for its arrival, who discovers his waste only at the very end of his life, when he also realizes that he has been too blind to see the escape through love that had been offered him by his fellow-watcher, May Bartram. Many critics work with this general understanding of the tale in the background as they focus on one or more specific features of the narrative. On style, for example, see Jane P. Tompkins, "'The Beast in the Jungle': An Analysis of Henry James's Late Style," *Modern Fiction Studies* 6 (1971): 185–92, and David Smit, "The Leap of the Beast: The Dramatic Style of Henry James's 'The Beast in the Jungle,'" *Henry James Review* 4 (1983): 219–30. On narrative technique, see Elizabeth Shapland, "Duration and Frequency: Prominent Aspects of Time in Henry James's 'The Beast in the Jungle,'" *Papers on Language and Literature* 17 (1981): 33–47, and Wayne C. Booth's discussion in *The Rhetoric of Fiction*, 2d ed. (Chicago: University of Chicago Press, 1983), pp. 278–81. For discussions of naming in the tale, see David Kerner, "A Note on 'The Beast in the Jungle,'" *University of Kansas City Review* 17 (1950): 109–18; Edward Stone, "James's Jungle: The Seasons," *UKCR* 21 (1954): 142–44; and Rachel Salmon, "Naming and Knowing in Henry James's 'The Beast in the Jungle': The Hermeneutics of the Sacred Text," *Orbis Litterarum* 36 (1981): 302–22. For a somewhat negative view of James's technique, see Allen Tate, "Three Commentaries," *Sewanee Review* 58 (1950): 1–15. And for a view that the tale is more ambiguous than most critics admit, see Janice H. Harris, "Bushes, Bears, and 'The Beast in the Jungle,'" *Studies in Short Fiction* 18 (1981): 147–54.

4. *The Novels and Tales of Henry James*, vol. 17 (New York: Scribner's, 1909), p. 61. Further references will be given in the text.

5. Mary Doyle Springer identifies this attribute as an important source of

our sympathy with Marcher. See *A Rhetoric of Literary Character* (Chicago: University of Chicago Press, 1978), p.219.

6. See Booth, *The Rhetoric of Fiction*, pp. 278–81.

7. This perhaps mealy-mouthed identification of the narrative as tragic is done advisedly; I do not want to enter discussions of whether Marcher is more like Lear or Willy Loman, or of whether "The Beast" is a genuine tragedy. My point is that if we abstract from the progression and think about a loose generic placement, tragedy is appropriate. Readers who are more concerned with stricter or tighter generic placements will soon see that my reluctance to be similarly concerned stems from what I regard as the special quality of the tale—and of James's use of Marcher's mimetic and thematic functions.

8. Interpretation, for Scholes, is itself the second step in a recommended three-step encounter with texts. The first step is reading, an activity concerned with focusing on the particulars of texts; Scholes recommends that one highlight especially salient particulars by considering alternative versions of the text, or as he says, producing "text within text." The third step is criticism, the activity of embracing or, more importantly, resisting the stance taken toward the cultural codes revealed by interpretation; Scholes's shorthand for criticism is "text against text."

9. Henry James, *The Ambassadors* (New York: Norton, 1964), p. 132.

10. This observation might be the starting place for Scholes's kind of criticism: does James's own anxiety of being like Marcher cause him to stack the deck against his protagonist, make him too easily the butt of the reader's and author's amusement so that we are left wondering why May would have anything to do with him in the first place? For more on what Scholes means by criticism and how it works, see his three chapters in *Textual Power* on "The Text in the Class," pp. 18–73.

11. Michael Coulson Berthold, "The Idea of 'Too Late' in James's 'The Beast in the Jungle,'" *Henry James Review* 4 (1983): 128–39.

12. For an example of evaluation and its attendant problems, see my discussion of Catherine Barkley in Chapter 6.

Chapter 3

1. Some of Fowles's critics—even some of his better ones such as Linda Hutcheon—take at face value the narrator's reference to Sarah as protagonist, citing the title of the novel as support for their position. From the vantage point provided by a concern with progression, however, that designation just will not hold up: Charles is the figure at the center of the instabilities; they all cluster around his life and his choices; the story of his progress in relation to Ernestina and Sarah is the story that takes the narrative and authorial audiences from the beginning to the end of the book. Hutcheon's discussion is in *Narcissistic Narrative* (Ontario: Wilfrid Laurier University Press, 1980), pp. 57–70.

2. Elizabeth D. Rankin, "Cryptic Coloration in *The French Lieutenant's Woman*," *Journal of Narrative Technique* 3 (1973): 193–207, has also noted the

connection between the metafictional Chapter 13 and the refusal to complete the portrait of Sarah. For other related discussions of Chapter 13 and the other metafictional elements of the narrative, see Hutcheon, *Narcissistic Narrative* cited above, and Philip Cohen, "Postmodernist Technique in *The French Lieutenant's Woman*," *Western Humanities Review* 38, 2 (1984): 148–61.

3. John Fowles, *The French Lieutenant's Woman* (Boston: Little, Brown, 1969), p. 10. Hereafter references will be made by page numbers in parentheses in the text.

4. For a useful detailed discussion of the narrator's temporal and spatial locations in the novel, see William Nelles, "Problems for Narrative Theory: *The French Lieutenant's Woman*," *Style* 18 (1984): 207–15. Nelles discusses the interesting combination of the narrator's temporal distance and his occasional spatial proximity to the characters. In effect, Fowles extends along both the spatial and temporal axes the privilege of the omniscient narrator to know whatever he wants and to tell us whatever he thinks is relevant.

5. Peter Rabinowitz, "Truth in Fiction: A Reexamination of Audiences," *Critical Inquiry* 4 (1977): 121–41. Rabinowitz's later essay, "Assertion and Assumption: Fictional Patterns and the External World," *PMLA* (1981): 408–19, also focuses largely on the different kinds of knowledge the different audiences have. In *Before Reading*, Rabinowitz develops some further consequences of the distinction, including its implications for the way we might understand realism, but he does not move the discussion in the direction I take here.

6. Most critics argue that the second ending is better because it is more in the spirit of the narrative's emphasis on the evolution of both characters toward the twentieth century. But Charles Scruggs's very fine defense of the plausibility of the first ending should, I think, make anyone who wants to reject it think twice. See his "The Two Endings of *The French Lieutenant's Woman*," *Modern Fiction Studies* 31 (1985): 95–113.

7. The next step for the rhetorical critic would be to ask about the possible sexist implications of Fowles's subordinating Sarah to Charles here. This is a complicated question because one does not want to legislate a principle that narratives cannot make male characters the primary focalizers of the narration, while what Fowles does here seems connected with his assumption that one can tell the story of the shift from the Victorian Age to the modern by focusing on the experiences of a man. As I noted above, I will take up a similar issue more fully and directly in Part III when I consider the problems raised by Hemingway's characterization of Catherine Barkley.

8. See, for example, Rankin, "Cryptic Coloration," William Palmer, *The Fiction of John Fowles* (Columbia: University of Missouri Press, 1974), and Peter Wolfe, *John Fowles, Magus and Moralist* (Lewisburg, PA: Bucknell University Press, 1976).

Chapter 4

1. Peter Brooks, *Reading for the Plot: Design and Intention in Narrative* (New York: Knopf, 1984). Hereafter page numbers will be given in parentheses in the text.

2. Reader-response criticism that wants to locate the meaning of narrative not in the text but in the individual reader will of course challenge this basic assumption of my rhetorical theory—and of Brooks's psychoanalytically based one. But to argue whether the meaning of a narrative is really, finally, ultimately, in the text or in the individual reader is, I think, to engage in a fruitless debate. Worthwhile criticism of very different kinds can proceed from each of the two different first principles. To the charge that one cannot do worthwhile criticism proceeding from the principle that the text is the basis for a rhetorical transaction between author and reader, my only reply here can be this book itself. Brooks's model and my own can be fruitfully· compared, however, because we share not only the assumption about the importance of the text but also the purpose of explaining the dynamics of reading narrative. For more on this problem of the relation of critical systems, see my "Data, Danda, and Disagreement," *Diacritics* 11 (Summer 1983), 39–50.

3. For a related discussion of the whole-part relationship in the processing of a text, see Chapter 3 of my *Worlds from Words* (Chicago: University of Chicago Press, 1981).

4. In this respect, the rhetorical framework that I am developing here rejects the formalist notion that the text is only its formal features. It seeks to combine an interest in those formal features with an interest in the way they reflect the shaping of an author and call for a response from a hypothetical reader. In that sense, the model is really triple-layered, but for most practical purposes, including doing criticism of the kind that the concept of progression invites, the distinction between the author's shaping of the formal features and the features themselves becomes unimportant.

5. In this respect progression leads beyond the story-discourse and fabula/ sjužet models of narrative structure. The idea of a synthesis between events, characters, setting, and the treatment of those events, as in Brooks's model, is not so much erroneous as incomplete. A narrative is a dynamic synthesis of all the materials of both story and discourse as well as the patterns of response built into the specific configuration of all those elements.

6. Charles Dickens, *Great Expectations* (New York: Holt, Rinehart, and Winston, 1972), p. 1. Further references will be given by page numbers in parentheses in the text.

7. For a useful discussion of the motif of reading, see Max Byrd, "'Reading' in *Great Expectations*," *PMLA* 91 (1976): 259–65.

8. Byrd's essay, cited above, has called my attention to this feature of the passage.

9. But even before we go our separate ways, there are significant differences. Brooks's division of the narrative into four plots (the major difference between his division and mine is that he divides the Satis House plot into two) and his distinction between official and repressed plots already signal his tendency to convert reading for the plot into reading for the themes in motion. The difference between the two Satis House plots he identifies is not a difference based on instability but one based on theme: the second "plot" simply identifies the not very hidden underside of Satis House. Similarly, the division into official and repressed plots gives an odd prominence to "bringing up by hand" as an official plot, since Pip never clearly honors his sister's

efforts: its prominence seems motivated more by Brooks's desires for his quadripartite division that allows him to make his points about the theme of plotting than by the narrative itself.

10. In addition to Brooks, see Julian Moynahan, "The Hero's Guilt: The Case of *Great Expectations*," *Essays in Criticism* 10 (1960): 60–79; Lawrence Jay Dessner, "*Great Expectations*: 'the ghost of a man's own father,'" *PMLA* 91 (1976): 436–49; Michal Peled Ginsburg, "Dickens and the Uncanny: Repression and Displacement in *Great Expectations*," *Dickens Studies Annual* 13 (1984): 115–24; and James L. Spenko, "The Return of the Repressed in *Great Expectations*," *Literature and Psychology* 30, 3–4 (1980): 133–46. These accounts, especially Spenko's, do, I believe, capture elements of Pip's character that are not readily explainable otherwise. More generally, the usefulness of the psychoanalytic perspective here illustrates the relation between psychoanalytic reading and rhetorical interpretation: the psychoanalytic perspective can be subsumed under the rhetorical on a case by case basis. The same principle applies to marxist, existential, anthropological and other "perspectival" accounts of character: when the authorial audience needs the perspective to understand the nature of the character, the rhetorical critic will welcome the perspective. See my comment on this point in the introduction, pp. 11–12.

11. This guilt is of course partly a consequence of his identification with the convict. Thus, although Pip *knows* that his sister is unjust to him, he nevertheless *feels* guilty, just as his knowledge that he is not responsible for assaulting her does not prevent him from feeling somehow guilty for what happens to her.

12. Spenko, in the essay cited above, demonstrates these connections at some length.

13. Lawrence Jay Dessner, in a thoughtful study of Wemmick's psychology, "*Great Expectations*: The Tragic Comedy of John Wemmick," *Ariel* 6, 2 (1975): 65–79, argues that the division between the two sides of Wemmick is not as great as first appears. But Dessner also says that his analysis "does not often correspond with the aesthetic experience of the reader" (p. 78). I think that the authorial audience does see Wemmick as sharply divided but is able to accept the "integration" of his character that I describe below. For a brief but useful discussion of Wemmick, see also Mary Ann Kelly, "The Functions of Wemmick of Little Britain and Wemmick of Walworth," *Dickens Studies Newsletter* 14, 4 (1983): 145–49.

14. For a fuller discussion of the way this repression works, see James L. Spenko, "The Return of the Repressed in *Great Expectations*," *Literature and Psychology* 30, 3–4 (1980): 133–46. For more on repression in the novel, see Michal Peled Ginsburg, "Dickens and the Uncanny: Repression and Displacement in *Great Expectations*," *Dickens Studies Annual* 13 (1984): 115–24.

15. In this respect, I part company with Brooks, who sees the second ending as suggesting an unbinding of the material of the Satis House plot, an indication that it has not been truly mastered. My point is that if the ending shows that both characters have mastered that material in their own ways, then the very fact of their union is not itself an unbinding. See Brooks, pp. 137–39. At a more general level, Brooks and I are in agreement that "the

choice between the two endings is somewhat arbitrary and unimportant in that the decisive moment has already occurred before either of these finales begins" (p. 137).

Chapter 5

1. Italo Calvino, *If on a winter's night a traveler*, trans. William Weaver (New York: Harcourt Brace Jovanovich, 1981), p.3. Hereafter references will be made by page numbers in parentheses in the text.

2. This differentiation of the flesh-and-blood reader from the "you" addressed in the sentence continues in the rest of the paragraph as that "you" begins to get located, however generally, in space: "Relax. Concentrate. Dispel every other thought. Let the world around you fade. Best to close the door; the TV is always on in the next room."

3. In "Readers in Texts," *PMLA* 96 (1981): 848–63, W. Daniel Wilson offers some good first steps in the analysis of what he calls "characterized readers." He distinguishes them from implied readers, but does not work, as I do, with their relation to narrative and authorial audiences.

4. Joseph Conrad, *Lord Jim* (New York: Norton, 1968), pp. 205–6.

5. Laurence Sterne, *Tristram Shandy* (New York: Norton, 1980), p.48.

6. William Makepeace Thackeray, *Vanity Fair* (Boston: Houghton Mifflin, 1963), p.87.

7. Since the characterized audience in the Sterne passage is clearly female and that in the Thackeray clearly male, they together raise the question of how the reader's own sex will influence his or her response to a characterized audience of a specific sex. To take just the most obvious question, will women have trouble accepting the use of the characterized audiences here since the first can be seen as employing a sexist stereotype and the second seems to relegate women to the secondary role of wife? Many women and some men will want to become what Judith Fetterley calls "resisting readers," and speak out against the assumptions upon which the characterized audiences are constructed as well as the attitudes toward women that reading in the authorial audience asks them to adopt. Needless to say, this kind of criticism is extremely significant. At the same time, I think that such a criticism comes most appropriately after the sort of analysis I am proposing here, one which takes as its first step the understanding of the five-sided communicative situation among author, narrator, characterized audience, narrative audience, and authorial audience. For much more extended discussion of these and related issues, see the collection *Gender and Reading*, ed. Elizabeth Flynn and Patrocinio Schweikart (Baltimore: The Johns Hopkins University Press, 1985).

8. Gerald Prince, "The Narratee Revisited," *Style* 19 (1985): 299–305. See also Prince, "Introduction to the Study of the Narratee," in *Reader-Response Criticism: From Formalism to Post-Structuralism*, ed. Jane Tompkins (Baltimore: The Johns Hopkins Press, 1980), 7–25.

9. For Wayne Booth, see the Afterword to the second edition of *The Rhetoric of Fiction* (Chicago: University of Chicago Press, 1983). For work on the narratee in addition to Prince's, see Mary Ann Piwowarczyk, "The Narratee

and the Situation of Enunciation: A Reconsideration of Prince's Theory," *Genre* 9 (1976): 161–77; William Ray, "Recognizing Recognition: The Intra-Textual and Extra-Textual Critical Persona," *Diacritics* 7 (Winter 1977): 20–33; and Robyn Warhol, "Toward a Theory of the Engaging Narrator: Earnest Interventions in Gaskell, Stowe, and Eliot," *PMLA* 101 (1986): 811–18.

10. See Peter Rabinowitz, "Truth in Fiction: A Reexamination of Audiences," *Critical Inquiry* 4 (1977): 121–41.

11. It is, I believe, for this reason that when Booth adopts Rabinowitz's model he leaves the ideal narrative audience behind and that Rabinowitz himself has silently dropped it out of his analyses. He makes no significant use of it in *Before Reading*.

12. The phrase is used by Barbara Herrnstein Smith in *Poetic Closure: A Study of How Poems End* (Chicago: University of Chicago Press, 1968) to refer to the way new or surprising information in the later lines of a poem will cause its readers to revise their interpretations of earlier lines.

13. Most of the narrators of the other titled chapters do, however, comment on their own narration without raising questions of whether they are themselves metafictionists.

14. Interestingly, the last two sentences of the chapter, which are again in the narrator's voice, are written not in second but in third person: "Actually, it seems the Reader really is about to leave. He will take with him *On the carpet of leaves illuminated by the moon* by Takakumi Ikoka to read on his journey" (p.198).

15. In Chapter 1, the narrator summarizes the Reader's preference for the kind of book he likes to read in a way that is analogous to, though not identical with, the Other Reader's expression of her preferences: "you go on and you realize that the book is readable nevertheless, independently of what you expected of the author, it's the book itself that arouses your curiosity; in fact, on sober reflection, you prefer it this way, confronting something and not quite knowing yet what it is" (p. 9).

16. For more on this point from somebody who finds tighter connections, see Marilyn Orr, "Beginning the Middle: The Story of Reading in Calvino's *If on a winter's night a traveler*," *Papers on Language and Literature* 21 (1985): 210–19.

Chapter 6

1. I take the term from Wayne C. Booth, *Critical Understanding: The Powers and Limits of Pluralism* (Chicago: University of Chicago Press, 1979), chap. 2 and passim. Booth, however, sometimes uses the term in a sense that I do not intend here: appropriating some one's text for one's own purposes. I use it to refer to a process that follows rather than supplants understanding. This activity of evaluation is similar to what Scholes calls "criticism" in *Textual Power* (New Haven: Yale University Press, 1985).

2. Judith Fetterley, *The Resisting Reader: A Feminist Approach to American Fiction* (Bloomington: Indiana University Press, 1978). Hereafter references to this book will be indicated by page numbers in parentheses in the text. Fet-

terley, of course, is not alone in her assessment of the book and Hemingway's treatment of Catherine. For example, Millicent Bell claims that in Catherine, Hemingway has created a "sort of inflatable rubber doll woman available at will to the onanastic dreamer." "*A Farewell to Arms:* Pseudoautobiography and Personal Metaphor," in *Ernest Hemingway: The Writer in Context,* ed. James Nagel (Madison: University of Wisconsin Press, 1984), p. 114. But Hemingway and Catherine also have their defenders, most notably Joyce Wexler, "E.R.A. for Hemingway: A Feminist Defense of Catherine Barkley," *Georgia Review* 35 (1981): 111–23, and Sandra Whipple Spanier, "Catherine Barkley and the Hemingway Code," paper delivered at Approaches to Hemingway Conference, San Diego State University, March 1987 (to be published in the Chelsea House volume on Hemingway edited by Harold Bloom). Virtually every commentator on the the novel acknowledges Hemingway's treatment as an issue that must be addressed. For another negative evaluation, see Edmund Wilson, "Hemingway: The Gauge of Morale," in *The Wound and the Bow* (New York: Oxford University Press, 1947). For some middle positions, acknowledging limitations but also justifying or minimizing them, see Daniel Schneider, "Hemingway's *A Farewell to Arms:* The Novel as Pure Poetry," *Modern Fiction Studies* 14 (1968): 283–96, Philip Young, *Ernest Hemingway: A Reconsideration* (University Park: Pennsylvania State University Press, 1966), and Carlos Baker, *Hemingway: The Writer as Artist,* 3d ed. (Princeton: Princeton University Press, 1963).

For a worthwhile study of the relation between Hemingway's wartime experience and the novel itself, see Michael Reynolds, *Hemingway's First War* (Princeton: Princeton University Press, 1976).

3. The larger point here is that the same material can be the basis for many different narratives with many different effects. The Second City comedy troupe does a wonderful rendition of *Hamlet* as a farce. It would be easy to make *The Ambassadors* into a melodramatic soap opera, and so on. These claims are very different from ones which would say that the covert story of *Hamlet* is farce, that of *The Ambassadors* melodrama.

4. Fetterley's analysis on this particular point also depends on an assumption that the introduction of the other text allows the interpreter considerable room to infer the applications of that text to the one under primary consideration. Fetterley, it seems to me, takes advantage of that free rein in seeing Catherine's allusion as a sign of Frederic's feeling. The trouble with the founding assumption is that it usually leaves room for a contradictory interpretation. In this case, one might with equal justice argue that the allusion to *Othello* reminds us that Frederic and Catherine can be considered among the company of those who "loved not wisely but too well."

5. Ernest Hemingway, *A Farewell to Arms* (New York: Charles Scribner's Sons, 1929), p. 3. Further references will be given in page numbers in parentheses in the text.

6. Eugene B. Cantelupe, "Statues and Lovers in *A Farewell to Arms,*" *Fitzgerald-Hemingway Annual* (1977): 203–05.

7. Spanier, "Catherine Barkley and the Hemingway Code."

8. Some critics see the Switzerland section not as an idyll but as a dead

end; Fetterley's comment that Catherine's death frees Frederic from the responsibilities of marriage, fatherhood, and family is related to this view. For the fullest articulation of it, see the essay by Bell cited in n. 2 above. I think that the progression both works against and leaves room for this view. In Switzerland, Frederic finally reaches the equivalent of the Abruzzi, the priest's homeland whose clear, cold, dry, and snow-covered landscapes are early set in opposition to the smoky cafés where Frederic spent most of his leave. But because Frederic and Catherine live there with the knowledge (on her part) and the feeling (on both of their parts) that they are living on borrowed time, there is something constrained and barren about the idyll. I think that Hemingway worked hard to have his readers sense Frederic and Catherine's own misgivings about their life with no future, but here his method of understatement finally does not serve him well. It works in the scene where Frederic and Catherine wake up and Frederic can't go back to sleep, but it does not work in many of their nonprogressive conversations.

9. Spanier, "Catherine Barkley and the Hemingway Code."

10. See Ralph Rader, "Fact, Theory, and Literary Explanation," *Critical Inquiry* 1 (1974): 221–45.

11. See Gerry Brenner, *Concealments in Hemingway's Fiction* (Columbus: Ohio State University Press, 1983), pp. 30–31. As his characterization of these passages suggests, Brenner's reading of the whole narrative is very different from mine. He sees it as an expression of Hemingway's belief in the irrationality of existence, an expression made through the untrustworthy tale of a narrator who is on the verge of suicide.

12. Sexists of course would claim that they are not denying full humanity to women but simply recognizing differences between the sexes—in this way, they claim not to be sexist. If they could be convinced that they were denying women full humanity, then they would be more likely to reform: such is the power of the norm that all humans be granted their humanity.

Conclusion

1. Norman Mailer, *The Armies of the Night: The Novel as History, History as a Novel* (New York: New American Library, 1968), p. 241. Hereafter citations will be made by page numbers in parentheses in the text.

2. Though developed independently and employing different terms, my analysis here is similar to that offered by Robert Merrill, *Norman Mailer* (New York: Twayne, 1978).

3. For a discussion of the metaphors in this section, see Wayne C. Booth, "Metaphor as Rhetoric: The Problem of Evaluation," *Critical Inquiry* 5 (1978): 49–72; 175–76.

4. George Eliot, *Middlemarch* (New York: Norton, 1977), p. 578. Further references will be given in page numbers in parentheses in the text.

5. "A Comparative Anatomy of Three Baggy Monsters," *Journal of Narrative Technique* (forthcoming, Spring 1989).

6. Such things would include accounting for Bulstrode's role in enhancing the power of the Lydgate plot, explaining the principles of Eliot's

interweaving—why she leaves off one story line and picks up another at any given point—and analyzing Farebrother's role as one who also contributes to the growing good of the world. I have made a start on these matters in "Elaboration and Economy in *Middlemarch*: Farebrother and the Final Paragraph," paper delivered at the International Conference on Narrative, Ann Arbor, Michigan, April 1987. Among the many accounts of the relations among the plots, most of which focus on the ideational similarities and contrasts, see especially Peter Garrett's discussion in the *Victorian Multiplot Novel* (New Haven: Yale University Press, 1978).

7. Virginia Woolf, *Mrs. Dalloway* (New York: Harcourt, Brace and World, 1925), p. 3. Hereafter page numbers will be cited in parentheses in the text.

8. Although I would not push the point too hard, I also think that honoring flexibility over predictive power is generally a methodological strength. When theories honor prediction over flexibility, further inquiry can often be short-circuited: the theory tells one in advance what the phenomena under investigation must be, how they must work, etc. Honoring flexibility is a way to privilege the a posteriori approach to new phenomena over the a priori (of course even the a posteriori will depend on some a priori decisions such as the categories for analyzing character, but these decisions are not conclusions about what one must find).

Index